Springer Series on Social Work

Albert R. Roberts, D.S.W., Series Editor

Graduate School of Social Work, Rutgers, The State University of New Jersey

Series volumes no longer in print are listed below.

1984   **Battered Women and Their Families:** Intervention Strategies and Treatment Programs, *Albert R. Roberts, D.S.W.*

1984   **Clinical Social Work in Health Settings:** A Guide to Professional Practice with Exemplars, *Thomas Owen Carlton, D.S.W.*

1986   **Elder Abuse and Neglect:** Causes, Diagnosis, and Intervention Strategies, *Mary Joy Quinn, R.N., M.A.,* and *Susan K. Tomita, M.S.W.*

1986   **Law and Social Work Practice,** *Raymond Albert, M.S.W., J.D.*

1987   **Information and Referral Networks:** Doorways to Human Services, *Risha W. Levinson, D.S.W.*

1988   **Social Work in the Workplace:** Practice and Principles, *Gary M. Gould, Ph.D.,* and *Michael Lane Smith, Ph.D.*

1988   **The Human Bond:** Support Groups and Mutual Aid, *Harry Wasserman, D.S.W.,* and *Holly E. Danforth, M.S.W.*

1988   **Social Work:** The Membership Perspective, *Hans S. Falck, Ph.D.*

1990   **Social Work Practice in Maternal and Child Health,** *Terri Combs-Orme, Ph.D.*

1990   **Program Evaluation in the Human Services,** *Michael J. Smith, D.S.W.*

1990   **Journeys to Recovery,** *Milson Trachtenberg, A.C.S.W., C.A.C.*

1990   **Evaluating Your Practice:** A Guide to Self-Assessment, *Catherine Alter, Ph.D.,* and *Wayne Evens, M.S.W.*

1990   **Violence Hits Home:** Comprehensive Treatment Approaches to Domestic Violence, *Sandra M. Stith, Ph.D., Mary Beth Williams, L.C.S.W.,* and *Karen Rosen, M.S.*

1991   **Breast Cancer in the Life Course:** Women's Experiences, *Julianne S. Oktay, Ph.D.,* and *Carolyn Ambler Walter, Ph.D.*

1991   **Victimization and Survivor Services:** A Guide to Victim Assistance, *Arlene Bowers Andrews, Ph.D.*

1992   **The Family Functioning Scale:** A Guide to Research and Practice, *Ludwig L. Geismar, Ph.D.,* and *Michael Camasso, Ph.D.*

1994   **Dilemmas in Human Services Management:** Illustrative Case Studies, *Raymond Sanchez Mayers, Ph.D., Federico Souflee, Jr., Ph.D.,* and *Dick J. Schoech, Ph.D.*

1994   **Managing Work and Family Life,** *Viola M. Lechner, D.S.W.,* and *Michael A. Creedon, D.S.W.*

1996   **Total Quality Management in Human Service Organizations,** *John J. Gunther, D.S.W.,* and *Frank Hawkins, D.S.W.*

1997   **Multicultural Perspectives in Working with Families,** *Elaine P. Congress, D.S.W.*

1997   **Research Methods for Clinical Social Workers:** Empirical Practice, *John S. Wodarski, Ph.D.*

Out of Print Titles:

1984   **Social Policy and the Rural Setting,** *Julia M. Watkins, Ph.D.,* and *Dennis A. Watkins, Ph.D.*

1984   **Social Work in the Emergency Room,** *Carole W. Soskis, M.S.W., J.D.*

1984   **Disability, Work, and Social Policy,** Models for Social Welfare, *Aliki Coudroglou, D.S.W.,* and *Dennis L. Poole, Ph.D.*

1984   **Foundations of Social Work Practice,** *Joseph Anderson, D.S.W.*

1985   **Task-Centered Practice with Families and Groups,** *Anne E. Fortune, Ph.D.*

1986   **Widow-to-Widow,** *Phyllis R. Silverman, Ph.D.*

John S. Wodarski, PhD, is Janet B. Wattles Research Professor and Director of the Doctoral Program and Research Center at the State University of New York at Buffalo. Among the top scholars in social work, he has authored or co-authored nearly 250 publications, including 22 books. Dr. Wodarski has a reputation as an excellent teacher and won a Social Work Professor of the Year award at the University of Georgia in 1988. His strengths are in child welfare and alcohol-abuse problems and his commitment to empirically based practice.

Research Methods for Clinical Social Workers

Empirical Practice

John S. Wodarski, PhD

HV
11
.W697
1997
WEST

 Springer Publishing Company

Springer Publishing Company, Inc.
536 Broadway
New York, NY 10012-3955

Cover design by Margaret Dunin
Production Editor: Pamela Lankas

97 98 99 00 01 / 5 4 3 2 1

Library of Congress Cataloging-in-Publication-Data

Wodarski, John S.
Research methods for clinical social workers : empirical practice
/ John S. Wodarski.
    p. cm.—(Springer series on social work)
Includes bibliographical references and index.
ISBN 0-8261-9650-0
    1. Social service—Research—Methodology. 2. Social case work.
I. Title. II. Series.
HV11.W697 1997
361.3'2'727—dc21   96-40362
                                                                CIP

Printed in the United States of America

Contents

Contributor   *vii*

1   Empirical Practice: An Introduction   1

2   Criteria for Choosing Knowledge and Assessing
    Empirical Intervention   29

3   Transforming Behavioral Science Knowledge
    into Practice Generalizations   39

4   Choice-of-Outcome Measures and Means for Assessment   72

5   Designs for Daily Practice Evaluation   107

6   Traditional Designs   127

7   Application of Statistical Techniques in the Evaluation
    of Practice   140

8   Advanced Statistical Techniques in Social Work
    Research   153
    Eileen M. Lysaught and John S. Wodarski

9   Preparing for Research   166

10   Competency-Based Agency Practice   182

11   Development of Management Information Systems
     for Human Services: A Practical Guide   205

12   Developing and Formulating Quality Proposals   225

13   The Research Practitioner: The Formulation
     of Process and Educational Objectives   234

14   Emerging Trends and Issues   246

Index   267

Contributor

Eileen Lysaught is a doctoral student in the School of Social Welfare at the State University of New York at Buffalo.

CHAPTER 1

Empirical Practice: An Introduction

W ithin the last three decades, the social work profession has responded to the challenge to base practice on empirical evidence to adequately meet client needs. In the majority of cases, most social workers would agree that the challenge has resulted in positive changes: for example, in the execution of relevant research studies; the incorporation of more research findings into practice; the development of a technology of interpersonal helping; an emphasis on the incorporation of new knowledge bases, such as sociobehavioral and systems theory, in the curricula of schools of social work; and the development of services to meet emerging client needs (Dulmus & Wodarski, 1996; Fraser, 1994; Wodarski, Thyer, Iodice, & Pinkston, 1991).

A past allegation about the lack of effectiveness of practice methods is no longer relevant with the accumulation of substantial empirical bases from many interpersonal helping strategies (Ammegman & Hersen, 1995). The minimal use of empirical methods to evaluate practice and the limited incorporation of relevant behavioral science knowledge in practice models are deficiencies of the profession, however. One of the ingenious proposals to meet this challenge is to train practitioners who can evaluate knowledge produced in the behavioral sciences and who, in turn, can translate such knowledge into practice principles (Bloom & Fischer, 1982; Gambrill, 1990; Wodarski, Feit, &

Green, 1995). Along those lines, this book proposes that bachelor's-level practitioners should be consumers of knowledge that facilitates effective practice, that master's-level practitioners should be sophisticated practitioners or managers, or both, and that doctoral-level practitioners should be producers and evaluators of knowledge.

In response to the call for empirically based practice, increased emphasis on research in practice has developed, that is, the use of evaluative research to provide a rational basis for the delivery of services (Alter & Evans, 1990). This volume aims to help practitioners understand the research process and equip them with the necessary tools and skills to (a) evaluate studies, (b) translate relevant behavioral science knowledge into practice principles, and (c) implement evaluation procedures in their daily practice.

RATIONALE FOR THE EMPIRICAL PRACTITIONER

The incorporation into social work practice of research methods and practice models based on behavioral science knowledge has increased during the last three decades. A primary reason for this move is the accumulating evidence that indicates the substantial effectiveness of empirically based interpersonal helping methods (Kilty & Meenaghan, 1995). Also, these therapeutic methods are easily evaluated. Likewise, research methodology provides the data necessary to make these methods empirical; reliable and valid measurements exist for adequately evaluating treatment outcomes for empirical intervention, in which the primary concern is changes in behavior through instructions to change overt behavioral patterns (Richey, Kopp, Tolson, & Ishisaka, 1987; Thomas, Bastien, Stuebe, Bronaon, & Yaffe, 1987). Another positive is the provision by federal agencies of adequate funding for projects to evaluate empirical practice interventions on a broad scale. The field is ready to employ the necessary sophisticated designs to evaluate traditional services adequately. Requisites of time, energy, money, and pilot investigations aimed at studying the methods that practitioners implement daily isolate those interventions that need further refinement (Barlow & Hersen, 1984; Cooper, 1990; Nuehring & Pascone, 1986). Moreover, new, brief, empirical technologies are available for effective practice, such as relaxation, social skills, relationship enhancement, and assertiveness training (Thyer, in press; Wodarski & Wodarski, 1993).

A concurrent positive development during this transitional period has been the profession's increasing commitment to base decisions about therapies and theories of human behavior on scientific principles and research data rather than on theoretical tradition and practice authority. Because many of the training programs in social work are based on globally defined objectives that cannot be used in the classroom or in fieldwork, social work educators have been searching for methodologies that will enable formalization of the training for practitioners (Wodarski et al., 1995). Competency-based social work education meets this need because it applies measurable concepts enabling evaluation of the training processes and indicating the practitioner's level of competence necessary to practice effectively (Camasso & Jagannathan, 1994; Menefee & Thompson, 1994; Rose, Cayner, & Edleson, 1977).

In research, the emphasis of the competency-based curriculum on the development of specific academic and practice competencies is a welcome addition. The evaluation of these competencies occurs through objective tests that adequately measure academic knowledge. The acquisition of practice skills is determined through the use of simulation training exercises, videotaping clinical interaction, and behavioral observations. Follow-up of different cohorts of trainees helps determine whether the clinical skills they learn in school are maintained and are relevant to the agencies in which they practice (Bernotavicz, 1994; McCowan, McGregor, & LoTempio, 1984; Reid, Parsons, & Green, 1989; Wodarski, Bricout, & Smokowski, in press).

Through external pressures at the federal and state levels and from professional organizations, attention has been placed on accountability of social work practice. Precision of worker interventions, use of concepts in observable events, collection of data to evaluate the treatment process, and inculcation of the scientific perspective in practitioners provide methods that verify practice techniques and, thus, provide the profession means of responding to the external pressures for accountability. This emphasis on accountability should ensure continued federal and state monetary and philosophical support.

No doubt social workers and other professionals working without empirically based practices are at risk for increased malpractice suits. Society has begun to demand proof that interventions work (Sanderson, 1995). Campbell (1994, p. 5) states: "When psychotherapists fail to maintain familiarity with the current literature, develop ill-conceived treatment plans, solicit the dependency of their clients, and confuse

them by creating imaginary problems, their negligence invites malpractice litigation."

Clinicians are not the only ones being held responsible for professional behavior. Universities are being challenged over their role in
educating incompetent practitioners. In Louisiana, a client successfully
sued her therapist and was awarded $1.7 million. The therapist was a
graduate of an education program with an emphasis in counseling
from Louisiana Tech's College of Education. Now a lawsuit is pending
as to whether the college adequately prepared this graduate (Custer,
1994). Is academia adequately preparing students to enter the field as
mental health clinicians? In referring to social work masters programs,
Hepler and Noble (1990, p. 126) state, "The quality of social work education ultimately affects practice competence and the social welfare of
citizens." Where then does responsibility end for the school and rest
with the graduate who is now a practitioner?

Many practitioners use continuing education to enhance their knowledge base to provide them with opportunities to remain current on new
research. As Houle, Cyphert, and Boggs (1987) state:

> It increases awareness that the appropriate goals broaden out to include
> all the needs for the growth of a profession, beginning with an aware-
> ness of its appropriate mission and continuing through a mastery of
> both its knowledge base and its methods of treatment, its internal struc-
> turing, its code of ethics, its relationships with allied professions, and its
> responsibilities to both its clients and its society (p. 90).

In many states, though, there is no requirement to maintain a minimal
amount of continuing education each year for some professions.

Managed care companies are also putting pressure on social workers and other mental health professionals to produce empirical treatment with proven outcomes. Managed care is an inescapable element
of mental health services in America today. Many private and public
insurers now utilize this cost containment program (Applbaum, 1993),
which often place caps on the number of outpatient mental health sessions allowed (Foos, Otten, & Hill, 1991). Thyer (1995) states, "To the
extent that a service provider can produce evidence that the services
he or she will be providing to children are well-supported by sound
clinical research studies, authorization for such treatments is enhanced.
If managed care programs produce incentives to select demonstrable
effective treatments, where these are known to exist, this will be to the

benefit of the profession and our child clients." As third parties make decisions regarding reimbursement for treatment for clients, practitioners will be forced to demonstrate outcome based on treatment.

Cost efficiency and treatment effectiveness are good arguments for group work (Randall & Wodarski, 1989). In 1980, three different approaches to family therapy were compared by Christenson, Johnson, Phillips, and Glascow: group method, individual mode, and minimal contact with the provision of reading material and brief personal intervention by the worker. Each approach was designed to improve parent effectiveness with problem children and had multiple measures to evaluate outcomes. Findings indicated that group and individual methods were best and equal to each other with the group condition requiring less than half as much professional staff time (Randall & Wodarski, 1989). Yalom (1995) reports a study by Toseland and Siporin which also supports that group therapy is at least as efficacious as individual therapy. This study indicated that group therapy was more effective than individual therapy in 25% of their cases. In the other 75%, there were no significant differences between group and individual therapy. In no study was individual therapy more effective. This indicates that group therapy may be the empirically proven treatment of choice with certain diagnoses; at the same time, group therapy may be cost effective for the client, agency, and third party payer.

As mental health professionals provide service to children and adolescents with mental health disorders, it is essential that they provide excellent assessments and match empirically proven treatment to diagnosis. This requires a working knowledge of all sections of the Diagnostic and Statistical Manual of Mental Disorders (DSM-IV) (American Psychiatric Association, 1994) as related to children and demands an ongoing quest for new knowledge and training for practitioners to enable them to provide the more effective treatments for their clients. Nothing less is ethically acceptable, with less possibly leading to legal implications. In addition, it is imperative to have an outcome-based practice so that clients can access treatment as needed through the third party gatekeeper called managed care.

FUNCTIONS OF RESEARCH

For the purposes of this volume, "research" is defined as the systematic application of empirical methods in social work practice for specifying worker interventions in scientific terminology (the independent variable). This all-encompassing definition includes interventions applied to individuals, groups, communities, organizations, and societies as a whole. Although few would argue the worthiness of this goal, the functions that research should serve in social work practice need to be put into proper perspective. The global assumption is that research will be the salvation of social work practice if only more of it is done and done well. The thesis of this volume is that certain ideas pertaining to research are dysfunctional and go beyond the scope of what is worthy of the investment. For example, the question whether casework is effective, which has occupied the time of many researchers and practitioners for the last three decades, cannot be properly determined through evaluative research (Dean & Reinherz, 1986; Kazdin, 1981; Proctor, 1990; Wodarski, 1981). The question is too general; it is not formulated in a specific manner that meets the basic requisites of evaluative research and, thus, the question is as inappropriate as asking whether the social work profession is relevant to society. The complex question for the evaluation of social work practice consists of six components: What client, what worker, what intervention, what context, how long, and what relapse-prevention procedures are necessary to increase the duration of the interpersonal changes at all levels of intervention?

Moreover, the profession can now equip the practitioner with effective psychosocial treatment that will substantiate empirical bases (Thyer, 1995). Historically, the social worker wants to provide a reason for service that has been questioned; thus the focus is on applying the technology of research to the evaluation of casework services. However, in order for evaluative research to assess social work services and help provide them on a more rational basis, the global question of whether social work practice is effective has to be restated thus: Is casework effective utilizing X, Y, and Z technique in X, Y, and Z context with X, Y, and Z therapist and X, Y, and Z client? For example, clinical research could yield the following proposition: A middle-aged, middle-class depressive male who has a good work history, a satisfactory marriage, a college education, and two children is most effectively treated through brief therapy consisting of structure, ventilation, and clarification in a series of eight sessions provided by a middle-aged male therapist who has had his MSW for at least 5 years and whose practice orientation has centered around the theoretical framework of brief therapy provided in a community mental health center. Relapse-prevention procedures are not considered necessary.

Thus, several crucial considerations must be dealt with before research can reasonably be expected to aid the planning and decision-making functions of practitioners, agencies, and institutions involved in the delivery of social services.

PLAUSIBLE STUDIES

Well-designed studies in social work practice should specify concretely what the unit of change is: for example, a client, a group, a community, or an organization. Empirically grounded terms also specify how this unit will change in some definable continuum. For example, the goal of increasing a client's social functioning would be defined in measurable behavioral objectives, that is, securing and maintaining employment. Likewise, the investigator would also specify how this unit will be changed: the composite interventive behaviors to be exhibited by a worker. At the same time, a study should specify in what context this interventive attempt will occur and the organizational characteristics of the context, such as agency size, number, and variety of services provided; fluidity of the agency's internal structure; its immediate social environment, administrative style, and supervisors; and so forth. Moreover, the characteristics of the person who will intervene should be clearly stated. For example, the *unit of change* may be 10 antisocial children between the ages of 11 and 12 who exhibit the following behaviors in a recreational group at a community center: hitting each other; damaging physical property; running away; climbing out of windows; making loud noises; using aggressive verbal statements; and throwing objects, such as paper, candy, erasers, and chairs. The *interventive approach* in this example is the group worker's choice of positive reinforcement to increase prosocial behavior; punishment and extinction to decrease antisocial behavior; and other behavior modification techniques, such as time-out, shaping, group contingencies, and so forth, as needed. The *context* is an open agency, a community center that offers primarily recreational, leisure time, and educational services for 16,000 enrolled members. Each year, the professional staff of the agency organizes approximately 200 clubs and classes for children and youths ranging in age from 6 to 18 years. The *change agent* is a young female between the ages of 18 and 24 who is in college, is highly motivated to work with children, has good verbal ability, is well adjusted, and is enrolled in an undergraduate social work program.

A well-designed study measures simultaneously client behavior and the amount of worker interventions through the duration of the study. The process would allow a better estimate of how the worker's interventions affect the client's behavior. Moreover, through repeated measures of client and worker behavior, the research practitioner can monitor change daily, and thus can acquire a more accurate estimate of the effects of worker interventions upon client behavior (Stein & Lambert, 1995; Wodarski, Feldman, & Pedi, 1974).

A significant past error in social work practice is to focus solely on what is to be changed in the client (the dependent variable) and to proceed only to measure it (Kazdein, 1994). Very seldom did we measure the interventions (the independent variable) employed. For example, a group worker providing services to children may utilize praise, directions, positive attention, criticism, positive physical contacts, time-out, holding, threats, and negative attention. The assumption is that the treatment, whether it be casework or group work, is a homogeneous coherent system of operations exhibited by each worker and is not influenced by the agency in which the treatment takes place or by other factors, such as a client's sex, race, or social class (Hollingshead & Redlich, 1958; Luborsky, Chandler, Auerbach, Cohen, & Bachrach, 1971). This deficiency in evaluative research hampers the researcher's ability to assess or control the quality of the interventive attempt. If treatment is not consistently implemented, no evaluation can take place.

WHAT SHOULD BE CHANGED AND WHY

It is essential that one understands that the determination of what should be changed involves constant value judgments or a series of them (Hudson & Nurius, 1994; Wodarski, 1994). This is obviously a complex and frequently difficult issue, but one that must be considered if services are to be provided on a rational basis. The practitioner immediately confronts the profession's code of ethics as a major determinant in what should be changed, but a code of ethics can only serve as a guide. Frequently, this is resolved by a formal or informal contract with the client, but contracts are a recent innovation in social work practice and probably represent the exception rather than the rule. The answer to what should be changed is not found in quantitative methods of research design technology but must be dealt with by a complex set of values and norms held or adhered to by the worker, the client, the agency, and society. If this issue is not adequately dealt with, it is highly probable that the remainder of the research either will be fruitless or will answer an inappropriate or trivial question (Jayarante & Levy, 1979; Stevenson, 1989; Thomas, 1978; Winett, 1991).

Most theoretical frameworks in social work show that change is usually defined by the normative structure of the society, whether the changes are in the client, a group of clients, a community, or an organization, such as a social agency. For example, role theory constructs are used to explain why clients are not performing well in roles as defined by society, and techniques are derived from role theory to modify clients' behavior so they assume their proper societal role. For instance, many young people do not adhere to the traditional values of society (Bennett & Westera, 1994; Erlich, 1971; Jacobs, Rettig, & Bovasso, 1991; Wheeler, 1971). Their behaviors are evaluated by traditional values and labeled as inadequate role performances, and specific socialization mechanisms are posited to correct these performances. Although societal norms cannot be flagrantly violated, the deficiency of this approach lies in the profession's tendency to seldom question the roles formulated by society, instead to accept them as given.

As with role theory, many psychodynamic theories define what should be changed in high-order constructs created to explain human behavior. Ego defenses, motivation, traits, personality configuration, conscience, and character are examples of terms linked together and formulated into a system that purports to explain why some succeed and others fail to achieve goals and tasks. However, notions of success and failure are heavily laden with valuative connotations, and the techniques derived from such theories are, again, often based on implicit societal norms that are accepted as given and seldom questioned. When a woman says to a worker that she wants to divorce her husband, the worker may translate this as a treatable psychological problem rather than a plea for guidance in securing financial and legal aid. The diagnosis may be entirely proper and correct, but if it is guided too much by the implicit norm that regards divorce as bad, the worker may be doing a grave disservice to the client, her children, the community, and the agency that hired the worker.

If one examines the goals of programs for the poor, delinquent, mentally ill, or developmentally disabled, it is evident that the focus of the 1990s is toward the attainment of middle-class values and is evaluated by middle-class criteria, such as having a "good" job, being married, having a "good" income, exhibiting proper social behaviors in particular contexts, and attaining more education. These outcome criteria, such as the current national philosophy of placing mothers who receive Aid to Families with Dependent Children (AFDC) back to work, are derived from the Protestant ethic of hard work, self-control, and good moral character. The objective of this volume is to question the suitability of these goals in practice research (Lysaught, Wodarski, & Feit, in press).

The majority of research executed in social work and related disciplines has continued to define the outcome criteria in such a way that the research starts with the assumption that it is an individual who must be changed, not their social system (Harrison, Wodarski, & Thyer, 1992). Research studies are needed that not only have well-grounded, empirically defined criteria when the service being evaluated is focused on the individual, but also studies focusing on adequately defined social system variables that may need to be changed to achieve the objectives of a program (Wodarski, Feit, Ramey, & Mann, 1995). For example, practice research might isolate behaviors involved in perpetuation of institutional racism and then determine whether interventions on the individual system, or both are necessary for effective change. Likewise, the rehabilitation of correctional offenders may involve not only programs to change the offender's behaviors, but also programs that change society's attitudes or provide decent jobs and housing. Research that focuses on the reciprocal quality of individual and environmental variables will begin to capture the interdependent factors of complex behavior and will lead to the development of empirical theories of human behavior, such as how a complex society increases the anxiety that relaxation tries to decrease (Wodarski, 1985).

Thus, it is the contention of Wodarski that the single most important consideration in the planning and design of practice research is the development, with adequate empirical assessment, of a clear and definitive statement or decision concerning what should be changed. If this issue is not adequately dealt with, undesirable consequences may result, such as the abuse of the client, ineffective intervention efforts, misguided use of personnel and facilities, failure to acquire needed information for planning, and inappropriate change in theory and practice. Yet in many research investigations, this issue is often wholly ignored or given only cursory attention. Thus, dependent and independent variables need to be specified (Finch, Nelson, & Ott, 1993; Wodarski et al., 1974). For example, it is extraordinarily common for a public-aid recipient, delinquent, or mental patient to confront a worker with three primary needs: a useful and minimally gratifying job, an adequate income, and, through these, an opportunity to acquire the minimal amenities compatible with dignity and health in modern society. Yet, in the past, it was decided that the client was deficient and required internal change, and he or she is given psychotherapy instead of training and social skills for specific employment, a job, and a set of opportunities that would come easily to many others (Wodarski & Wodarski, 1993). In short, the worker in such cases has decided that what should be changed is the client, when a more appropriate option in many cases is to change the structure of job opportunities.

THE INTERVENTIVE APPROACH AND THE CHANGE AGENT

Once a practice problem has been defined and a decision is made concerning what should be changed, the question arises as to what will bring about the desired change. Earlier studies failed to consider this critical component, Reid and Shyne (1969) executed a worthy study that compared the effectiveness of brief casework to the effectiveness of extended casework. As they defined it, examination of brief casework is based on nine separate operations, and the question remains concerning what accounted for the observed changes. Hudson (1971) reported an experiment with preschool children and their parents that showed intensive casework was effective in changing certain performance abilities, but was merely defined as more frequent contacts and smaller caseloads and not as techniques that would differentiate intensive from other forms of casework. Meyer, Borgatta, and Jones (1965) defined treatment methods in an analogous manner with the additional stipulation that intensive casework was also "professional" casework. Currently, various treatment interventions are available with empirically validated manuals for anxiety, depression, and so forth, which contain step-by-step procedures, including social skills, relaxation therapy, problem-solving skills, systematic desensitization, and parenting skills (Jongssma & Peterson, 1995).

Moreover, these manuals facilitate the training of practitioners through exact specifications of directions. The previous approach to defining and conceptualizing practice research is no longer adequate. The question of which specific operations accounted for the change in these and other practice research studies remains (Billingsley, White,

& Munson, 1980; Vermilyea, Barlow, & O'Brien, 1984). Even though certain globally defined services were better than others, the exact nature or processes responsible for their success remain unknown. One might claim that casework is casework, be it intensive or regular, brief or extensive, professional or nonprofessional. But we know better than that. We are not concerned with the simple truism that workers are different and quality of training differs. We know, too, that we would do well to take into account such differences. One could argue that it really does not matter. In this age of increasing costs in the delivery of social services, however, it seems to be an ethical obligation to find the most effective components of any seemingly efficacious method of change (Wodarski, Smokowski, & Feit, in press). Likewise, a profession committed to helping people achieve more adequate levels of living has no right to continue aspects of service that are not related directly to client change (Feldman, 1970, 1971; Hayes & Varley, 1965; National Association of Social Workers, 1967, Wakefield & Kirk, 1996). Thus, research investigations should help isolate those programs that will help clients increase their level of functioning and answer such critical questions as, What is adequate treatment; that is, what are the critical components? Where should it be provided? What qualities should the change agent possess? How long should treatment be provided? What happens if there is no change in the client? Are relapse-prevention procedures necessary (Bergin & Garfield, 1994; Wodarski, 1980)?

In the past, most of the independent variables (social work services provided by workers) of concern in social work were too globally conceptualized to be relevant to clients or to be evaluated by research methods thus yielding more significant findings in the evaluation of practice. In most research studies, services were broadly defined as operations of specific departments in specified agencies: for example, casework offered by workers with master's degrees in social work. The author directed a 5-year research investigation of three different types of group work—behavior modification, traditional, and group centered—with antisocial boys ages 8 to 18. If one type of group work used in the study, such as behavior modification, was shown to be "better" than the others, it would still remain unknown what, within that method, was responsible for the change (i.e., structuring group contingencies, use of material reinforcers, using praise, punishment, extinction, time-out, or shaping) (Feldman, Caplinger, & Wodarski, 1983).

A behaviorist could argue that all this is not pertinent and that it is sufficient to show only differential results. However, this attitude has certain drawbacks. First, research methods are used in this context in a purely combative context ("my mother/dad is smarter than your mother/dad," or "continue or expand our program because we've shown that casework works") rather than isolating the important components of the change process. Replication is another concern, and is the cornerstone of training and research. It is difficult to replicate an experiment if the worker cannot precisely specify the nature and magnitude of the intervention; that is a principal reason for the ambiguous outcomes that occur upon replication of an experiment. A third reason, closely allied with the second, is that if one cannot specify the precise nature and magnitude of the intervention, one does not contribute to building a practice science, even though a positive outcome may be achieved. In other words, if researchers demonstrate that treatment-intervention is successful but they cannot point to the elements of treatment known to be responsible for the positive outcomes, they are not able to teach others how to improve their treatment skills on the basis of their research findings (Blythe & Tripodi, 1989; Fischer, 1978; Kazdin, 1980). Moreover, clients have a right to the least restrictive and least costly methods, as do taxpayers.

All of the above points are evidence of a major weakness frequently observed in evaluative research—a general failure to conduct adequate definition and measurement of the independent variable. Many experimental social scientists make careful plans and heavy investments in defining and measuring one or more dependent variables and, by comparison, ignore the independent variable altogether. This problem deserves elaboration. For example, a worker conducts an experiment to test the hypothesis that professional casework services will effectively reduce the number of illegitimate births among a group of adolescent girls in a vocational high school. To test this hypothesis, girls are randomly assigned to either a control group or an experimental group because random assignment is one of the best known means for holding all other extraneous effects constant. The worker may then proceed believing that it is not necessary to define or measure further the proposed intervention (professional casework services) because all other extraneous effects are held constant or averaged out. In this example, the term *professional casework* is not an appropriately specified independent variable but is merely a vehicle through which the independent variable will be administered. For professional casework, the terms "solution-focused therapy," "problem-solving skills," the "strengths perspective," "behavioral modification," or "medical treatment" could be substituted and the same assertion would hold. All of these are only treatment modalities, not proper independent variables; they make available to practitioners a "bag of tricks"—tools, techniques, ideas, and behavior—that could be used as interventive approaches.

The specified manuals for relaxation and systematic desensitization are examples of properly specified independent variables that can be taught to practitioners. Actually, the example just cited represents a case that cannot be adequately dealt with even after specifying the interventive approach or independent variable that will reduce illegitimate births. Not even the dependent variable has been adequately specified. The general problem of reducing illegitimate births contains several important features. Obviously, illegitimate births occur only when people fornicate out of wedlock. Is the proper thing to be changed the act of sexual intercourse or the out-of-wedlock status? To reduce illegitimate births, should the professional casework service be directed to reducing sexual contact or should it aim at effecting a marriage between the sexual partners? Either choice would likely imply a different set of treatments. Another option would be to theorize that the real source of the problem is the moral degeneracy of the female partner (this supports the dual standard in this country that appears to be an accepted norm) and subject her to socialization training. This implies a different interventive approach. Another theorist might say that all the foregoing are incorrect, that what is needed is the simple recognition that the sexual partners have the right to govern their own bodily functions and that the proper method of dealing with the problem of illegitimate births is to take care of the "birth" part of the problem through instructions in birth-control techniques. This would make sense based on the fact that many couples now live together for 1–10 years before getting married. A radical solution, so repugnant that it must be rejected, would consist of a program of involuntary sterilization. Abortion will also put an end to illegitimate births.

In short, the events that cause illegitimate births are the same as those causing legitimate births, and there are two means of reducing births: reduce or eliminate sexual activity and interrupt the normal birth process. There are many ways of accomplishing either of these, but from a research point of view, it is important to recognize that there is nothing inherent in professional casework that will apparently stop illegitimate births. This does not mean that casework is not a proper means for dealing with certain aspects of this problem. Regardless of the professional treatment modality, researchers must specify the independent variable. In this example, some of the variables that might be considered are training in birth-control techniques, abortion, psychotherapy to modify a deficient superego, a reinforcement schedule designed to extinguish sexual impulses and/or behavior, separation or isolation of the sexual partners, counseling aimed at effecting a marriage, sterilization, and change of society's views toward illegitimate births.

Much of this discussion pertains to issues relating to proper specification of the independent and dependent variables and value judgments concerning what should be changed (Hudson, 1982). Once these have been dealt with, the researcher is in a much better position to select an intervention, but the choice is not then guaranteed. Indeed, at this point, research technology can be of considerable use to professional social work practice. From a purely blind experimental point of view, the social worker could randomly choose an intervention and then test it to see if it produced the desired change, surely a wasteful process. A better procedure is to rely upon both available theory and prior knowledge to identify those interventions that presumably offer to effect the desired change. Once these interventions have been identified, research technology can then be used to test each of them and compare the outcome by which had any or the greater effect on the dependent variable.

The crucial issue at this point is to decide, using theory and prior knowledge, which interventions can be expected to bring about the desired change. Using, for example, the problem of illegitimate births, what is there about "casework" that can reasonably reduce birth? The proper answer to such a question must be that no one knows. On the other hand, if the researcher has decided that sexual partners have the right to regulate their own bodily functions, it might reasonably be claimed, based on prior knowledge, that training in contraception will reduce the frequency of pregnancy. No doubt, qualified caseworkers may be selected to provide this training and assist couples or single individuals to get medical examination, treatment, prescription, and medical supervision. Not all caseworkers are qualified to give such training, and practitioners should be measured or tested to determine that they have the knowledge base necessary for successful administration of the interventive method—in this case, training in use of contraceptives (Wodarski & Wodarski, 1995).

An effective interventive method cannot be specified in global, general terms. It must be specific and directly related to the problem. However, the necessary specificity of the intervention cannot be achieved until the practitioner has dealt explicitly with the evaluative issue of what should be changed, and on that basis has specified the proper dependent variable in measurable terms. After all that is done, the worker must be certain that the intervention has been so defined and measured as to assure that the intended treatment will be successfully administered. If the worker decides that contraceptive training is the appropriate treatment, the chance of failed treatment and an erroneous research conclusion is possible unless it is determined that the worker has an adequate knowledge to conduct the training.

CRITERIA FOR POSITIVE ASSESSMENT: THE AMOUNT OF CHANGE

In many research studies, the traditional means of judging the adequacy of social work treatment was to compare an experimental group with a control group or no-treatment group. A treatment is successful if the change is statistically significant. Indeed, this difference from the control, or no-treatment group must be considered a necessary outcome before it can be concluded that treatment has produced a "better" or positive outcome. However, the criterion by itself is neither sufficient nor adequate. Many clients can be statistically different after treatment on a measure used to compare clients in control and experimental groups. However, if these participants judge the significant change as having a trivial impact on their lives, then the treatment was wholly unworthy of the money, time, and effort they and others invested.

Thus, the important question is: Does a statistical difference on the measure employed really mean something to the client? In other words, how relevant, important, and meaningful are the criteria for change for the client? For example, many clinical research endeavors have used self-inventories as a basis for evaluating client change. Self-inventories by themselves may be inadequate criteria. For instance, in a well-designed program to change the attitudes of welfare clients toward their work, their attitudes may change but their work habits may remain the same. Likewise, children who are antisocial may perceive significant amounts of change after being involved in treatment even though their behaviors may remain relatively the same. Additionally, using traditional statistical techniques for evaluation of change does not enable the researcher to assess which clients have changed statistically because traditional designs are based on the evaluation of group data that do not reflect individual change. The objective in social work practice is not to change group scores but to change the behavior of individuals. Here again, the question is posed: What amount of change is necessary to be truly relevant to meeting client needs? In many instances, a highly significant finding may not lead to the improvement of the client's life (Plutchik, 1974).

Statistical significance is a very important criterion, for it is used to "rub out" the hypothesis that observed change could be attributed to chance. However, it tells us virtually nothing about whether the observed change is important. Moreover, the social scientist can nearly always ensure statistically significant outcomes merely by increasing sufficiently the size of one's sample. Thus, it is claimed that statistical significance is not a proper criterion for assessing a positive outcome in clinical research. It is necessary but inadequate. Only after achieving statistically significant results can the researcher properly ask: Was the treatment effective? When researchers demonstrate statistically significant results, they have effectively ruled out chance (within certain error limits) as one hypothesis to account for the observed outcome, but they have not shown the treatment was effective.

What then is meant by "effective" in the context of practice research? That is precisely the issue that must be decided in advance of conducting the study or at least before the results are in. An experiment, for example, might be conducted to determine whether supportive therapy, positive reinforcement, punishment and deprivation, or intensive psychoanalysis is the preferred modality for improving the performance of underachieving children in a school system. How can positive outcome be judged in these cases? As I have said before, it is not sufficient to show that a statistically significant result was obtained. Suppose, for the sake of argument, that two of the treatments were statistically significant when compared with a no-treatment control group. That finding, as stated earlier, merely shows that chance is unlikely to account for the observed gains. But how large are the gains? One of the significant treatments may have produced only a 2% gain while the other produced a 4% gain in performance on relevant criterion variables. One treatment is twice as effective as the other. But how important is a 4% gain? Unfortunately, that is the kind of question that simply cannot be answered by statistical and scientific methods—it involves a value judgment. (This does not mean that value judgments cannot be treated scientifically; they can.) The researchers, the sponsors of the research, the users of the research, and the clients themselves may all have to decide how large a significant (real) observed gain must be before a treatment can be effective. Should an overall gain of specified score points be required, or should it be demanded that the mean score of the target group exceed a specified cutting point, or should it be required that every member of the target group obtain a score that exceeds a specified cutting point? A treatment or treatments in clinical research must be judged effective or not by well-defined and specific criterion or criteria set at the beginning rather than the end of the research. This is not an easy task; the investigator must determine how much of an effect must be achieved using a set of explicit values. It is extremely difficult sometimes to disclose the underlying real values that motivate a research study. For example, 2 successes out of 10 in child abuse may be reasonable to continue interventive services. However, such success rates may not be statistically significant. Success in social work needs to be reexamined and set at realistic levels (Howing, Wodarski, Kurtz, & Gaudin, 1993).

A solution to the myth of statistical significance is not to rely on this criterion alone when evaluating the impact of a social treatment. The treatment effect should be interpreted by how the client perceives the change and various other criteria. Thus, use of multiple criteria for evaluation of change may alleviate many of the dysfunctional aspects of the sole use of statistical significance. Multiple criteria evaluation allows for the measurement of multidimensional behavior. For example, in evaluating a treatment program for antisocial children, a number of criteria could be employed. Various inventories designed to measure antisocial behavior could be completed by children, parents, group therapists, and other significant adults, such as teachers or ministers. Additionally, the attainment of behavioral observational data enables comparisons between perceived behavioral change and actual behavior. Likewise, the subjective evaluation of the interventions by clients, practitioners, and significant others through interviews should be used to assess the practical importance of the interventive attempts. By employing multiple criteria for evaluation, the investigator increases the probability that strong aspects of each assessment procedure are included. Thus, by securing data from various sources, a more accurate evaluation of the study can take place.

Another issue in assessing positive outcome centers around different outcome sources that will be utilized for evaluation of treatment effects. At the end of treatment, the client may be very dissatisfied with the outcome, but the worker may feel that considerable and important changes have been made. How are such potential conflicts to be managed or dealt with? More often than not, these conflicts arise when the experimenter's goals, or those of the sponsors, are being served rather than the goals of the client. For example, legal assistance for the poor may be judged as an ineffective program by the client because the program disallows the client's spouse to pay for a divorce in order to permit the client to remarry someone else whom the client is currently living with. Change at certain levels and not others shows the factorial complexity of human behavior.

Obviously, the cost of the various treatments must also be weighed when deciding which ones are effective; that is, which produced the largest gain and the least cost. Rarely is the treatment that meets or exceeds the established change criteria also the least expensive in dollar costs or duration, and rarely is the treatment that produces the largest gain at the cheapest cost the treatment of choice. Oftentimes the problem of competing objectives must be faced: saving money or helping the client. In many cases, one objective can be achieved only at the expense of the other. For example, a treatment may help the client considerably but the cost of doing so would bankrupt the agency. On the other hand, the agency might survive indefinitely if treatment expenditures are not allowed to rise above a specified level, but the treatment that can be given at such costs is ineffective according to the established change criteria. This is referred to as the minimax principle—minimize losses and maximize gains. However, this is only a principle, and even if it is achievable, it may not be adequate. Five different treatments, for example, may produce statistically significant results and may vary in cost and duration. One of those treatments may produce the largest gain at the lowest unit cost over the shortest duration (a rare outcome), and it still may be judged as ineffective by any or all of the a priori criteria established for the experiment.

The above examples show that selection of the criteria to be used in assessing the outcomes of evaluative research cannot be isolated from the issues previously discussed: What should be changed, what is the properly defined and measured dependent variable(s), and what is the properly defined and measured independent variable(s)? However, the criteria against which an evaluative study is to be assessed are, more often than not, multiple and require value judgments that rarely, if ever, can be dealt with by using the tools of science. If the practice values concerning what should be changed and the values undergirding the criteria for determining which treatments are effective are not dealt with, it is unlikely that research technology will be of any significance in developing a practice science.

THE EMPIRICAL PRACTITIONER

For the empirical practitioner, practice theories are chosen from empirical data that support their use. Such an approach to understanding human behavior begins in the scientific laboratories where researchers employ experiments to test their beginning formulations about the possible causes of behavior. As experimentation progresses, empirically derived laws are developed according to the existing database. Following the systematic collection of substantial data and the replication of numerous experiments that support a law, experiments are undertaken in natural environments to test whether the principles in laboratories can be generalized (Powers & Osborne, 1976; Thomas, 1978).

Such a sequential process in theory development and testing, which characterizes applied social psychology and small-group and behavioral practice, is dramatically different, however, from the manner in which traditional practice theories that social workers employ are developed. Early theories began with global descriptions of human behavior without experimental data to support their postulates about human behavior. Adequate testing of the ability of these theories to alter human behavior has not occurred, perhaps because of their structural unsoundness, lack of internal consistency, conceptual vagueness, and procedural weakness (Hall & Lindzey, 1970; Nelson, 1981, 1984). Basic tenets and concepts of these theories have not been constructed in a logical, consistent, and testable fashion that would enable the prediction of human behavior. Moreover, appropriate behaviors that should be exhibited by the worker to facilitate client changes have not been elaborated. Neither has the duration of the intervention nor the relapse-prevention procedures necessary to ensure the success of behavioral change been specified (Fischer, 1971, 1973; Wodarski & Feldman, 1973). Although these theories do not lack descriptive richness and explanatory potency, they fail to offer highly specific and individualized treatment techniques, and their ability to reliably predict the future behavior of individuals remains to be demonstrated empirically. Predictive rather than descriptive theories give the research practitioner the necessary conceptual tools to change behavior.

The empirical practitioner in social work views practice as an experiment. Each interventive technique is offered as a tentative hypothesis awaiting verification; global statements about causes of behavior, diagnosis and/or assessment, and treatment are avoided. The concepts used to explain and predict the behavior of the client and the worker are always described in observable concrete terms so that communication is clear, open, and concise, not only between the worker and the client, but also between the worker and the other professionals who may be working concurrently with the client (Fischer & Corcoran, 1994).

The behaviors of the social worker and the client must always have observable referents; any behavior must be described in such a manner that two or more persons can observe the behavior and agree that it has occurred. This procedure is essential if appropriate treatment procedures are to be devised and effectiveness documented. Data must be secured in all therapeutic interventions so that the worker can determine what effect the treatment attempts have produced. This provides the worker with the feedback necessary to assess whether a specific technique should be continued, treatment discontinued, or a given intervention program revised. Through such an approach, evaluation becomes a central aspect of social work process and a means for practitioners to contribute to the knowledge necessary for effective practice.

COMPETENCIES OF THE EMPIRICAL PRACTITIONER

It is necessary to specify objectives for training empirical practitioners if social work is to produce personnel capable of evaluating new services to clients; planning, designing, and evaluating adequate service delivery systems; systematically delineating targets for intervention; rigorously assessing methods of change; and finally, understanding the burgeoning research base of social work and facilitating the dissemination of such knowledge.

The empirical practitioner's repertoire of intervention skills involves the systematic application of practice techniques derived from behavioral science theory and supported by empirical evidence to achieve behavior change in clients. The empirical practitioner must possess theoretical knowledge and empirical perspective regarding the nature of human behavior, the principles that influence behavioral change, and the empirical data that provide the rationale for the interventions. The worker also must be capable of translating this knowledge into concrete operations for practical use in different practice settings. In order to be an effective practitioner, therefore, the social worker must possess a solid behavioral science knowledge base and a variety of research skills. Moreover, a thorough grounding in research methodology enables the worker to evaluate therapeutic interventions, a necessary requisite of scientific practice. Because the rigorous training of social workers with scientific perspective equips them to assess and evaluate any practice procedure that has been instituted, there is continual evaluation providing corrective feedback to practitioners. For the empirical social worker, theory, practice, and evaluation are all part of one intervention process, and the arbitrary division of theory, intervention, and research, which does not facilitate therapeutic effectiveness or improve practice procedures, is eliminated. To be effective, the bachelor's-level practitioner should be the consumer of human knowledge, the master's-level practitioner should be an effective practitioner and/or manager, and the doctoral-level practitioner should be the producer of knowledge (Wodarski et al., 1995).

Knowledge Base

The central emphasis is on employing empirically supported procedures aimed at the solution of the client's difficulties. The body of knowledge that the practitioner needs to possess to be an effective change agent includes the following:

1. A thorough understanding of the scientifically derived theories of behavioral science as they relate to human behavior, personality formation, the development and maintenance of interpersonal relationships, behavior change, and practice intervention.
2. The ability to translate behavioral science knowledge into practice technology.
3. The skills necessary to assess a study in terms of its internal and external validity and the implications it has for social work practice.
4. The ability to evaluate objectively any practice procedure and outcome and formulate new practice strategies when those that had been formulated originally have proven ineffective.
5. A working knowledge of a wide variety of research designs, experimental approaches, and statistical procedures, and the ability to utilize them appropriately for the critical evaluation of one's inter-

ventive attempts, whether these interventions take place on the micro- or macrolevels of society.
6.   The knowledge of relapse-prevention procedures.

Although clients are given the knowledge and the tools with which to modify their own behavior, practitioners still take full responsibility in the helping process because their contractual obligations require that they assist the client modify those specific problems for which professional assistance originally was sought. The social workers' knowledge of the principles of human development and behavior change and their training in practice evaluation enable them to evaluate objectively the outcomes of any intervention program they have devised for a particular client. If a program has been proven ineffective in alleviating a client's distress, the social worker is ethically bound to investigate the reasons for its failure and develop other means of altering the behavior based on evidence (Wodarski, 1980).

OVERVIEW

The scientific approach to social work practice offers much promise for the social work profession. Based on empirical data and scientific findings, it makes available concrete tools for effective intervention, and, most important, builds into the intervention process a problem-solving and evaluative component needed in social work.

The chapters that follow discuss how research methodology can be incorporated into the practicing repertoires of clinical social workers. Chapter 2 covers the use of scientific and practice criteria to evaluate the relevance of behavioral science knowledge and empirical studies for social work practice. Chapter 3 reviews the use of behavioral science knowledge to create therapeutic services in terms of answering the questions of implementation of change strategy (where, by whom, why, for how long, on what level, and relapse-prevention procedures). Securing baselines and operationalizing outcome concepts to be used in evaluating practice are covered in Chapter 4. Building adequate studies through the use of appropriate designs is discussed in Chapters 5 and 6. Chapter 7 describes the statistical procedures necessary for deciding whether a treatment significantly improved clients' functioning. Complex multivariate statistics are reviewed in Chapter 8. Practical aspects of doing research are reviewed in Chapter 9. Chapter 10 explains a model for the beginning training of empirical practitioners in schools of social work. Requisites for competency-based agency practice are reviewed in Chapter 11. Chapter 12 shows how grants facilitate the evaluation of effective social work services. The use of computers and technology is described in Chapter 13. The concluding chapter emphasizes the emerging trends in the field of practice research.

REFERENCES

Alter, C., & Evans, W. (1990). *Evaluating your practice: A guide to self-assessment.* New York: Springer Publishing Co.

American Psychiatric Association. (1994). *Diagnostic and statistical manual of mental disorders* (4th ed). Washington, DC: American Psychiatric Press.

Ammerman, R. T., & Hersen, M. (1995). *Handbook of child behavior therapy.* New York: Wiley.

Appelbaum, P. S. (1993). Legal liability and managed care. *American Psychiatrist, 24,* 67–90.

Barlow, D. H., & Hersen, M. (1984). *Single-case experimental designs: Strategies for studying behavior chance* (2nd ed.). New York: Pergamon.

Bennett, L. & Westera, D. (1994). The Primacy of relationships for teens: issues and responses. *Family & Community Health, 17,* 60–69.

Bergin, A. E., & Garfield, S. L. (1994). *Handbook of psychotherapy and behavior change* (4th ed). New York: Wiley.

Bernotavicz, F. (1994). A new paradigm for competency-based training. *Journal of Continuing Social Work Education, 6*(2), 3–9.

Billingsley, F., White, S. C., & Munson, R. (1980). Procedural reliability: A rationale and an example. *Behavioral Assessment, 3,* 229–243.

Bloom, M., & Fischer, J. (1982). *Evaluating practice: Guidelines for the accountable professional.* Engelwood Cliffs, NJ: Prentice Hall.

Blythe, B. J., & Tripodi, T. (1989). *Measurement in direct practice.* Newbury Park, CA: Sage Publications.

Camasso, M. J., & Jagannathan, R. (1994). The detection of AFDC payment errors through MIS and quality-control data integration: An application in the state of New Jersey. *Administration in Social Work, 18,* 45–68.

Campbell, T. W. (1994). Psychotherapy and malpractice exposure. *American Journal of Forensic Psychology, 12,* 5–40.

Christensen, A., Johnson, S. M., Phillips, S., & Glascow, R. E. (1980). Cost effectiveness in behavioral marital therapy. *Behavior Therapy, 11,* 208–226.

Cooper, M. (1990). Treatment of a client with obsessive-compulsive disorder. *Social Work Research and Abstracts, 26*(2), 26–32.

Corcoran, K., & Fischer, J. (1987). *Measures for clinical practice: A sourcebook.* New York: Free Press.

Dean, R. G., & Reinhertz, H. (1986). Psychodynamic practice and single-system design: The odd couple. *Journal of Social Work Education, 22*(2), 71–81.

Dulmus, C. N., & Wodarski, J. S. (1996). Assessment and effective treatments of childhood psychopathology: Responsibilities and implications for practice. *Journal of Child and Adolescent Group Therapy, 6*(2), 75–99.

Erlich, J. L. (1971). The turned-on generation: New antiestablishment action roles. *Social Work, 16,* 22–27.

Feldman, R. A. (1970). Professional competence and social work values: An empirical study of Turkish social workers. *Applied Social Studies, 2,* 145–153.

Feldman, R. A. (1971). Professionals and professional values: A cross-cultural comparison. *International Review of Sociology, 1,* 1–13.

Feldman, R. A., Caplinger, T. E., & Wodarski, J. S. (1983). *The St. Louis conundrum: The effective treatment of antisocial youths.* Englewood Cliffs, NJ: Prentice Hall.

Finch, A. J., Nelson, W. M., & Ott, E. S. (1993). *Cognitive Behavioral Procedures with Children and Adolescents.* Boston: Allyn & Bacon.

Fischer, J. (1971). A framework for the analysis and comparison of clinical theories of induced change. *Social Service Review, 45,* 110–130.

Fischer, J. (Ed.). (1973). *Interpersonal helping: Emerging approaches for social work practice.* Springfield, IL: Charles C Thomas.

Fischer, J. (1978). Does anything work? *Journal of Social Service Research, 1*(3), 215–243.

Fisher, J., & Corcoran, K. (1994). *Measures for clinical practice* (2nd ed., vol. 2). New York: Free Press.

Foos, J. A., Ottens, A. J., & Hill, L. K. (1991). Managed mental health: A primer for counselors. *Journal of Counseling & Development, 69,* 332–336.

Fraser, M. W. (1994, Spring/Summer). Scholarship and research in social work: Emerging challenges. *Journal of Social Work Education, 30,* 252–266.

Gambrill, E. (1990). *Critical thinking in clinical practice.* San Francisco: Jossey-Bass.

Hall, C. S. & Lindzey, G. (1970). *Theories of personality.* New York: Wiley.

Harrison, D. F., Wodarski, J. S., & Thyer, B. A. (1992). *Cultural diversity and social work practice.* Springfield, IL: Charles C Thomas.

Hayes, D. B., & Varley, B. K. (1965). Impact of social work education on students' values. *Social Work, 10,* 40–46.

Hollingshead, A. B., & Redlich, F. C. (1958). *Social class and mental illness.* New York: Wiley.

Houle, C. O., Cyphert, F., & Boggs, D. (1987). Education for the professions. *Theory into Practice, 26,* 87–93.

Howing, P. T., Wodarski, J. S., Kurtz, D., & Gaudin, J. M. (1993). *Maltreatment and the school-aged child: Developmental outcomes and system issues.* New York: Haworth Press.

Hudson, W. H. (1982). *The clinical measurement package: A field manual.* Homewood, IL: Dorsey Press.

Hudson, W. W. (1971). An autotelic teaching experiment with ancillary casework services. *American Education Research Journal, 8,* 467–483.

Hudson, W. W., & Nurius, P. S. (1994). *Controversial issues in social work research.* Needham Heights, MA: Allyn & Bacon.

Jayarante, S., & Levy, R. (1979). *Empirical clinical practice.* New York: Columbia University Press.

Jacobs, J. Rettig, S., & Bovasso, G. (1991). Change in moral values over three decades, 1958-1988. *Youth & Society, 22,* 468–481.

Jongssma, A. E., & Peterson, L. M. (1995). *The complete psychotherapy treatment planner.* New York: Wiley.

Kazdin, A. E. (1980). *Research design in clinical psychology.* New York: Harper & Row.

Kazdin, A. E. (1981). Drawing valid inferences from case studies. *Journal of Consulting and Clinical Psychology, 49,* 183–192.

Kilty, K. M., & Meenaghan, T. M. (1995). Social work and the convergence of politics and science. *Social Work, 30,* 445–453.

Luborsky, L., Chandler, M., Auerbach, A. H., Cohen, J., & Bachrach, H. M. (1971). Factors influencing the outcome of psychotherapy: A review of quantitative research. *Psychological Bulletin, 75,* 145–185.

Lysaught, E. M., Wodarski, J. S., & Feit, M. D. (in press). Workfare programs: Issues and recommendations. In proceedings: *34th National Workshop on Welfare Research and Statistics.*

McCowan, R. J., McGregor, E., & LoTempio, S. (1984). Competency-based evaluation of social services training. *Journal of Continuing Social Work Education, 2*(31), 12–13.

Menefee, D. T., & Thompson, J. J. (1994). Identifying and comparing competencies for social work management: A practice-driven approach. *Administration in Social Work, 18*(3), 1–25.

Meyer, H. J., Borgatta, E. F., & Jones W. C. (1965). *Girls at Vocational High: An experiment in social work intervention.* New York: Russell Sage Foundation.

National Association of Social Workers. (1967). *Code of ethics.* Washington, DC: National Association of Social Workers.

Nelsen, J. C. (1981). Issues in single-subject research for nonbehaviorists. *Social Work Research and Abstracts, 17*(2), 31–37.

Nelsen, J. C. (1984). Intermediate treatment goals as variables in single-case research. *Social Work Research and Abstracts, 20,* 3–10.

Nuehring, E. M., & Pascone, A. B. (1986). Single-subject evaluation: A tool for quality assurance. *Social Work, 31,* 359–365.

Nurius, P., & Hudson, W. H. (1989). Computers and social diagnosis: The client's perspective. *Computers in Human Services, 5*(1), 21–35.

Plutchik, R. (1974). *Foundations of experimental research.* New York: Harper & Row.

Powers, R. B., & Osborne, J. G. (1976). *Fundamentals of behavior.* New York: West.

Proctor, E. (1990). Evaluating clinical practice: Issues of purpose and design. *Social Work Research and Abstracts, 26,* 32–40.

Randall, E., & Wodarski, J. S. (1989). Theoretical issues in clinical social group work. *Small Group Behavior, 20,* 475–499.

Reid, D. H., Parsons, M. B., & Green, C. W. (1989). *Staff management in human services: Behavioral research and application.* Springfield, IL: Charles C Thomas.

Reid, J. W., & Shyne, A. W. (1969). *Brief and extended casework.* New York: Columbia University Press.

Richey, C. A., Kopp, J., Tolson, E., & Ishisaka, H. (1987). Practice evaluation in diverse settings. In N. Gottlieb (Ed.), *Perspectives on director practice evaluation.* Seattle: Center for Social Welfare Research.

Rose, S. D., Cayner, J. J., & Edleson, J. L. (1977). Measuring interpersonal competence. *Social Work, 22*(2), 125–129.

Sanderson, W. C. (1995, March). Which therapies are proven effective? (Shared perspectives). *APA Monitor,* p. 4.

Stein, D. M., & Lambert, M. J. (1995). Graduate training in psychotherapy: Are therapy outcomes enhanced? *Journal of Consulting and Clinical Psychology, 63,* 182–196.

Stevenson, L. (1989). Is scientific research value-neutral. *Inquiry, 32,* 213–222.

Thomas, E. J. (1978). Research and service in single-case experimentation: Conflicts and choices. *Social Work Research and Abstracts, 14*(4), 20–31.

Thomas, E. J., Bastien, J., Stuebe, D., Bronaon, D. E., & Yaffe, J. (1987). Assessing procedural descriptiveness: Rationale and illustrative study. *Behavioral Assessment, 9,* 43—56.

Thyer, B. A. (1995). Effective psychosocial treatments for children: A selected review. *Early Child Development and Care, 106,* 137–147.

Thyer, B. A. (in press). *Effective psychosocial treatments for children: A selected review.*

Vermilyea, B. B., Barlow, D. H., & O'Brien, G. T. (1984). The importance of assessing treatment integrity: An example in the anxiety disorders. *Journal of Behavioral Assessment, 6,* 1–11.

Wakefield, J., & Kirk, S. (1996). Unscientific thinking about scientific practice: Evaluating the scientist-practitioner model. *Social Work Res, 20,* 83–95.

Wheeler, G. R. (1971). America's new street people: Implications for the human services. *Social Work, 16,* 19–24.

Winett, R. (1991). Caveats on values guiding community research and action. *Journal of Applied Behavior Analysis, 24,* 637–639.

Wodarski, J. S. (1980). Legal requisites for social work practice. *Clinical Social Work Journal, 8*(2), 90–98.

Wodarski, J. S. (1981). *Role of research in clinical practice.* Baltimore, MD: University Park Press.

Wodarski, J. S. (1985). An assessment model of practitioner skills: A prototype. *Arete, 10*(2), 1–14.

Wodarski, J. S. (1994). Should policy decisions be based predominantly on empirical evidence of effectiveness? In W. W. Hudson & P. S. Nurius (Eds.), *Controversial issues in social work research.*

Wodarski, J. S., Bricout, J., & Smokowski, P. R. (in press). Making interactive videodisc computer simulation accessible and practice relevant. *Journal of Teaching in Social Work.*

Wodarski, J. S., Feit, M. D., & Green, R. K. (1995). Graduate social work education: A review of two decades of empirical research and considerations for the future. *Social Service Review, 69,* 108–130.

Wodarski, J. S., Feit, M. D., Ramey, J. H., & Mann, A. (1995). *Social group work in the 21st century.* New York: Haworth Press.

Wodarski, J. S., & Feldman, R. (1973). The research practicum: A beginning formulation of process and educational objectives. *International Social Work, 16,* 42–48.

Wodarski, J. S., Feldman, R., & Pedi, S. (1974). Objective measurement of the independent variable: A neglected methodological aspect of community-based behavior research. *Journal of Abnormal Child Psychology, 2,* 239–244.

Wodarski, J. S., Thyer, B. A., Iodice, J. D., & Pinkston, R. (1991). Graduate social work education: A review of empirical research. *Journal of Social Service Research, 14*(314), 23–44.

Wodarski, J. S., Smokowski, P. R., & Feit, M. D. (in press). Preventive health service for adolescents: A cost-benefit analysis. *Preventive Human Services.*

Wodarski, J. S., & Wodarski, L. A. (1993). *Curriculums and practical aspects of implementation: Preventive health services for adolescents.* Lanham, MD: University Press of America.

Wodarski, L. A., & Wodarski, J. S. (1995). *Adolescent sexuality: A peer/family curriculum.* Springfield, IL: Charles C Thomas.

Yalom, I. (1995). *The theory and practice of group psychotherapy* (2nd ed.). New York: Basic Books.

CHAPTER 2

Criteria for Choosing Knowledge and Assessing Empirical Intervention

$\mathbf{T}$wo critical skills practitioners must develop to base their practice on a rational, empirical basis are the ability to evaluate research studies and the ability to translate research into practice generalizations (Fischer, 1978a, 1978b; Briar, 1990; Kirk, 1990). This chapter reviews the criteria that may aid practitioners in the assessment of behavioral science research, the use of scientific and practice criteria that can be used to determine the relevance of a study for social work practice, and the characteristics of effective treatment programs for use in comparative evaluations.

SCIENTIFIC CRITERIA FOR THE EVALUATION OF RESEARCH STUDIES

Following initial acquaintance with the research process, which can be accomplished through a basic social work research course, practitioners should begin to review research studies in their chosen areas of specialization and evaluate them according to the following criteria:

1. *Testability.* Are the basic premises of the study stated in a manner that allows them to be tested adequately? Are the concepts linked to observable events? If not, the basic premises cannot be tested. Moreover, are the key concepts logically interrelated in a consistent, clear, and explicit manner? What are the basic questions and hypotheses of the study? Are the independent variables specified? Is the question linked in a logical and consistent manner to relevant literature and concepts contained within a particular conceptual framework?

2. *Internal consistency.* How well integrated are the various procedures composing the study? All procedures must be logically consistent. Are concepts operationalized well, experimental treatments validated, samples adequately derived, and data inferences checked? Is the study constructed in such a manner that enables answering of the question?

3. *Subsumptive power.* To what extent does the study draw on the available knowledge in the literature? This is easily assessed through timeliness, relevancy, and sufficiency in number of references cited. Are questions formulated in a manner that will add to the available knowledge of social work practice?

4. *Parsimony.* Are the basic relationships between theoretical concepts stated and tested simply and clearly? Practitioners should ask themselves: Do I really know what is happening in this study?

5. *Communicability.* To what extent can the findings of the study be communicated to other professionals without distortion and vagueness? Can another practitioner read the study and derive the same conclusions and practice applications? Is there clear, concise communication of the data? Science is a cumulative social process; hence, it is essential for communications to be clear.

6. *Stimulation value.* To what extent does the study generate other research? How often is it cited in the literature? This criterion reflects the usefulness of a study for a field in incentives for other investigators to develop new insights, to generate discoveries, and to restructure their research endeavors in more profitable ways. How much stimulus value does this study have for me?

7. *Rival factors.* How easily can the basic findings of the study be accounted for by events other than the posited ones, such as history, maturation, testing, instrumentation, regression, selection, mortality, interaction of selection and maturation, interaction of testing and the experimental variable, reactive arrangements and multiple experimental variable interference (Campbell, 1967; Campbell & Stanley, 1967)? These factors are discussed in Chapter 6.

8. *Procedural clarity.* How explicit is the study regarding agreement among various assumptions, relationships, hypotheses, measurement devices, data collection procedures, data analysis, and conclusions? Generally, how well does the study hold together? How well does the study read?

CRITERIA FOR THE EVALUATION OF RESEARCH STUDIES FOR SOCIAL WORK PRACTICE

Social work practice involves helping clients increase behaviors and decrease certain others. Therefore, the following criteria are relevant in determining whether a study adds to practice knowledge.

1. Does the study lead to development of knowledge to explain and predict worker and client behaviors in interactional situations in which services are to be provided? Are client and worker variables that influence the interactional situation, such as sex, age, ethnic background, and other relevant social attributes specified?

2. Does the study lead to knowledge that explains what is involved in forming the relationship? What are the basic features of relationship formulation in eye contact, verbal behavior, or sex of each participant? Maintenance procedures must also be explained. Are these procedures specified for other practitioners?

3. What are the behaviors that are involved in the attempt to influence? How and when should these behaviors be exhibited by the worker? Are criteria clear as to when the different intervention techniques are to occur: how to proceed, at what pace, how long, and when to terminate?

4. Are treatment techniques related to outcome variables? How valid are the assumptions of the study about explaining and predicting behavior? How accurately measured is the amount of change that took place? Is treatment related to behavioral change?

5. If a study provides relevant practice principles, how useful to workers is the knowledge in terms of the accessibility of the variables involved? Can the variables be identified and manipulated? Is the cost–benefit ratio too great? Does the knowledge violate the values and ethics of the profession?

6. Are procedures for relapse prevention addressed? What procedures are specified to ensure the maintenance and generalization of changed behaviors? Have the change agents programmed the environment to maintain the change by substituting "naturally occurring" reinforcers, training relatives or other individuals in the client's environment, gradually removing or fading the contingencies, varying the conditions of training, using different schedules of reinforcement, and using delayed reinforcement and self-control procedures (Kazdin, 1975; Wodarski, 1980)? Such procedures will be employed in future sophisticated and effective social service delivery systems (Wodarski, in press)?

CHARACTERISTICS OF THE EFFICACIOUS THERAPEUTIC PROGRAM

Conceptualization and Operationalization of Treatment

Appropriate conceptualization and operationalization of treatment interventions are imperative for the development of effective programs. Workers must be able to specify which behaviors to implement for a given treatment strategy. This represents a difficult requirement for many theoretical frameworks. Usually, therapeutic services are described on a global level and are assigned a broad label, such as transactional analysis, behavior modification, or family therapy. However, such labels are valuable only so long as they specify the operations involved in implementing the services. For instance, the global label of behavior modification can be separated into the following distinct behavioral acts: directions, positive contact, praise, positive attention, holding, criticism, threats, punishment, negative attention, time-out, and application of a token economy (Rosen & Proctor, 1978; Wodarski, Feldman, & Pedi, 1974; Wodarski & Pedi, 1977). Moreover, essential attributes of the change agent that facilitate the implementation of treatment should be delineated.

Rationale for Service Provided

The rationale for offering a program should be based primarily on empirical grounds. The decision-making process should reflect that the change agents have considered what type of agency should house the service. Additional questions also should be posited: How can the program be implemented with minimal disruption? What new communication structures need to be added? What types of measurements can be used in evaluating the service? What accountability mechanisms need to be set up? What procedures can be utilized for monitoring execution of the program (Feldman & Wodarski, 1974; Reid, 1978; Wodarski, 1975; Wodarski & Feldman, 1974)?

Duration

No empirical guidelines exist on how long a service should be provided; that is, when client behavior has improved qualitatively and quantitatively, some criteria should indicate that services are no longer necessary. Such criteria should be established before the service is provided. These criteria should indicate how the program will be evaluated, should enable workers to determine whether or not a service is meeting the needs of the client, and should help reveal the particular factors involved in deciding whether a service should be terminated. The more concrete the guidelines, the less this evaluation process will be based on subjective factors.

Adequate Specification of Behaviors and Baselines

An adequate treatment program must take into account the need for reliable specification of target behaviors or those behaviors that are to be changed. For example, a treatment program to alleviate antisocial behavior might employ behavioral rating scales where the deviant behaviors are concretely specified. These could include such observable behaviors as hitting others, damaging physical property, running away, climbing and jumping out of windows, throwing objects, and making loud noises and aggressive or threatening verbal statements. A prerequisite for the adequate evaluation of any therapeutic service is securing a baseline before treatment. This enables the investigator to assess how treatment interventions compare with no treatment interventions.

Measures of Therapist and Client Behaviors

Various measures, such as checklists filled out by children and significant others (group leaders, parents, referral agencies, or grandparents) and behavioral time-sampling schedules, can be utilized to assess change in clients (Wodarski & Rittner, 1995). Likewise, behavioral rating scales can be used to assess the behaviors exhibited by a change agent. These and other measures are reviewed in Chapter 4.

The literature of the last decade has called for multicriteria measurement processes for the evaluation of therapeutic services. However, the few investigators who have used multicriterion measurement indicate that many changes secured on certain inventories do not correspond necessarily with results of other measurement processes utilized. For example, studies by Wodarski and colleagues (Wodarski & Buckholdt, 1975; Wodarski, Feldman, & Pedi, 1976a, b; Wodarski & Pedi, 1977, 1978) found little correlation between self-inventory and behavioral rating scales. In many instances, a change can occur on one of the measurements and not on another measurement. The strongest data are derived from behavioral observation scales because observers are trained for long periods of time to secure reliable and accurate data. Thus, a major question to ask of any research study is: Does it employ multicriteria measurement, behavioral observations, or self-inventories that have adequate reliability and validity?

SPECIFICATION OF CRITERIA FOR EVALUATION OF TREATMENT EFFICACY

Any therapeutic program should specify the criteria by which the service will be evaluated. This should be done before the treatment is implemented. For example, evaluation may occur through behavioral observations provided by trained observers and through the use of checklists filled out by children and other significant adults. Because of the multidimensional nature of human behavior, it seems necessary for professionals to evaluate more than a single criterion in order to develop a comprehensive and rational basis for the provision of services. Moreover, highly sophisticated treatment programs will quantify the extent of behavioral change targeted and actually achieved and the social relevance of changes that have occurred; do these programs really matter in the client's ability to function in his or her environment (Kazdin, 1977).

Treatment Monitoring

Having met all prior prerequisites, it then becomes necessary to monitor the implementation of treatment throughout so that necessary adjustments can be made over time if the quality of treatment varies. If behavioral change is obtained and the investigator can provide data to indicate that treatments were differentially implemented, the change agents can claim with confidence that their treatment has been responsible for the observed modifications in behavior. However, if such data cannot be provided when client change has occurred, many rival hypotheses can be postulated to account for the results (Wodarski & Pedi, 1977).

Reliable Measures

Reliable measures must be used in evaluating a program. Without this basic scientific requisite, evaluative efforts may be ill spent and data secured may not be assured to be consistent. The reliability requirement is often disregarded on the interpersonal research-helping process, thus allowing for the postulation of rival hypotheses to account for the findings (Wodarski & Buckholdt, 1975).

Designs

It has frequently been assumed that the only way therapeutic services can be evaluated by employing classical experimental designs—those where participants are assigned randomly to one or more experimental or control groups. However, such designs may have many deficits and may not be the most appropriate for the evaluation of services. In implementing these designs, they may be costly in money, energy, and administration (Wodarski & Buckholdt, 1975). Moreover, the criterion of random assignments of subjects is usually hard to meet in the evaluation of services provided to clients. New time-series designs, however, are emerging from behavior modification literature (see Chapter 5). The designs are easily implemented in social work; they cost less money, energy, and administrative execution. These designs provide pilot data on which to base costly experimental studies and data that enable a worker to determine if interventions have had an effect on client behaviors.

The emphasis in the evaluation of services in social work on the use of traditional experimental designs, which involves grouping clients into experimental and control groups, is diametrically opposed to a basic practice assumption, namely, that every individual is unique and needs to be considered in his or her own gestalt. The single-case study, which has been championed in recent behavior modification research, may alleviate many of the measurement problems discussed. In this approach, the client serves as his own control, and a client's change is evaluated against data provided by himself during a baseline period that precedes the application of treatment. Chapters 5 and 6 provide criteria upon which the worker can evaluate the appropriateness of the design chosen for evaluation.

Statistics

Evaluation involves several means of assessing whether significant change has taken place. Evaluation of therapeutic services entails the construction of tables and graphs of client and therapist behaviors. Usually graphs are constructed from measures of central tendencies, such as the mean, mode, or median. A common error in social work practice is to focus solely on what is to be changed in the client and to proceed only to measure that change. Sophisticated evaluation programs measure the behaviors of the client and the change agent simultaneously to enable the assessment of what effects the change agent's behavior has had on the client.

Guidelines on acceptable levels of change are being developed. They will indicate whether a program has had a positive effect in the investment of professional effort, financial resources, and significance for the client (Gottman & Leiblum, 1974; Masters, Garfinkel, & Bishop, 1978; Wodarski, Hudson, & Buckholdt, 1976). To aid in the evaluation endeavor, computer programs are available that summarize, graph, and place data in tabular form. Two critical questions are: Can I easily understand the results? How appropriate were the tables, graphs, and statistical procedures in the communication of the findings?

FOLLOW-UP

The proper assessment of any therapeutic program with clients involves follow-up, a procedure employed by surprisingly few investigators. Crucial questions answered by follow-up include whether a therapeutic program has changed behaviors in a desired direction, how long these behaviors were maintained, and to what other contexts they generalized (Wodarski, 1992–1993). Have the change agents programmed the environment to maintain the change in substituting "naturally occurring" reinforcers, training relatives or other individuals in the client's environment, gradually removing or fading the contingencies, varying the conditions of training, using different schedules of reinforcement, and using delayed reinforcement and self-control procedures (Kazdin, 1975; Wodarski, 1980)? Such procedures will be employed in future sophisticated and effective social service delivery systems. Pertinent questions remain concerning when and where a follow-up should occur, for how long it should last, and who should secure the measurement.

Empirical guidelines for these questions are yet to be developed. Usual procedures include follow-ups one and two years after service has been provided. Failure to provide an adequate follow-up period is a major deficiency of many evaluative studies executed in the social sciences (Wodarski, 1980).

SUMMARY

This chapter equips practitioners with the tools to evaluate studies and assess whether or not the knowledge is relevant to social work practice. A set of criteria are provided that enable the evaluation of treatment programs reported in the literature. As the knowledge produced by the behavioral sciences increases, such criteria will be part of a skill repertoires to aid empirical practitioners in choosing the complex knowledge needed in practice.

REFERENCES

Briar, S. (1990). Empiricism in clinical practice: Present and future. In L. Videka-Sherman & W. Reid (Eds.), *Advances in clinical social work research*. Silver Spring, MD: NASW Press.

Campbell, D. T. (1967). From description to experimentation: Interpreting trends as quasi-experiments. In C. W. Harris (Ed.), *Problems in measuring change* (pp. 112–142). Madison, WI: The University of Wisconsin Press.

Campbell, D. T., & Stanley, J. C. (1967). *Experimental and quasi-experimental designs for research*. Chicago: Rand-McNally.

Feldman, R., & Wodarski, L. S. (1974). Bureaucratic constraints and methodological adaptations in community-based research. *American Journal of Community Psychology, 2,* 211–224.

Fischer, J. (1978a). Does anything work? *Journal of Social Service Research, 1,* 215–243.

Fischer, J. (1978b). Effective casework practice: An eclectic approach. New York: McGraw-Hill.

Gottman, J. M., & Leiblum, S. R. (1974). *How to do psychotherapy and how to evaluate it*. New York: Holt, Rinehart, & Winston.

Kazdin, A. E. (1975). Behavior modification in applied settings. Homewood, IL: Dorsey.

Kazdin, A. E. (1977). *The token economy*. New York: Plenum Press.

Kirk, S. (1990). Research utilization: The substructure of belief. In L. Videka-Sherman & W. Reid (Eds.), *Advances in clinical social work research* (pp. 1–7). Silver Spring, MD: National Association of Social Workers.

Masters, S., Garfinkel, I., & Bishop, J. (1978). Cost-benefit analysis in program evaluation. *Journal of Social Service Research, 2,* 79–93.

Reid, W. J. (1978). The social agency as a research machine. *Journal of Social Service Research, 1978, 2,* 11–23.

Rittner, B., & Wodarski, J. S. (1995). Clinical instruments. Assessing and treating children and families. *Early Child Development and Care, 106,* 43–58.

Rosen, A., & Proctor, E. K. (1978). Specifying the treatment process: The basis for effectiveness research. *Journal of Social Service Research, 2,* 25–43.

Wodarski, J. S. (1975). Use of videotapes in social work. *Clinical Social Work Journal, 3,* 120–127.

Wodarski, J. S. (1980). Procedures for the maintenance and generalization of achieved behavioral change. *Journal of Sociology and Social Welfare, 7,* 298–311.

Wodarski, J. S. (1992–1993). Teaching adolescents about alcohol and driving: An empirically validated program for social workers. *Research on Social Work Practice, 4,* 28–39.

Wodarksi, J. S. (1993). Cognitive and behavioral treatment: Uses, issues, and future directions. In D. K. Granvold (Ed.), *Cognitive and behavior social work treatment.* Belmont, CA: Wadsworth Publishing Company.

Wodarski, J. S., & Buckholdt, D. (1975). Behavioral instruction in college classrooms: A review of methodological procedures. In J. M. Johnson (Ed.), *Behavior research and technology in higher education.* Springfield, IL: Charles C Thomas.

Wodarski, J. S., & Feldman, R. A. (1974). Practical aspects of field research. *Clinical Social Work Journal, 2,* 182–193.

Wodarski, J. S., Feldman, R. A., & Pedi, S. J. (1974). Objective measurement of the independent variable: A neglected methodological aspect of community-based behavioral research. *Journal of Abnormal Child Psychology, 2,* 239–244.

Wodarski, J. S., Feldman, R. A., & Pedi, S. J. (1976a). The comparison of antisocial and prosocial children on multicriterion measures at summer camp. *Journal of Abnormal Child Psychology, 50,* 256–272.

Wodarski, J. S., Feldman, R. A., & Pedi, S. J. (1976b). The comparison of prosocial and antisocial children on multicriterion measures at summer camp: A three-year study. *Social Service Review, 3,* 255–273.

Wodarski, J. S., Hudson, W., & Buckholdt, D. R. (1976). Issues in evaluative research: Implications for social work. *Journal of Sociology and Social Welfare, 4,* 81–113.

Wodarski, J. S., & Pedi, S. J. (1977). The comparison of antisocial and prosocial children on multicriterion measures at a community center: A three-year study. *Social Work, 22,* 290–296.

Wodarski, J. S., & Pedi, S. J. (1978). The empirical evaluation of the effects of different group-treatment strategies against a controlled treatment strategy on behavior exhibited by antisocial children, behavior of the therapist, and two self-ratings measuring antisocial behavior. *Journal of Clinical Psychology, 34,* 471–481.

Wodarksi, J. S., & Rittner, B. (1995). Clinical instruments—Assessing and treating children and families. *Early Child Development and Care, 106,* 43–58.

CHAPTER 3

Transforming Behavioral Science Knowledge into Practice Generalizations

The preceding chapter focused on criteria for selecting knowledge from the behavioral sciences for social work practice. This chapter illustrates how knowledge from the social sciences can be utilized to form beginning practice generalizations. Use of the criteria for choosing knowledge is elaborated in Chapter 2. These criteria must be applied in the selection of research data for answering the following essential questions on the nature of practice: worker and client characteristics, type of treatment intervention, type of context, duration, and relapse-prevention procedures.

The sheer volume of studies makes the translation of behavioral science knowledge into practice principles a difficult task (Maas, 1979). This chapter provides an example of how such translations may take place and serves as a prototype for future endeavors as illustrated by selected and classic studies.

WORKER CHARACTERISTICS

Similarity of Client and Worker

Worker variables, such as social class, race and ethnicity, religion, age, sex, and verbal skills, have been related to therapeutic outcome. One practice generalization taken from the literature is that differences between clients and workers should be minimal. The data point to a homogeneous grouping of worker and clients on various characteristics (Garfield & Bergin, 1986; Gurman & Razin, 1977). Research also indicates, however, that practice experience reduces the significance of this relationship (Durlak, 1979). Until more studies are conducted to delineate the exact parameters of these practice interactions, it is recommended that inexperienced practitioners work with clients who are similar to themselves on relevant attributes. Support for this proposition is derived also from literature on attraction, which indicates that similarity between worker and client on certain variables increases the attractiveness of the therapeutic context, thus increasing the probability that clients would remain in therapy, a necessary condition for behavioral change (Shapiro, 1974; Yutrzenka, 1995).

Professionals versus Paraprofessionals

Earlier studies that evaluated services offered by professionals as compared to those offered by paraprofessionals have found that professionals did not necessarily give better service (Durlak, 1979; Emrick, Lassen, & Edwards, 1977). These studies along with more recent ones suggest that the reason the paraprofessional does as well as, or better than the professional may revolve around the paraprofessional being closer to the client on various attributes, thus enabling the client to identify with the worker, to place more trust in the worker, and to feel less alienation to the worker (Beutler & Kendall, 1995; Stein & Lambert, 1995).

Research has shown consistently that workers who exhibit warmth, accurate empathic understanding, and genuineness lay the foundation for effective therapy. Beyond the nurture of the therapeutic alliance, however, there is research evidence that highlights the effectiveness of one intervention procedure over another (Patterson, 1986). This fact has plagued the psychotherapeutic profession for the past 50 years. It is called the "placebo" problem, which contends that therapeutic techniques do not show superior effectiveness compared with the spontaneous remission occurring without treatment (Eysneck, 1994). This places reliance squarely on the qualities of the therapist rather than upon the intervention "technologies." As Patterson (1986) concludes:

> What is identified as characteristic behavior of an effective therapist cannot be used as a technique. It is not the behaviors which lead to effective therapy, but the effective therapist who tends to behave in certain ways in implementing his or her attitudes of concern, respect, and genuineness and who attempts to understand empathically (p. 555).

This may partially explain the research finding that after graduation, only a third of the professionally trained workers possess acceptable levels of warmth and empathy (Wodarski, Pippin, & Daniels, 1988; Wodarski, Feit, & Green, 1995). The relationship between these attributes and professional education is not clear (Garfield, 1971).

Communications Regarding Expectations for Change and Competence

Research has shown that the worker who communicates positive expectations of change facilitates therapeutic outcome because the client's expectations are powerful determinants of counseling effectiveness. The client should be helped to expect benefits from the operations involved in therapeutic practice. The client expects the worker to be experienced, genuine, accepting, and to exhibit expert and trusting behaviors. Client expectation frequently is not realized because the client often sees trainees rather than experienced practitioners (Goldfried & Davison, 1994; Rosenthal, 1976; Tinsley & Harris, 1976).

The worker's ability to convey credible abilities and treatment techniques is a significant variable. Studies indicate that a worker can show credibility by being organized, by providing structure in the client's and worker's role in therapy, by suggesting appropriate topics for beginning discussions, and by engaging in proper nonverbal communication; the worker can establish trust by being attentive, by leaning toward the client, by having responsive facial expressions and appropriate head nods, and by maintaining an attentive posture (Corrigan, Dell, Lewis, & Schmidt, 1980; Schmidt & Strong, 1970; Shealy, 1995).

Positive Communications

Extensive research shows therapeutic attractiveness is increased if the worker indicates to the client that verbal statements are being received and processed accordingly (Duehn & Proctor, 1977). The worker can signal that messages have been received through appropriate verbal statements and through nonverbal means, such as proper eye contact. These operations signify to the client that the worker has been listening, a rewarding process that should increase the probability of continuance in the relationship (Seabury, 1980; Horvath & Greenberg, 1989). These component variables are conceptualized as "verbal congruence." The foregoing would suggest again the efficacy of homogeneous grouping of clients and workers, especially concerning language ability, age, and social class. Should a given treatment modality favor heterogeneous grouping, this postulate, at the minimum, would point to the desirability of pretherapy tutoring or coaching for selected clients and workers, or both.

"Content relevance" refers to the extent to which the content of an interactive response is perceived by participants as relevant and admissible to their own definition of the interactional situation. It can be postulated that expected content in an interaction is likely to be highly reinforcing to all concerned and, consequently, the situation itself will be evaluated positively by the participants. This postulate has been supported by much social work literature concerning the compatibility of role expectations held by clients and therapists (Aronson & Overall, 1966; Mechanic, 1961; Oxley, 1966; Rosen & Lieberman, 1972; Rosenfeld, 1974; Sapolsky, 1970; Thomas, Polansky, & Kounin, 1967).

Practice Recommendations

Many researchers have studied worker variables and their relationship to therapeutic outcome. Many variables are mentioned in repeated studies and are substantiated. The studies are conclusive and should be applied to the training of workers. Thus, empirical statements can be made regarding worker variables and their influence on practice. On the basis of the available consistent data, I recommend the following points.

1. Client and worker should be grouped according to similar attributes to facilitate the attractiveness of the worker. Extreme differences should be avoided. The matching for beginning practitioners is necessary to ensure the good fit between the inexperienced worker and the appropriate client.

2. All workers should possess acceptable levels of empathy, warmth, and genuineness.

3. Practitioners should possess communication skills in verbal congruence: they should communicate clearly and consistently (Seabury, 1980); and they should possess nonverbal skills including appropriate facial expressions and correct body posture.

4. Practitioners should exhibit credibility and show acceptance of the client by being personable. They should be able to provide support and structure and to create the expectation that the therapeutic process will produce desired changes.

Table 3.1 summarizes the common factors of the effective worker based on replicated studies (Shealy, 1995).

CLIENT VARIABLES

It has been suggested that client and therapist be matched by age, sex, race and ethnicity, values, attitudes, and socioeconomic status (Harrison, Wodarski, & Thyer, 1992). The following sections provide an overview of selected research studies aimed at determining the effects of these variables on intervention outcome.

Table 3.1   Common Factors of Worker Efficacy

Congruency

Acceptance/unconditional positive regard

Empathy

Understanding/communicate understanding

Encourage autonomy; responsibility

Ability to relate/develop alliance

Well-adjusted

Interest in helping

Provide treatment as intended

Exploration of client

Expectation for improvement

Emotionally stimulating/challenging/not afraid of confrontation

Firm, direct; can set limits

Work hard for client/persistent

Nurturing

Age

There are not many studies on the variable of age and its effect on the client–counselor relationship. Pilot work in this area by Lasky and Salomone (1977) suggested, however, that there is a relationship between age similarity and therapist status with regard to interpersonal attraction in the psychotherapy dyad. Three groups of male psychiatric inpatients were formed according to the following age classifications: those under 30, those between 30 and 45, and those over 45. Each client was given an audiovisual presentation in which four slides were used to depict age and status of therapists. Each patient chose which therapist he would rather be with in therapy. Those under 30 were more attracted to younger, low-status therapists than older, low-status therapists, or any therapist in the high-status condition. Those between 30 and 45 were not attracted to the younger therapist any more than to the older therapist or status. Those 45 and older were attracted to the high-status therapist, regardless of therapist age. Results indicate that age is more significant for younger patients and status is more significant for older patients.

An interesting study of older psychiatrists showed that they saw a higher proportion of older patients, they advocated more comprehensive treatment for older patients, and they found older patients to be more interesting and gratifying. However, psychiatrists who had an outpatient orientation were less interested in the elderly than were the institutional psychiatrists (Garetz, 1975).

According to Harrison and Dziegielewski (1992), growing old in general continues to be viewed negatively in our society not only by those who are younger but also by many health-care and mental-health-care professionals. These authors view the elderly as victims of societal attitudes that devalue old age.

> Many individuals (young and old) will do almost anything to avoid or deny old age. Such prejudices are the result of both rational and irrational fears. Rational fears of declines in health, income, losses of loved ones, and social status can be exaggerated by our negative stereotypes of the elderly and the irrational fears of changes in appearance, loss of masculinity, femininity, and perceived mental incompetence. The elderly continue to be oppressed by myths and misinformation and by real obstacles imposed by various biological, psychological, social and economic factors. (p. 209)

Harrison and Dziegielewski (1992) suggest that social workers, at a minimum, need to examine their own attitudes toward aging and the older people. They should not, directly or indirectly, discriminate based on age; this attitude results in ineffective and unethical practice. Practitioners need to recognize the aged as a valuable resource in society, and to provide services and advocacy that will maximize the older person's degree of life satisfaction and well-being.

Sex

Recent evidence suggests a bias toward female clients by male workers. Male workers tend to keep female clients in therapy longer, and to diagnose proportionately more pathology among women who showed deviation from traditional sex roles (Dailey, 1980; Safer, 1975). Before working with females, male workers need to examine and to evaluate their attitudes and stereotypes regarding females that may influence the therapeutic relationship, and the duration, goals, and outcome of therapy (Cowan, 1976).

Research has consistently indicated that mental health practitioners generally hold different mental health standards for men and women, and see traditional male behavior as more healthy than traditional female behavior (Aslin, 1977; Broverman, Broverman, Clarkson, Rosencrantz, & Vogel, 1970; Hampton, Lambert, & Snell, 1986; Kabacoff, Marwit, & Orlofsky, 1985; Kravetz & Jones, 1981). Undoubtedly, every currently identified psychological construct has been examined for its differential distribution between the sexes. Many of these examinations have revealed statistically significant differences, some on quite consistent bases (e.g., locus of control). In examining the meta-analytic reviews (i.e., additional reviews of studies) of this research, however, Deaux (1984) noted ". . . 5% may approximate the upper boundary for the explanatory power of subject-sex main effects in specific social and cognitive behaviors" (p. 108). In other words, 95% of the variance was not explained by sex differences. As is typically the case, males and females display much more similarity than dissimilarity when considering the distribution of individual attributes.

Research has also demonstrated sex differences in the patterns of psychopathology (Leland, 1982; Myers et al., 1984; Robins et al., 1984; Schaffer, 1981; Travis, 1988; Widom, 1984). Specifically, women's rates of depression and anxiety (including panic disorders, phobias, and obsessive-compulsive disorders) are found to be two to three times higher than those of men, while rates of alcoholism, drug dependence, and personality disorders of men are five to six times higher than those of women. Women attempt suicide at a rate 2.3 times higher that of men, but men kill themselves 2.3 times more than women (Steffensmeier, 1984). Women are also more likely than men to suffer from eating disorders, including obesity (Attie & Brooks-Gunn, 1987).

Race and Ethnicity

Racial influences on treatment have received renewed attention in the literature, with more than a fourfold increase in studies over the past 10 years. These studies, however, have been mainly descriptive. Problems of small sample size and unreliable measures are prevalent. Many articles are simply reviews of the literature based on theoretical knowledge with data derived only from nonsystematic recordings of the author's clinical experiences.

The data suggest that racial differences seem to have a negative effect upon psychotherapy. Black clients in treatment with white therapists view therapy as less beneficial than white clients do; black clients are less self-disclosing than white clients are, regardless of social class. Racial similarity led to greater self-disclosure and higher ratings of rapport with the therapist (Garfield, 1971).

Greene (1975), however, reports results differing from his colleague's propositions. He investigated the interactive effects of counselor race and level of functioning (provision of appropriate levels of empathy, unconditional positive regard, and warmth) with client race as measured by client self-exploration during the initial interviews. Results showed that racial biases and prejudices within the counseling interview do not significantly affect levels of client self-exploration. If the counselor offers high levels of facilitative conditions, the client experiences greater self-exploration regardless of the counselor and client racial combination.

In a review of the effects of race in clinical interactions, Siegel (1974) sums up his and other findings rather succinctly. He suggests that competence is more important than race to blacks who were asked for hypothetical preferences for professional service-givers. There is evidence that, for optimal results, black patients should be paired with black staff for the intake interview. However, despite much clinical speculation about the possibility that white clinicians are less effective than black clinicians with black patients, there is little evidence to sug-

gest that this is the case. In fact, there is no research comparing therapeutic outcome using black versus white therapists with black patients
(Kadushin, 1972).

In summary, the data are inconclusive regarding the influence of race
on therapeutic outcome. Some studies suggest race is not a factor; others suggest that racial differences create problems in the interview and
with the relationship, but that racial congruence is not an essential element. Data suggest that worker competence and knowledge of the
client's problems are more important than race. More research needs
to be done on the possible effects of clinician race on the black, as well
as the white, patient. Such research should focus especially on therapeutic process and outcome.

Cole and Pilisuk (1976) conducted research to investigate the differences in the provision of mental health services to various ethnic groups.
Services to clients in an outpatient mental health clinic were examined
for possible differences in care according to ethnicity. The sample consisted of 32 whites, 50 African Americans, 9 Mexican Americans, 2
Asian Americans, and 1 Mid-Easterner. A major finding was the clear
and consistent differences in treatment given to nonwhite men versus
white men. White men were more likely to be diagnosed as neurotic or
less seriously ill, to be given more individual and long-term psychotherapy, to be treated without medication, to be accountable in terminating
treatment themselves, and to be described as bright and verbal. Nonwhite men were more likely to be described as hostile and paranoid
and to be attributed other negative characteristics. Nonwhite clients
usually received more serious diagnoses of mental pathology, received
more supportive or mechanical therapies than intensive psychotherapy,
received a shorter duration of treatment, and received not the same
range of services extended to white clients. African American men in
particular had difficulty obtaining the most needed and most preferred services.

Gardener, Kirby, Pablow, and Castillo (1975) described several cases
in which patients showed psychotic symptoms in interviews held in
their native language but not in interviews held in the secondary language. They suggested that the effort of communicating in another
language produces unconscious vigilance over the emotions.

Acosta and Sheehan (1976) studied preferences and attitudes toward
therapists among Mexican Americans and Anglo-Americans. Ninety-
four Mexican Americans and 93 Anglo-American community college
students listened to one of two matched audiotapes. The therapist was

identified as being one of four categories: Anglo-American professional, Anglo-American nonprofessional, Mexican American professional, or Mexican American nonprofessional. Both ethnic groups attributed more skill, understanding, trustworthiness, and attractiveness to Anglo-American professionals and to the Mexican American nonprofessionals than to the Mexican American professional. Mexican American students showed a more favorable attitude toward the usefulness of therapy than did Anglo-Americans.

This pilot literature suggests that ethnic variables play a major role in therapeutic outcomes. More studies need to be conducted in order to examine the specific impact.

Socioeconomic Status

Numerous articles and studies describe the impact of socioeconomic status on the therapeutic relationship. From the available data, it can be concluded that generally the social class of the client can determine the specific therapy intervention, duration of treatment, and use of available resources in a community. Ultimately, the socioeconomic status of the client affects the outcome of therapy; this relationship has been evident in the literature since the late 1950s.

Siassi and Messer's (1976) article "Psychotherapy with Patients from Lower Socioeconomic Groups" discusses how patients of low socioeconomic status (SES) are infrequently considered for individual psychodynamic therapy. They mention that the problems of their population are perceived as primarily economic. Recommendations, therefore, are geared toward social and political action aimed at securing jobs, housing, and political power for their clients. Workers also believe that clients of lower SES are less verbal and unable to postpone gratification necessary for long-range gains. Poor people do not feel that personal problems can be solved by discussion. Instead, lower SES individuals want medication, direction, and advice offered by action-oriented, judgmental, and persuasive therapists. Lengthy individual therapy is not used with these patients because they would terminate therapy, thereby wasting the therapist's time. The authors state further that therapists' attitudes toward the lower SES patients tend to be negative and to be fraught with stereotypes and biases. It is not surprising that studies in the past have found that lower-class patients usually have a more negative attitude than middle-class patients toward therapy.

Fischer and Miller (1973) discussed in their paper, "The Effect of Client Race and Social Class on Clinical Judgments," how lower-class patients are looked at differently than middle-class patients; therefore, workers believe the lower-class patients should be treated differently than middle-class patients. Moreover, they believe lower SES patients are looked down on by their therapists. These researchers believe social deficits affect clinical judgments. Therapists' treatment for lower SES patients is different from higher SES patients. The authors conclude that race and social class do make a difference in therapists' attitudes, and that these attitudes affect treatment.

In his article titled "Social Work Techniques with the Poor," Pierson (1970) suggests that therapists be flexible in their treatment techniques when working with lower SES clients. Pierson believes that newer techniques can be discovered to help these people and challenges social workers to break from habitual ideas long enough to consider them. Feelings, he believes, are very private to the lower-class client. Instead of verbalizing feelings, lower-class people express their feelings through actions. Additionally, the poor have their own standards of conduct for social relationships, and it is harder for them to develop relationships. Pierson maintains that treatment must take these characteristics into account if it is to be effective.

A consistent theme throughout these writings is that when working with lower class clients, the worker requires flexibility and the ability to change the therapy to meet their needs. Most articles confirm the belief that the typical practice interventions based on psychoanalytic and ego psychology do not work with lower class clients (Briar, 1968).

A contributing consequence or ongoing pattern of prejudice and discrimination is the disproportionate number of African Americans living in impoverished conditions. Many of the African American clients with whom social workers practice experience multiple problems often associated with poverty, including addictions, unemployment, mental illness, and poor physical health. Myths about the disproportionate participation of African Americans in the welfare system, including welfare dependency and defrauding the system, are widespread in our society.

Asian Americans also suffer from societal myths. This ethnic group is often viewed as the "model minority," implying a smooth assimilation into the dominant culture. This stereotype tends to minimize the problems faced by members of this group. Many Asian Americans arrive in this country as refugees in need of numerous social services (e.g., Southeast Asians).

Hispanics are the fastest-growing ethnic group in our country. An increase in this group is a result of high birth and immigration rates.

Although many Hispanics are bilingual, others speak only Spanish. Additional social workers will be needed who are culturally sensitive and who can communicate with the increasing number of Hispanic clients.

Historically, Native Americans have suffered injustices by our government. Today, conditions on many reservations include high rates of substance abuse, poverty, and substandard housing. Yet as a profession, social work has paid little attention to the concerns of this client group.

Members of all of these racial and ethnic groups experience subtle and overt forms of prejudice and discrimination. Social workers who are involved with clients from diverse racial backgrounds need to be sensitive to the unique issues facing these individuals. Practitioners also need to be aware of ways social forces contribute to the problems experienced by African American, Asian American, Hispanic, and Native American clients (Kropf & Isaac, 1992).

YAVIS versus Non-YAVIS

Psychiatrists, psychologists, and social workers prefer clients to be similar to themselves (Luborsky, Chandler, Auerbach, Cohen, & Bachrach, 1971) and that their clients be young, attractive, verbal, intelligent, and successful (YAVIS) (Henry, Sims, & Spray, 1971, 1973; Schofield, 1964). As a result of these biases, the bulk of therapy has been geared toward YAVIS clientele.

In 1964, William Schofield published a book containing the results of an interesting survey of psychiatrists, psychologists, and social workers who were involved in private practice. Participants were asked to describe their case load with variables descriptive of their "typical" clients and also the characteristics of their "ideal" clients. On the average, more than half of each sample of therapists expressed a distinct preference with respect to the ideal client's age, marital status, and educational and occupational levels. Sex preference, however, was not as clear. Less than one-third of the psychiatrists and one-fourth of the psychologists expressed a preferred sex, but those who did selected females predominantly. In each therapist group, 60% to 70% selected the 20–40-year age range as ideal. None of the groups considered widowed or divorced clients as ideal; psychiatrists and social workers had a marked preference for married clients. Nearly half of the psychologists preferred single clients, however. At least three-fourths of each group preferred clients whose educational level included no less than high school and no more than an undergraduate college degree. Three-fourths of the psychologists and psychiatrists preferred clients from professional and managerial occupations. Social workers had no clear occupational preference, although one-fifth of the social workers in the study liked skilled laborers. When comparing the compatibility of "typical" versus "ideal" clients, social workers' caseloads deviated most from their "ideal." Psychiatrists followed, with psychologists experiencing the best match.

Schofield was intrigued by the characteristics of the nonpreferred client who was equally rejected by all three groups of therapists. This group included those who were extremely young (under age 15), older (over 50), were widowed or divorced, had limited education (less than high school) or too much education (postgraduate training), or were employed in service occupations, agriculture, fishery, or forestry, or were semiskilled, or unskilled laborers. He suggested that therapists tend systematically to select clients who present the YAVIS syndrome.

This concept of the YAVIS client has stimulated research on the importance of client variables in the outcome of psychotherapy. Luborsky et al. (1971), in their article titled "Factors Influencing the Outcome of Psychotherapy," state that when a patient and psychotherapist agree to meet, what follows is unpredictable because only a few of the factors influencing the fate of the individual patient in psychotherapy can be discerned. Even after a thorough initial evaluation and several early sessions, they report that some patients improve and some do not. This same study revealed those patient factors that were most often significantly associated with improvement. These include

1. adequate psychological health or personality functioning,
2. absence of schizoid trends,
3. high motivation,
4. high intelligence,
5. low anxiety, and
6. educational and social assets.

The characteristics Luborsky found to be associated with improvement typify and reinforce the YAVIS client profile. It is possible that regular therapy is geared toward YAVIS clientele who are mostly middle-class, and that for those who do not meet these criteria, therapy remains problematic or possibly ineffective. Is Schofield correct in hypothesizing that optimal conditions for successful psychotherapeutic outcome prevail when client and therapist belong to the same social class (more similar values between client and worker) and thus enhance communication?

Jennings and Davis conducted a study (1977) to determine if a structured learning approach for non-YAVIS clients significantly enhanced therapy. The experimental design consisted of 40 lower socioeconomic children and adolescents in a residential hospital. The subjects were randomly assigned to two groups—one experimental and one control—and were matched on subject characteristics of age and sex. The control condition was a time-and-attention placebo procedure designed to appear credible to the subjects.

Data from the study support the hypothesis that a relationship exists between therapeutic success and client preparation for initial therapeutic encounters. According to Jennings and Davis, behaviors such as attentiveness, expression of feelings, and answering questions are attractive to the worker in the therapeutic relationship and are judged to elicit positive consequences. Moreover, knowing what to expect in therapeutic situations and exhibiting behaviors that increase attraction between themselves and the worker are conducive to positive therapeutic outcome. This indicates that client in-therapy behavior, and, hence, attractiveness to the worker, should no longer be left to chance; data support the approach of actively teaching lower socioeconomic clients those behaviors that workers expect during therapy. Inasmuch as psychotherapy, in which both client and therapist participate, is considered a viable tool for behavior change, it seems inefficient to train only one member of the dyad. Data continue to support these early propositions (Wodarski, 1995).

Practice Recommendations

The following practice generalizations can be derived from results of studies cited in this section:

1. The worker should be trained to recognize the effects of client characteristics, such as age, race, ethnicity, and socioeconomic status, on therapeutic outcome. For example, the finding that male workers tend to prolong work with female clients and see more pathology in them, the more they deviate from traditional roles needs to be elucidated for white male middle-class workers.

2. If client and worker are significantly different on relevant variables, there should be pretraining for the client on what is to be expected.

TREATMENT COMPONENTS

Length of Therapy

A substantial number of evaluative studies have been produced in the last three decades that have had a profound impact on traditional therapeutic practice. Major changes have come about as a result of these studies, one in particular being the length of therapy (Fischer, 1978). In the past, therapy was considered to be a long and involved process. Current trends, however, indicate that the optimal number of visits is between 8 and 16. Current research indicates that brief directive interventions have a consistent outcome advantage in the treatment of a multitude of disorders (Giles, Prial, & Neims, 1993). Reid (1978), Stuart (1974), and others provide a rationale for the development of a short-term model of therapy for social work practice. Moreover, managed health care will support only payment for empirically based treatments that are of a short duration, the rationale being that more evidence supports short-term care except for a few significant chemical problems (Johnstone et al., 1995; Nickelson, 1995).

Behavior Acquisition

A second focus involves helping clients learn new behaviors to deal with their specific situations. This emphasis is the opposite of changing attitudes or motivation first and positing that behavioral change would follow. Research evidence is accumulating to indicate that if clients are taught behaviors that enable them to influence their external and internal environments (self-management procedures, appropriate assertive behavior, and problem solving), their social functioning increases.

Development of behaviors is believed to occur optimally in structured therapeutic contexts; that is, where intervention procedures follow a sequential pattern to develop and maintain socially relevant behaviors. Such patterns usually consist of mutually agreed upon contracts that include goals, methods, termination criteria, and the rights and responsibilities of client and worker. Two examples of historically empirically based treatment technologies are task-centered casework and behavioral approaches.

Task-Centered Casework

Task-centered casework is a theoretical system of short-term intervention that emerged in 1972 with the publication of *Task-Centered Casework* by Reid and Epstein. Reid and Epstein (1977) published a follow-up book, *Task-Centered Practice,* and in another book, *The Task-Centered System,* Reid (1978) nicely elucidated the relevant aspects of the task-centered approach. Task-centered casework is unique in development since researchers and practitioners have worked together to specify its constructs and have tested various aspects of the total intervention package.

In 1975, Reid took a major step in placing task-centered casework on firm empirical grounds by operationalizing the variable of task performance in a five-step plan called task implementation sequence (TIS). TIS is a progressive treatment sequence that includes "enhancing commitment, planning task implementation, analyzing obstacles, modeling, rehearsal, guided practice, and summarizing," with the goal of eliciting specific client behaviors. The introduction of "operational tasks" is part of a beginning effort to specify the model's constructs and thereby place the paradigm on firmer scientific ground by specifying the unit of attention—the task—in more measurable terms. Three keys to the success of task-centered casework may be the structural elements of the model, its emphasis on short-term service, and the specification of goals to be achieved by the client in concrete steps.

Behavioral Approaches

Along with the development of the task-centered approach, corresponding and enhancing treatment technologies have been developed. These consist of behavioral approaches to the solution of interpersonal problems. Numerous data-based behavioral technologies are available for workers to use in helping clients acquire necessary behaviors to operate in their environments. Every year more data support the successful history of behavior modification practice with children classified as hyperactive, autistic, delinquent, and retarded, and adults classified as antisocial, retarded neurotic, and psychotic (Davison & Neale, 1994; Glass and Arnkoff, 1992; Goldfried, Greenberg, & Marmar, 1990; Thyer, 1995).

The following is a categorization of the areas of possible application of behavioral technology in social work practice. Each application has substantial empirical support. A further elaboration of theory, research, and illustrations of the application of the techniques is available in *Behavioral Social Work* (Wodarski & Bagarozzi, 1979).

Children

1. *Foster care* helps natural and foster parents acquire appropriate parenting skills and develop behavior-management programs. Helping parents to use contingency contracts, stimulus control, and time-out procedures to facilitate their children's development of social skills needed for effective adult functioning.

2. *Schools* help decrease absenteeism; increasing appropriate academic behavior, such as reading comprehension, vocabulary development, and computational skills; increasing interpersonal skills, such as the ability to share and cooperate with other children and adults; and decreasing disruptive behaviors.

3. *Juvenile courts* help decrease deviant behavior and increase prosocial behavior by contingency contracting, programming significant adults to provide reinforcement for prosocial behavior, and developing programs for training children in those behavioral skills that will allow them to experience satisfaction and gain desired reinforcements through socially acceptable means.

4. *Community centers* help children develop appropriate social skills, such as working together, participating in decision making, making plans, discussing, and completing plans successfully.

5. *Outpatient clinics* help clients reduce anxiety, eliminate disturbing behavioral problems, define goals of career and lifestyle, increase self-esteem, gain employment, solve problems (both concrete and interpersonal), develop satisfying lifestyles, and learn skills necessary for successful adult functioning in society.

Adults

1. *Family service* helps develop marital interactional skills for effective problem-solving and goal-setting behaviors, development of better parenting behaviors, and development of clearer communication structures to facilitate interaction among family members.

2. *Community mental health centers* help individuals reduce anxieties through relaxation techniques. Teaching self-control to enable clients to alter certain problem-causing behaviors. Offering assertiveness training as one means of having personal needs met. Helping in the acquisition of behaviors to facilitate interaction with family, friends, and coworkers.

3. *Psychiatric hospitals* use token economies to help clients acquire necessary prosocial behaviors for their effective reintegration into society. Structuring clients' environments through provision of reinforcement by significant others for the maintenance of appropriate social behaviors, such as self-care, employment, and social interactional skills. Analogous emphasis indicated for working with the retarded in institutions.

4. *Public welfare* helps clients achieve self-sufficiency; learn effective child management and financial management procedures; and develop social behaviors, skills, and competencies needed to gain employment.

5. *Corrections* use token economies to increase prosocial behaviors, learn new job skills, and develop self-control and problem-solving strategies that are not antisocial.

Implementation of Change Strategy: Level of Intervention

Social work has been characterized historically as a profession that emphasizes a one-to-one relationship with clients to achieve behavioral change (Glenn & Kunnes, 1973; Levine & Perkins, 1987; Ryan, 1971; Wodarski, 1995). The profession has seldom addressed itself adequately to the appropriateness of the various service-delivery mechanisms for certain types of clients, however. Few empirical studies have delineated the parameters or criteria for determining whether one-to-one or group-level treatment is best for achieving behavioral change in a given situation.

Individual Treatment versus Group Treatment

Even though recent years have witnessed a growing emphasis on group treatment for clients as a result of various conceptualizations that place a heavy emphasis on the roles that clients' peers and significant others play, relatively few clients are treated in this manner as compared with those treated in casework. Yet, there are a number of obvious deficiencies in placement of clients in casework services. The casework relationship is unlike most situations faced in daily interaction. In contrast, the provision of services in groups offers the following benefits: The group interactional situation more frequently typifies many kinds of daily interactions. Services facilitating the development of behaviors that enable people to interact in groups are likely to better prepare them for participation in larger society, that is, to help them learn social skills necessary to secure reinforcement (Feldman & Wodarski, 1975). For example, training in relaxation, systematic desensitization, assertiveness, and parenting skills can all occur in one-to-one contexts. From a social learning theory perspective, however, it is posited that if a behavior is learned in a group context, it is likely to come under the control of a greater number of discriminative stimuli, therefore, greater generalization of the behavior can occur for a broader variety of interactional contexts. There are additional substantiated rationales for working with individuals in groups. Groups provide a context where new behaviors can be tested in a realistic atmosphere. Clients can get immediate peer feedback regarding their problem-solving behaviors. They are provided with role models to facilitate the acquisition of requisite social behavior. Groups provide a more valid locus for accurate diagnosis and a more potent means for changing client behavior (Meyer & Smith, 1977; Rose, 1977).

These theoretical rationales indicate that treating clients in groups should facilitate the acquisition of socially relevant behavior. Criteria need to be developed concerning who can benefit from group treatment, however. Such knowledge will only be forthcoming when adequately designed research projects are executed in which clients are assigned randomly to individual and group treatment to control for confounding factors, such as type of behavior, age, sex, income level, and academic abilities.

In instances where an individual does not possess the necessary social behaviors to engage in a group, a one-to-one treatment relationship may provide the best treatment. For example, many antisocial children would be lost quickly in a group simply because they do not have the essential social behaviors for interaction. Likewise, with hyperactive children, it may be necessary to work on an individual basis until their dysfunctional behaviors are controlled enough to allow them to participate in a group context. As soon as they develop the necessary social skills, however, therapeutic changes are likely to be further facilitated if they can be placed in a group (Jacobs & Spradlin, 1974).

Macrolevel Interventions

If, following an assessment, a change agent decides that a client is exhibiting appropriate behaviors for his social context but that a treatment organization or institution is not providing adequate reinforcers for appropriate behaviors, or that it is punishing appropriate behavior, the change agent must then decide to engage in organizational or institutional change. This may mean changing a social policy, changing bureaucratic means of dealing with people, or other strategies. To alter an organization, the worker will have to study its reinforcement contingencies and assess whether or not he or she has the power to change these structures so that the client can be helped.

In social work practice, the primary focus has been on changing the individual. Practitioners must restructure their thinking. "Inappropriate" behavior exhibited by a client must be examined according to who defined it as inappropriate and where requisite interventions should take place. Future research should provide various means of delineating how human behavior can be changed by interventions on different levels, thus providing the parameters for micro- and macrolevel interventions. The obvious question that will face social workers is how to coordinate these multilevel interventions (Goldfried & Davison, 1994).

Generalization and Maintenance
of Behavioral Change

Interventions at the macrolevel are increasingly more critical, since follow-up data collected 5 years later on antisocial children who participated in a year-long behavior modification program, which produced extremely impressive behavioral changes in the children, indicate that virtually none of the positive changes were maintained (McCombs, Filipczak, Rusilko, Koustenis, & Wodarski, 1977; McCombs, Filipczak, Friedman, & Wodarski, 1978). Possibly, maintenance could be improved when change is also directed at macrolevels.

Considerable study is needed to delineate those variables that facilitate the generalization and maintenance of behavior change. These may include substituting "naturally occurring" reinforcers, training relatives or other individuals in the client's environment, gradually removing or fading the contingencies, varying the conditions of training, using different schedules of reinforcement, and using delayed reinforcement and self-control procedures (Kazdin, 1975; Wodarski, 1993). Such procedures will be employed in future sophisticated and effective social service delivery systems.

Home visits, which were once the focus of practice, may also be employed in the future. Positive features of home visits include providing the opportunity to assess family interactions more adequately, increasing in the probability of involving significant others in the treatment process, providing the opportunity to delineate attitudinal differences and their effect on therapy, increasing the worker's influence potential, and so on (Behrens & Ackerman, 1956; Chappell & Daniels, 1970; Freeman, 1967; Hollis, 1972; Mickle, 1963; Moynihan, 1974; Richmond, 1917).

Practice Recommendations

On the basis of the available data, the following generalizations may be made about treatment components:

1. Human services should be time limited.
2. Services should involve substantially structured roles for worker and client.
3. Techniques that have an accumulated database should be utilized.
4. Appropriate intervention strategies should be used: individual, group, or societal.
5. Behaviors acquired in clients as a result of therapy must be maintained once therapy is concluded. Therefore, appropriate maintenance procedures must be considered.

TREATMENT CONTEXT

Interpersonal helpers usually provide therapeutic services in environments different from where the problematic behavior occurs. If new behaviors are acquired in these situations, the different contexts create artificial barriers for their generalization and maintenance. This section reviews literature on the effects of architectural and physical factors on treatment interventions, a topic seldom addressed but nevertheless one that pilot data suggest is relevant. Professionals now accept that context and environment influence one's behavior, and thus will influence a client's response to treatment interventions. The concept that the atmosphere of a particular setting can facilitate or impede communication is central to all modes of interpersonal helping.

A number of studies have been executed that attempt to define relationships between the particulars of treatment settings and the quality of treatment interventions. Yet, little is known about how the physical environment affects therapeutic and social interactions, and, understandably, there are no generally accepted principles of what social/therapeutic conditions are most beneficial in the treatment of a specific mental illness. A number of researchers attempting to learn more in this area have limited their investigations to patients in mental hospitals or nursing homes, or have used analogous clinical situations, usually involving freshmen psychology students. One seriously questions whether the latter studies will generalize to any other group of people or even to a real treatment interaction. Inadequate experimental design in other studies deters drawing useful conclusions from their results. Nonetheless, a few practice principles from the available data can be made.

Seating Arrangements

Sommer (1959, 1961, 1962) studied the seating arrangements tending to promote the most conversation by residents of a Saskatchewan mental hospital. The studies, though essentially observational in nature, are widely quoted. It was found that people conversed more when sitting across from each other than when sitting side by side, except when the distance across exceeds the limits of comfortable conversation. Women preferred to sit closer than men. People in chairs arranged around square tables had much more verbal interaction than those seated in rows. Thus, Sommer concluded that people sitting corner-to-corner interact more than those side-by-side or face-to-face.

McClannahan (1973a, 1973b) noted another aspect of seating patterns that influences verbal interaction. Seating arranged near busy front entrances seemed to result in more conversations than the common hospital situation where seating is provided in quiet, peripheral areas. Holahan (1972) supports McClannahan and Sommer, saying that seating patterns exert a powerful influence over the amount and quality of social interaction among hospital patients.

Osmond (1957) coined the terms "sociofugal" and "sociopetal" to characterize different types of space/furniture arrangements. He defines sociofugal as semifixed feature space that tends to keep people apart and inhibit interaction. Sociopetal space encourages interaction, such as close and angular seating arrangements. Griffin, Mauritzen, and Kasmer (1969) noted that hospital staff, in their quest for order and neatness, may tend to put seats in rows, by that producing sociofugal arrangements that discourage conversation and interaction.

All of the above are important factors to keep in mind if one accepts the premise that increased social interaction promotes better mental health in patients. A more sociopetal arrangement may encourage members to remain in group therapy, the result of which might be improved mental health. Likewise, nursing home personnel can use information from studies showing that extended periods of inactivity and isolation can decrease verbal and self-care skills and thus hasten the need for total nursing care in the older people (McClannahan & Risley, 1975). Manipulation of seating arrangements, in this case, is one factor that can discourage helpless "old" behavior.

Conversational Distance

Several studies have been done on optimal conversational distance, and a few have focused on ideal therapist–client distance. Sommer

(1962) claimed the limit for comfortable conversation is a nose-to-nose distance of 5½ feet. Hall (1966) broke down that distance into what he calls *intimate* distance, about 18 inches; *personal* distance, 18 inches to 4 feet; social distance at 4½ feet; and *public* distance at greater than 12 feet. Hall (1959, 1960) noted that cultural background influences these standards. He said, for example, that for Arabs, the normal conversation distance is where one can smell the breath of the other person. Holahan's (1972) observational data seem to go along with Hall's, indicating that there are differences in the quality, personal nature, trust, and intimacy of conversations held at different distances and from different seating arrangements.

Sommer (1962) pointed out that in large rooms, like hospitals, comfortable conversational distance is about 3 ft. In smaller rooms, however, such as in private houses, even as far as 8 feet is a comfortable distance. In a study using diverse client groups with college students as controls, Kelly (1972) found that a client-therapist interaction distance of 39 in communicated a more positive attitude from the therapist to the client than did distances of 55 or 80 in. Dinges and Oetting (1972) found that distances of 30 in and 88 in, in hypothetical clinical interactions involving college students, provoked more anxiety in clients than did intermediate distances. Unfortunately, no data exist that relates the distance variable to treatment outcome.

Hampe (1967) stressed the necessity of respecting clients' wishes concerning client–therapist distance. He refers especially to adolescent girls who, he claims, fear penetration, invasion, submission, and fusion with the therapist if he threatens the distance between them.

In addition to client-therapist distance preferences, clients have feelings about the space around them. According to Haase and Dimattea (1970), clients prefer spatial arrangements that are protected. McClannahan (1973a, 1973b) added that people prefer to sit with their backs to walls and other tangible barriers, rather than in open spaces.

Room Size

Another dimension of treatment context that has been considered is room size. In one of the few studies attempting to relate contextual factors directly to some kind of treatment outcome, Haase and Dimattea (1970) compared room size, client-therapist distance, and furniture arrangements to degree of success in meeting a treatment goal. They employed an operant conditioning paradigm, using verbal reinforcement to increase positive client self-referent statements. The authors concluded that room size most significantly affected the conditioning process. The smaller room (7.67 m², or about 9 ft x 9 ft) seemed to inhibit the conditioning. The apparently more facilitative room was the larger one, measuring 13.39 m² (or about 12 ft x 12 ft). Unfortunately, replication or comparative studies to substantiate their findings are not available.

Furniture

The presence or absence of desks in therapy situations has been the subject of a number of studies. Haase and Dimattea (1970) found furniture arrangement effects to be of little significance although clients tended to prefer having a desk intervene between themselves and the therapist. In a less rigorous study, Pricer (1971) separated the sexes and found that women preferred a desk between themselves and the therapist, who in every case was a male. Male clients preferred no desk. In 1953, White, a cardiologist, wrote that 55% of his patients were at ease when conferring without a desk in his office, while only 11% were at ease with a desk interposed. He drew these conclusions from his observations of patients' posture while seated in his office. Widgery and Stackpole (1972) studied the effect of desks on perceived interviewer credibility, which may or may not relate to social worker credibility. They concluded that highly anxious subjects, who in this case were students, perceived credibility to be higher without a desk, while less anxious subjects perceived credibility higher with a desk. The authors reasoned that the desk may act as a symbol of the interviewer's high status, thus aggravating an anxious student's anxiety. For low-anxiety students, they thought that the desk could be an "energizer" of interviewer credibility. Relationship of this variable to treatment outcomes has not been investigated. Again, in the absence of empirical data, these conclusions must be received as speculation only.

Interior Design

Pricer (1971) and Mintz (1956) were interested in the effects of a decorated room versus a bare room on a clinical interaction. Pricer concluded that a decorated setting reflected a less positive counselor relationship than a drab setting. He speculated that the decorated room might have stimulated some stereotype in the clients (college students) that inhibited relationship formation. The study was not controlled for a number of compounding variables. In reference to the effect on workers, Mintz found that two examiners working in "ugly" rooms had reactions of fatigue, headache, discomfort, and irritability, whereas the examiner in the "beautiful" room felt pleasure, enjoyment, importance, energy, and the desire to continue his activity.

Griffin et al. (1969) cautioned that a room's attractiveness has no simple effect on moods of psychiatric patients. Price and Moos (1975) pointed out another connection between room decor and effects on mental illness: They stated that schizophrenics in an overdecorated, overstimulating environment will tend to increase their bizarre symptoms.

In an unusually well-constructed hospital study, Holahan and Saegert (1973) compared patient mood and behavior in a newly decorated and brightly painted ward to that in an unchanged control ward in the same hospital. They found that patients demonstrated more positive attitudes in the new ward and that patients socialized more in the redecorated and equipped ward, with the most pronounced differences occurring in the dining room and corridors.

One other physical factor should be mentioned in reference to the treatment process. Spivack (1967) described the auditory and visual distortions caused by the elongated tunnels and polished corridors prevalent in many psychiatric hospitals. His concern was that the auditory reverberations and accentuation tend to produce anxiety and frustration in the mentally ill.

Availability of Equipment and Materials

Another aspect of physical setting that influences the treatment process is the availability of equipment and materials in the setting. Children's social behavior is influenced by the nature of available play materials (Quilitch & Risley, 1973). "Social" toys, such as playing cards, seesaws, and wagons, led to increased social play, whereas amusements like gyroscopes and crayons did not. Similarly, the social behavior of nursing home residents and mental hospital patients has been found to be influenced by the quality and availability of materials (McClannahan & Risley, 1975). If increased social interaction is a criteria for therapeutic progress, it does seem, as Holahan and Saegert say, that the setting and availability of materials and equipment can inhibit or facilitate such progress.

Atmosphere

In the last decade, instruments have been developed to assess systematically social environmental characteristics of treatment contexts, particularly in mental hospitals. The instruments consist of scales designed to measure the dimensions of environmental contexts. One such scale is the Community-Oriented Program Environment Scale (COPES). This scale is designed to measure 10 dimensions of the treatment environment of psychiatric programs. These include staff and patient involvement, support, spontaneity, autonomy, practical orientation, personal problem orientation, anger and aggression, order and organization, program clarity, and staff control. The patients' and staff's perception of the extent of these dimensions in their program is measured. COPES has been found to be a useful instrument in the identification of factors that relate to favorable and unfavorable treatment outcomes, and to act as a feedback mechanism to facilitate social change and systems design (Bromet, Moos, & Bliss, 1976).

The Moos (1974) Standardized Ward Atmosphere Scale (WAS) was developed and employed by Moos (1972) in his extensive examination of 15 Veterans Administration hospitals. He and his colleagues attempted to discover the correlations between ward climate, as perceived by patients and staff, and treatment outcome, as defined by dropout rates, high turnover rates, and length-of-time-out-of-hospital rates. He found that certain items rated similarly by patients and staff on the WAS correlated significantly with those certain outcomes:

1. Wards with high dropout rates were perceived as low in personal involvement and feelings of support on the part of either patients or staff and low in organization and clarity.
2. Wards with higher rapid-release rates were perceived as relatively well organized and clear with moderately high staff control, but with little emphasis on open, spontaneous expression of feelings and little sense of support.
3. Wards most successful in helping patients remain out of the hospital were perceived as emphasizing patient autonomy and independence, high in organization and clarity, and encouraging open expression of feelings, such as anger.

Practice Recommendations

The following conclusions may be drawn from the literature on treatment context:

1. Seating arrangements that facilitate interaction should be encouraged.
2. Correct distance should be employed in interviews to facilitate verbal interactions.
3. Room size should be appropriate to the goals of therapy.
4. Appropriate furniture, such as a desk and a couch, should be employed to facilitate the therapeutic endeavors.
5. Atmosphere of therapeutic context should be assessed periodically to ensure personal involvement, support, independence, organization, autonomy, and expressions of feelings.

SUMMARY

This chapter illustrates how research studies can be used to answer six complex questions by social work practice. The future will witness more elaborate applications that reflect the factorial complexity of social work practice.

REFERENCES

Acosta, F., & Sheehan, J. G. (1976). Preferences toward Mexican American and Anglo-American psychotherapists. *Journal of Consulting and Clinical Psychology, 44,* 272–279.

Aronson, H., & Overall, B. (1966). Treatment expectations of patients in two social classes. *Social Work, 11,* 35–41.

Aslin, A. (1977). Feminist and community mental health center psychotherapists' expectations of mental health for women. *Sex Roles, 3,* 537–544.

Attie, I., & Brooks-Gunn, J. (1987). Weight concerns as chronic stressors in women. In R. C. Barnett, L. Biener, & G. K. Baruch (Eds.), *Gender and stress.* New York: Free Press.

Behrens, M., & Ackerman, N. (1956). The home visit as an aid in family diagnosis and therapy. *Social Casework, 37,* 11–19.

Beutler, L. E., & Kendall, P. C. (1995). Introduction to the special section: The case for training in the provision of psychological therapy. *Journal of Consulting and Clinical Psychology, 63,* 179–181.

Briar, S. (1968). The casework predicament. *Social Work, 13,* 5–11.

Bromet, E., Moos, R. H., & Bliss, F. (1976). The social climate of alcoholism treatment programs. *Archives of General Psychiatry, 33,* 910–916.

Broverman, I. K., Broverman, D. M., Clarkson, F. E., Rosencrantz, P. S., & Vogel,

S. R. (1970). Sex role stereotypes and clinical judgments of mental health. *Journal of Consulting and Clinical Psychology, 34,* 1–7.

Chappell, J., & Daniels, R. S. (1970). Homevisiting in a black urban ghetto. *American Journal of Psychiatry, 126,* 1455–1460.

Cole, J., & Pilisuk, M. (1976). Differences in the provision of mental health services by race. *American Journal of Orthopsychiatry, 46,* 510–525.

Corrigan, J. O., Dell, D. M., Lewis, K. N., & Schmidt, L. E. (1980). Counseling as a social influence process: A review. *Journal of Counseling Psychology, 27,* 395–441.

Cowan, G. (1976). Therapist judgments of clients' sex–role problems. *Psychology of Women Quarterly, 1,* 115–124.

Dailey, D. M. (1980). Are social workers sexists? A replication. *Social Work, 25,* 46–50.

Davison, G. C., & Neale, J. M. (1994). *Abnormal psychology* (6th ed.). New York: Wiley.

Deaux, K. (1984). From individual differences to social categories: Analysis of a decade's research on gender. *American Psychologist, 39,* 105–116.

Dinges, N., & Oetting, E. (1972). Interaction distance anxiety in the counseling. *Journal of Counseling Psychology, 19,* 146–149.

Duehn, W. D., & Proctor, E. K. (1977). Initial clinical interaction and premature discontinuance in treatment. *American Journal of Orthopsychiatry, 47,* 284–290.

Durlak, J. A. (1979). Comparative effectiveness of paraprofessional and professional helpers. *Psychological Bulletin, 86,* 80–92.

Emrick, C. D., Lassen, C. L., & Edwards, M. T. (1977). Nonprofessional peers as therapeutic agents. In A. S. Gurman & A. M. Razin (Eds.), *Effective psychotherapy.* New York: Pergamon Press.

Eysneck, H. J. (1994). The outcome problem in psychotherapy: What have we learned? *Behavior Research and Therapy, 32,* 477–495.

Feldman, R. A., & Wodarski, J. S. (1975). *Contemporary approaches to group treatment.* San Francisco: Jossey-Bass.

Fischer, J. (1978). *Effective casework practice.* New York: McGraw Hill.

Fischer, J., & Miller, H. (1973). The effects of client race and social class on clinical judgments. *Clinical Social Work Journal, 1,* 100–109.

Freeman, R. D. (1967) The home visit in child psychiatry: Its usefulness in diagnosis and training. *Journal of the American Academy of Child Psychiatry, 6,* 276–229.

Gardener, R. C., Kirby, D. M., Pablow, R. Y., & Castillo, E. S. (1975). Ethnic stereotypes: Role of language. *Journal of Social Psychology, 96,* 3–9.

Garetz, F. (1975). The psychiatrists's involvement with aged patients. *American Journal of Psychiatry, 132,* 63–65.

Garfield, S. L. (1971). Research on client variables in psychotherapy. In A. Bextin & S. Garfield (Eds.), *Handbook of psychotherapy and behavioral change: An empirical analysis.* New York: Wiley.

Garfield, S. L., & Bergin, A. E. (Eds.). (1986). *Handbook of psychotherapy and behavior change* (3rd ed.). New York: Wiley.

Giles, T. R., Prial, E. M., & Niems, D. M. (1993). Evaluating psychotherapies: A comparison of effectiveness. Special series: Evaluation in treatment methods in psychiatry. *International Journal of Mental Health, 22,* 43–65.

Glass, C. R., & Arnkoff, D. B. (1992). Behavior therapy. In D. K. Freedheim (Ed.), *History of psychotherapy: A century of change* (pp. 587–628). Washington, DC: American Psychological Association.

Glenn, M., & Kunnes, R. (1973). *Repression or revolution.* New York: Harper Colophon Books.

Goldfried, M. R., Davison, G. C. (1994). *Clinical behavior therapy.* New York: Wiley.

Goldfried, M. R., Greenberg, L. S., & Marmar, C. (1990). Individual psychotherapy: Process and outcome. *Annual Review of Psychology, 41,* 659–688.

Greene, J. (1975). Interactive effects of counselor race and level of functioning with client race and advantagement as measured by client self-exploration during the initial interview. *Dissertations Abstracts International, 35*(8-A), 451–459.

Griffin, W., Mauritzen, J., & Kasmer, J. (1969). The psychological aspects of the architectural environment: A review. *American Journal of Psychiatry, 125,* 1057–1061.

Gurman, A. S., & Razin, A. M. (Eds.). (1977). *Effective psychotherapy.* New York: Plenum.

Haase, R., & Dimattea, D. (1970). Counselor, administrator, and client preference for sitting arrangement. *Journal of Counseling Psychology, 17,* 319–325.

Hall, E. T. (1959). *The silent language.* New York: Doubleday.

Hall, E. T. (1960). The language of space. *Landscape, 10,* 41–45.

Hall, E. T. (1966). *The hidden dimension.* New York: Doubleday.

Hamblin, R. L., Buckholdt, D., Ferritor, D., Kozioff, M., & Blackwell, L. (1971). *Humanization process.* New York: Wiley.

Hampe, W. (1967). Territory defense and fear of the therapist. *Voices, 3,* 47–52.

Hampton, B., Lambert, F. B., & Snell, W. R. (1986). Therapists' judgments of mentally healthy beliefs for women and men. *Journal of Rational–Emotive Therapy, 4,* 169–179.

Harrison, D. F., & Dziegielewski, S. F. (1992). Social work practice with the aged. In D. F. Harrison, J. S. Wodarski, & B. A. Thyer, (Eds.), *Cultural diversity and social work practice* (pp. 181–213). Springfield, IL: Charles C Thomas.

Harrison, D. F., Wodarski, J. S., & Thyer, B. A. (1992). *Cultural diversity and social work practice.* Springfield, IL: Charles C Thomas.

Henry, W. E., Sims, J. H., & Spray, S. L. (1971). *The fifth procession: Becoming a psychotherapist.* San Francisco: Jossey-Bass.

Henry, W. E., Sims, J. H., & Spray, S. L. (1973). *Public and private lives of psychotherapists.* San Francisco: Jossey-Bass.

Holahan, C. (1972). Seating patterns and patient behavior in the day-room. *Journal of Abnormal Psychology, 80,* 115–124.

Holahan, C., & Saegert, S. (1973). Behavioral and attitudinal effects of large scale variation in the physical environment of psychiatric wards. *Journal of Abnormal Psychology, 82,* 454–462.

Hollis, F. (1972). *Casework: A psychosocial therapy.* New York: Random House.

Horvath, A. O., & Greenberg, L. S. (1989). Development and validation of the working alliance inventory. *Journal of Counseling Psychology, 36,* 223–233.

Jacobs, A., & Spradlin, W. W. (1974). *The group as agent of change: Treatment, prevention, personal growth in the family, the school, the mental hospital, and the community.* New York: Behavioral Publications.

Jennings, L. R., & Davis, S. C. (1977). Attraction-enhancing client behaviors: A structures-learning approach for non-YAVIS. *Journal of Consulting and Clinical Psychology, 45,* 135–144.

Johnstone, B., Frank, R. G., Belar, C., Berk, S., Bieliauskas, L. A., Bigler, E. D., Caplan, B., Elliott, T. R., Glueckauf, R. L., Kaplan, R. M., Kreutzer, J. S., Mateer, C. A., Patterson, D., Puente, A. E., Richards, J. S., Rosenthal, M., Sherer, M., Shewchuck, R., Siegel, L. J., & Sweet, J. J. (1995). Psychology in health care: Future directions. *Professional Psychology: Research and Practice, 26,* 341–365.

Kabacoff, R. I., Marwit, S. J. & Orlofsky, J. L. (1985). Correlates of sex-role stereotyping among mental health professionals. *Professional Psychology: Research and Practice, 16,* 98–105.

Kadushin, A. (1972). *The social work interview.* New York: Columbia University Press.

Kazdin, A. E. (1975). *Behavior modification in applied settings.* Homewood, IL: Dorsey Press.

Kelly, R. D. (1972). Communicational significance of the therapist's proxemic cues. *Journal of Consulting and Clinical Psychology, 39,* 345.

Kravetz, D., & Jones, L. E. (1981). Androgyny as a standard of mental health. *American Journal of Orthopsychiatry, 51,* 502–509.

Kropf, N. P., & Isaac, A. R. (1992). Cultural diversity and social work practice: An overview. In D. F. Harrison, J. S. Wodarski, & B. A. Thyer (Eds.), *Cultural diversity and social work practice* (pp. 3–12). Springfield, IL: Charles C Thomas.

Lasky, R. G., & Salomone, P. R. (1977). Attraction to psychotherapy: Influences on therapist status and therapist-patient age similarity. *Journal of Clinical Psychology, 33,* 511–516.

Leland, J. (1982). Gender, drinking, and alcohol abuse. In I. Al-Issa (Ed.), *Gender and psychopathology.* New York: Academic.

Levine, M., & Perkins, D. V. (1987). *Principles of community psychology: perspectives and applications.* New York: Oxford University Press.

Luborsky, L., Chandler, M., Auerbach, A., Cohen, J., & Bachrach, H. (1971). Factors influencing the outcome of psychotherapy: A review of quantitative research. *Psychological Bulletin, 75,* 145–185.

Maas, H. S. (1979). Assessing family and child welfare practice. *Social Work, 24,* 365–372.

McClannahan, L. (1973a). The therapeutic and prosthetic living environments for nursing home residents. *The Gerontologist, 13,* 424–429.

McClannahan, L. (1973b). Recreation programs for nursing home residents: The importance of patient characteristics and environmental arrangements. *Therapeutic Recreation Journal, 7,* 26–31.

McClannahan, L., & Risley, T. R. (1975). Design of living environments for nursing home residents: Increasing participation in recreation activities. *Journal of Applied Behavior Analysis, 8,* 261–268.

McCombs, D., Filipczak, J., Rusilko, S., Koustenis, G., & Wodarski, J. S. (1977, December). *Follow-up on behavioral development with disruptive juveniles in public schools.* Paper presented at the 11th annual meeting of the Association for the Advancement of Behavior Therapy, Atlanta, GA.

McCombs, D., Filipczak, J., Friedman, R., & Wodarski, J. S. (1978). Long-term follow-up on behavior modification with high-risk adolescents. *Criminal Justice, 5,* 21–34.

Mechanic, D. (1961). Role expectations and communications in the therapist-patient relationship. *Journal of Health and Human Behavior, 2,* 190–198.

Meyer, R. B., & Smith, S. S. (1977). A crisis in group therapy. *American Psychologist, 32,* 638–643.

Mickle, J. (1963). Psychiatric home visits. *Archives of General Psychiatry, 9,* 379–383.

Mintz, N. B. (1956). Effects of esthetics surroundings. II. Prolonged and repeated experience in a "beautiful" and an "ugly" room. *Journal of Psychology, 41,* 459–466.

Moos, R. H. (1972). Size, staffing, and psychiatric ward treatment environment. *Archives of General Psychiatry, 26,* 414–418.

Moos, R. H. (1974). *Ward atmosphere scale manual.* Palo Alto, CA: Consulting Psychologist Press.

Moynihan, S. K. (1974). Home visits for family treatment. *Social Casework, 55,* 612–617.

Osmond, H. (1957). Function as a basis of psychiatric ward design. *Mental Hospitals* (Architectural Supplement), *8*(4), 23–29.

Oxley, G. B. (1966). The caseworker's perceptions and client motivation. *Social Casework, 47,* 432–438.

Patterson, C. H. (1986). *Theories of counseling and psychotherapy.* New York: Harper & Row.

Pierson, A. (1970). Social work techniques with the poor. *Social Casework, 51,* 481–485.

Price, R., & Moos, R. (1975). Toward a taxonomy of inpatient treatment environments. *Journal of Abnormal Psychology, 84,* 181–188.

Pricer, R. D. (1971). The effect of contextual variables on client perception of the initial counseling session. (Doctoral dissertation, University of Mississippi, 1971.) *Dissertation Abstracts International, 32,* 5B, 303.

Quilitch, H., & Risley, T. (1973). Effects of play material on social play. *Journal of Applied Behavior Analysis, 6,* 573–578.

Reid, W. J. (1975). A test of a task-centered approach. *Social Work, 20,* 3–9.

Reid, W. J. (1978). *The task-centered system.* New York: Columbia University Press.

Reid, W. J., & Epstein, L. (1972). *Task-centered casework.* New York: Columbia University Press.

Reid, W. J., & Epstein, L. (Eds.). (1977). *Task-centered practice.* New York: Columbia University Press.

Richmond, M. E. (1917). *Social diagnosis.* New York: Russell Sage Foundation.

Robins, L. N., Helzer, J. E., Weissman, M. M., Orvaschel, H., Gruenberg, E., Burke, J. D., & Regier, D. A. (1984). Lifetime prevalence of specific psychiatric disorders in three sites. *Archives of General Psychiatry, 41,* 949–958.

Rose, S. D. (1977). *Group therapy: A behavioral approach.* Englewood Cliffs, NJ: Prentice Hall.

Rosen, A., & Lieberman, P. (1972). The experimental evaluation of interview performance of social workers. *Social Science Review, 46,* 395–412.

Rosenfeld, J. M. (1974). Strangeness between helper and client: A possible explanation of nonuse of available professional help. *Social Service Review, 38,* 17–25.

Rosenthal, R. (1976). *Experimenter effects in behavioral research.* New York: Irvington.

Ryan, W. (1971). *Blaming the victim.* New York: Vintage Books.

Safer, J. (1975). Effects of sex of patient and therapist on length of therapy. *International Mental Health Research Newsletter, 17,* 12–13.

Sapolsky, A. (1970). Relationship between patient-doctor compatibility, mutual perception, and outcome of treatment. *Journal of Abnormal Psychology, 17,* 115–118.

Schaffer, K. F. (1981). *Sex roles and human behavior.* Cambridge, MA: Winthrop.

Schmidt, L. D., & Strong, S. R. (1970). Expertness and influence in counseling. *Journal of Counseling Psychology, 17,* 81–87.

Schofield, W. (1964). *Psychotherapy: The purchase of friendships.* Englewood Cliffs, NJ: Prentice Hall.

Seabury, B. A. (1980). Communication problems in social work practice. *Social Work, 25,* 40–43.

Shapiro, R. J. (1974). Therapist attitudes and premature termination in family and individual therapy. *Journal of Nervous and Mental Disease, 159,* 101–107.

Shealy, C. G. (1995). From *Boys Town* to *Oliver Twist:* Separating fact from fiction in welfare reform and out-of-home placement of children and youth. *American Psychologist, 50,* 565–580.

Siassi, I., & Messer, S. B. (1976). Psychotherapy with patients from lower socioeconomic groups. *American Journal Psychotherapy, 30,* 29–40.

Siegel, J. M. (1974). A brief review of the effects of race in clinical interactions. *American Journal of Orthopsychiatry, 44,* 555–561.

Sommer, R. (1959). Studies in personal space. *Sociometry, 22,* 247–260.

Sommer, R. (1961). Leadership and group geography. *Sociometry, 24,* 99–110.

Sommer, R. (1962). Distance for comfortable conversation. *Sociometry, 25,* 111–116.

Spivack, M. D. (1967). Sensory distortions in tunnels and corridors. *Hospital and Community Psychiatry, 18,* 24–30.

Stein, D. M., & Lambert, M. J. (1995). Graduate training in psychotherapy: Are therapy outcomes enhanced? *Journal of Consulting and Clinical Psychology, 63,* 182–196.

Stuart, R. B. (1974). *Trick or treatment.* Champaign, IL: Research Press.

Thomas, E. J., Polansky, N. A., & Kounin, J. (1967). The expected behavior of a potentially helpful person. In E. J. Thomas (Ed.), *Behavioral science for social workers.* New York: Free Press.

Thyer, B. A. (1995). Effective psychosocial treatments for children: A selected review. *Early Child Development and Care, 106,* 137–147.

Tinsley, H. E., & Harris, D. J. (1976). Client expectations for counseling. *Journal of Counseling Psychology, 23,* 173–177.

Travis, C. B. (1988). *Women and health psychology: Mental health issues.* Hillsdale, NJ: Lawrence Erlbaum Associates.

White, H. (1953). The patient sits down. *Psychosomatic Medicine, 15,* 256–257.

Widgery, R., & Stackpole, C. (1972). Desk position, interviewee anxiety, and interviewer credibility. *Journal of Counseling Psychology, 19,* 173–177.

Widom, C. S. (Ed.). (1984). *Sex roles and psychopathology.* New York: Plenum.

Wodarski, J. S., & Bagarozzi, D. (1979). *Behavioral social work.* New York: Human Sciences.

Wodarski, J. S., Feit, M. D., & Green, R. K. (1995, March). Graduate social work education: A review of two decades of empirical research and considerations for the future. *Social Service Review, 69,* 108–130.

Wodarski, J. S., Pippin, J. A., & Daniels, M. (1988). Effects of graduate social work education on personality, values, and interpersonal skills. *Journal of Social Work Education, 24,* 266–277.

Wodarski, J. S. (1995). Cognitive and behavioral treatment: Uses, issues, and future directions. In D. K. Granvold (Ed.), *Cognitive and behavior social work treatment.* Belmont, CA: Wadsworth Publishing Company.

Wodarski, J. S. (in press-a). The empirical and legal bases of intervention provided by social workers. In B. Thyer (Ed.), *Controversial issues in social work practice.*

Wodarski, J. S. (in press-b). Uses, issues, and future directions. In D. K. Granvold (Ed.), *Cognitive and behavior social work treatment.* Belmont, CA: Wadsworth Publishing Company.

Yutrzenka, B. A. (1995). Making a case for training in ethnic and cultural diversity in increasing treatment efficacy. *Journal of Consulting and Clinical Psychology, 63,* 197–206.

CHAPTER 4

Choice-of-Outcome Measures and Means for Assessment

Previous chapters have addressed how research can be used to help the practitioner provide better services to clients. The chapters to follow cover basic research methodology, designs, and statistics needed for practitioners to begin to use research in their empirical practice.

CLIENT OUTCOMES

Examples are drawn from the classic study of antisocial children, *The St. Louis Conundrum: Effective Treatment of Antisocial Youth* (Feldman, Caplinger, & Wodarski, 1983). The first requisite for the use of research in practice is the delineation of the possible outcomes for the client with whom the clinician is working. The specification of outcomes is critical because they determine what data will be measured and what criteria will be needed on which an empirical intervention is evaluated (Graycar, 1979; Lindsey, Wodarski, & Streever, 1986; Rossi & McLaughlin, 1979; Wodarski, Hudson, & Buckholdt, 1976). Discussions about the appropriateness of various outcomes with other professionals and an adequate review of the available literature help make possible the elucidation of outcomes. From the discussion in Chapter 1, it is evident that professional and client values, theoretical orientation, agency goals, socio-political factors, available resources, and practice context affect the chosen outcomes.

Once outcomes are decided, the basic question is how to measure the specified outcomes. Basically, there are four means of collecting the necessary data: behavioral observations, self-inventories, interviews, and unobtrusive measures. (Unobtrusive measures have not yet been used in interventive research, thus their use will not be reviewed.) Two critical questions must be asked of the methodology chosen: (1) Can the necessary data be secured reliably? and (2) How costly, in terms of time, money, energy, and administration, is it to secure the data that is needed?

This chapter discusses the types of measurements that can be used and reviews the pros and cons of each measurement device. Examples of each measurement process from the author's research endeavors are provided in the appendices to this chapter.

MEASURES OF WORKER AND CLIENT BEHAVIOR

Various measures, such as interview schedules, checklists filled out by clients and significant others (group leaders, parents, referral agencies, and grandparents), and behavioral observations (time-sampling schedules), can be utilized to assess change in clients. Likewise, behavioral rating scales can be used to assess the behaviors exhibited by a change agent. There are excellent publications available describing the various measures that can be used (Bloom & Fischer, 1982; Corcoran & Fischer, 1987; Johnson, 1976; Reynolds, 1975; Robinson & Shaven, 1973). They specify particular items measured, appropriate clientele, types of data provided, reliability, and procedures involved in administration. The type of measurement process selected depends on the behaviors chosen for modification; availability of technical equipment; cost of securing various types of data; context of measurement; and frequency, duration, and intensity of the target behavior. (For an excellent discussion of measurement techniques, see Bijou, Peterson, Harris, Allen, & Johnston, 1969; Thomas, 1974.) The focus in this chapter is on the general features that should be considered essential to any measure chosen for practice evaluation.

SINGLE versus MULTIPLE
CRITERION MEASUREMENT

The literature indicates that most empirical evaluations use single measures of behavioral change (Conger & Cole, 1975; Empey & Erickson, 1972; Empey & Lubeck, 1971; Sarri & Selo, 1974; Segal, 1972; Shireman, Mann, Larsen, & Young, 1972; Wodarski & Bagarozzi, 1979). Single measures are used even though they do not isolate all of the possible dimensions of change in human behavior and do not capitalize on all the new methodological advancements in the social sciences that tap various levels of measurement. Multicriterion measurements on the other hand tap all possible avenues of change; for this reason, many researchers over the past decade have encouraged using them to evaluate therapeutic services to maximize the possibility of capturing change in the various dimensions of human behavior. For example, in multicriterion measurements, self-assessment, assessment by others, and behavioral observations should be used concurrently for a more comprehensive evaluation of client change (Luborsky, Mintz, & Christoph, 1979).

Unfortunately, the few investigators who have used multicriterion measurements indicate that many changes secured on certain inventories do not correspond to other measurement processes used in a study; that is, correlation between measures is low. For example, Wodarski, Feldman, and Pedi (1975a, 1975b; 1976a, 1976b), Wodarski and Pedi (1977), Caplinger, Feldman, and Wodarski (1979), and Feldman et al. (1983) found little correlation between inventories completed by children and significant others and behavioral rating scales. In many instances, a change occurs on one of the measurements and not on another measurement.

Consumer assessment of benefits should be considered in the evaluation of outcomes even though such an assessment is a difficult methodological issue to resolve when outcomes differ from the criteria established by researchers (Wodarski, 1981). In our case, consumer evaluation of two community-based treatment programs for antisocial children was very favorable. Similar responses are reflected in data obtained from parents evaluating both community-based treatment programs for predelinquent and delinquent children (Wodarski, 1981). In both cases, however, consumer assessments were not compatible with other data, indicating that the consumer may use criteria for evaluation different from those of researchers.

CHOICE OF MEASURES

The decision concerning which of the various types of measures should be used rests on the aims of the empirical evaluation. Both self-inventories and behavioral scales have certain advantages and obvious drawbacks. Self-inventories have low reliability but they cost less; also, they may measure behavioral tendencies that behavioral scales do not measure. Behavioral scales provide highly reliable data but are more costly and, depending on the breadth of observation, may provide data that are limited to a specific social context. The strongest data are derived from behavioral observation scales simply because observers are trained for long periods of time to secure reliable and accurate data. If an appropriate behavioral observation scale is not available, then investigators can develop their own scale by observing clients systematically and then defining the relevant behaviors in such a way that two people can consistently agree that these behaviors have occurred.

If questionnaires and interview schedules are to be used, they should involve minimal interpretation and should have been adequately pretested. Interview schedules are excellent devices in beginning empirical evaluation when research questions are not clearly formulated. Interview schedules should be constructed with the rationale for collection clearly resolved by the empirical researchers. Questions for interviews and questionnaires should be stated in a manner that facilitates the ease of responses and requires little interpretation by the clients. Both measures should be brief to prevent fatigue for the investigator and client. As the evaluation becomes more clearly specified, the researcher should give the measures a clearer structure to increase reliability.

ADEQUATE SPECIFICATION OF BEHAVIOR AND BASELINES

An adequate treatment program must take account of the need for reliable specification of target behaviors that are to be changed by whatever means used to measure them—questionnaires, interviews, or behavioral observations. For example, a treatment program to alleviate antisocial behavior might employ behavioral rating scales in which the deviant behaviors are highly specified. These could include such observable behaviors as hitting others, damaging physical property, running away, throwing objects, climbing and jumping out of windows, and making loud noises and aggressive or threatening verbal statements.

Whatever the mode of measurement, the investigator must secure a baseline before implementing treatment for the adequate evaluation of any therapeutic service. This baseline enables the investigator to assess how the treatment interventions compare with no treatment interventions. The best type of baseline measure is secured by trained behavioral observers. Usually these observers have been trained to establish reliability on behavioral categories through an extensive training procedure. If observations on behaviors cannot be secured by trained observers, there are other less desirable data sources, such as baselines taken by the client himself or by significant others in his environment. These baselines, even though less reliable, many times are necessary because of various organizational or other environmental constraints. Some of these constraints may be lack of money for trained observers or lack of investigation of behaviors that occur at times when they are not readily observable by others. When the practitioner uses baseline data not secured by a trained observer, the data should be obtained from two or more independent sources in order to check consistency.

The following are considerations that should be addressed before a practitioner decides on the exact procedure for securing a baseline. First, context should be chosen in which the individual's target behavior occurs at a high frequency. If the behavior occurs in more than one context, baselines may be secured for each context if possible. Such a procedure enables the assessment of a broader range of contexts where the behavior occurs, contributes to the determination of whether or not behavioral changes in one context are analogous to those changes in another context, and provides a more accurate measure of behavior (Wodarski, 1977). Another consideration is the accessibility of the behavior. If the behavior is readily observable, this will not be a problem. If it is inaccessible, such as a behavior that occurs late at night or in contexts where observation is not possible, the investigator must use reports by the clients or others who are present when the behavior occurs to secure the data. In any case, an observer who is consistent and reliable should be chosen. Finally, whether the person who secures data is a trained observer or someone else, periodic reliability checks must be made to ensure that the data being provided are consistent (Nelson, Lipinski, & Black, 1975).

CRITERIA FOR EVALUATION MEASURES

Reliability

When choosing a particular measure, the practitioner should ask two questions: Is the measure reliable and is it valid? One of the major deficiencies of behavioral science research is failing to report the reliability or validity of the measures used in a study (Garfield & Bergin, 1978; Wodarski & Bagarozzi, 1979). *Reliability* refers to the consistency of the measure. If used again, the measure provides data similar to previous data. *Intrareliability* refers to how consistently an individual fills out an outcome measure. *Interreliability* refers to how consistently more than one individual completes the assessment process. Such distinctions are necessary because in many instances perceptions by various practitioners are used as the major means of assessing client change. Means of determining reliability include the following techniques: test–retest, alternate forms, split-half or odd-even, and consistency between scales that measure the same phenomenon.

1. *Test–Retest.* This tool uses a second administration of the assessment measure to the individual within a reasonable time period, usually a period of 1 to 2 weeks after its first administration. The basic idea is that the passage of time should not affect the attribute being measured.

2. *Alternate forms.* A large pool of items is developed from which two scales of items are composed through random selection to determine on which scale an item will appear. If the scales are consistent in the measurement of the attribute, then agreement should be good between them.

3. *Split-half or odd-even.* If an instrument is measuring the same attribute throughout the inventory, consistency should occur between the odd and even items or between the first half and last half of the items of the scale.

4. *Consistency.* Finally, if any inventory is already known to measure a phenomenon reliably, then reliability can be established for another inventory by determining the consistency between the two.

Validity

It is essential to use instruments that are reliable because a measure must provide consistent data before it can be valid. If a measure is valid, the inventory measures what it purports to measure. Fewer reports of validity occur in behavioral science than of reliability. This severe deficiency may be due to the substantial time and energy required to execute various validations. Types of validity procedures include face, predictive, concurrent, content, convergent and discriminative, and construct.

1. *Face.* The clinician looks at an inventory and determines if this scale contain items that reflect the phenomenon of interest? For example, an inventory used to report delinquent behavior among youth should contain items relating to such activities as stealing, drinking, aggressive assaults, and drug usage.

2. *Predictive.* An instrument should be able to predict the future behavior of the individual. The use of grades, Graduate Record Examination scores, letters of reference, interviews, and Miller's Analogy Scores to help predict performance in graduate social work education are familiar examples. The ability to predict dangerous behavior based on historical factors is one challenge that faces the helping professions.

3. *Concurrent.* This procedure relates the scores of one assessment inventory with an inventory on which validity has already been established. Thus, if an inventory such as the Jesness (1969), which has an established reputation for tapping antisocial behavior, agrees with scores derived from a checklist measuring specific types of antisocial behavior, validity of the latter inventory may be inferred.

4. *Content.* An instrument should have enough items to adequately measure the phenomenon of interest. For example, content can be assessed in a measurement of antisocial behavior by asking whether enough items are contained in the instrument to measure the various aspects of the behavior, such as gross motor behaviors, physical contacts, verbalizations, throwing objects, or other distracting behaviors.

5. *Convergent and discriminative.* Tests that measure the same phenomena should correlate; tests that do not measure the same phenomena should not correlate. For example, no substantial differences should occur between results of the various classical measures of delinquency, such as Jesness, Gold, and Gough; whereas results of such inventories should not correlate highly with scales measuring marital satisfaction.

6. *Construct.* A theoretical framework is chosen and client behavior is predicted. If the predictions are accurate, the assumption is made that the inventory measures the attribute. For example, it is predicted that neurotics are more anxious than psychotics. If, when testing the two groups, you find that neurotics previously designated by formal

criteria such as a diagnosis by professionals score much higher on an anxiety scale than psychotics, then the prediction is accurate and you assume that the measure of anxiety has validity.

ASSESSMENT PROCEDURES

Behavioral Observation (Time Sampling): Children

A nonparticipant observational technique may be used to measure the frequency of behavior exhibited by clients. This procedure is frequently implemented in social work practice. In the St. Louis study, this assessment process was used with antisocial and prosocial children at a community center and summer camp (Feldman et al., 1983). The observer was to remain as unobtrusive as possible and to avoid virtually all social interactions with the group. Upon his introduction, the children were informed that the observer would not interfere with the group in any way; all information obtained would be confidential and would be reviewed only by the research team, and they could help the observer do his job by ignoring him as best as possible.

A checklist that yielded highly reliable data was used to tabulate the incidence of prosocial, nonsocial, and antisocial behaviors observed. Checklist reliability was established through simultaneous ratings of behavior recorded on videotapes illustrating the small-group behavior of similar children. The tapes included numerous illustrations of antisocial behavior. Observers also were trained by videotapes. The training sessions were completed when each observer could reliably agree on behavioral coding with one of the investigators and the other observers at a level of 0.90 or above, utilizing the rating categories described in Appendix A of this chapter. Observations were made in a fixed order every 10 s for one of the children, then for another child, and so on, until all the children had been observed. The procedure was repeated for the duration of the group meeting or group activities at the summer camp. In each instance, the first behavioral act observed for a child was rated as prosocial, nonsocial, or antisocial. To minimize bias due to the observers' expectations, the observers were not informed of the hypothesized changes for each experimental condition or any particular subject.

To ensure consistent agreement among the observers during the 3-year study, 189 separate reliability checks were performed on the ratings at the community center and at summer camp. These checks were made by having the observers simultaneously rate the interactions of children on videotapes. Different tapes illustrating children interacting in various types of situations, such as discussing difficulties (at school and with parents, drugs, sex, girls, or boys), painting, playing ball, or building a campfire, were used in each reliability session to prevent the observers from rating a child solely on the basis of previous acquaintance with the videotape. The tapes included numerous illustrations of antisocial behavior. The following formula yielded a ratio of interobserver agreement, interval by interval:

$$\text{Ratio of interobserver agreement} = \frac{\text{number of agreements}}{\text{number of agreements} + \text{number of disagreements}}$$

The mean of the reliability ratios was 92.25, with a range of 84 to 99. All observers were required to have a reliability rating that was consistently above 0.90.

To systematize observers' ratings, a recording scheme was devised based on the assessment of three types of subject behaviors: antisocial behavior, prosocial behavior, and nonsocial behavior. Observer ratings were based solely on those three behavioral categories. (See Appendix A for instructions on administration of the scale and definitions of behavioral categories.)

Strengths

- Provides highly reliable data. Research indicates that time-sampling behavior represents actual frequencies of behavior (Wodarski et al., 1975a; Bijou et al., 1969).
- Permits comparison of individual and group data.
- Provides large amount of longitudinal data to enable assessment of change over time.

Weaknesses

- High cost of securing the data in financial assets, energy of the researchers, and administrative constraints.
- Data that are limited to a specific context.
- All behaviors equally rated.
- Possibility that some behaviors may not have been included in the definition or have occurred so infrequently as to not have been observed.

Behavioral Observation (Time Sampling): Therapists

Observers rated the behaviors of the leaders in the community center as well as those of the children. After rating the behaviors of all the children in the group, the observer then rated the behavior of the leader before proceeding to rate the children again. This procedure produced between 60 to 120 observations of leader behavior per session (2 hr). Financial and administrative concerns permitted this type of sampling procedure only infrequently. The ideal situation would have been to observe the worker after each observation of a child. Such a process would enable direct isolation of the effects of worker behavior on the child. Reliability for this part of the checklist was established in the same manner as described for the other part of the checklist. The training sessions were completed when each observer could agree with the others at a level of 0.85 or above, utilizing the rating categories to be described shortly. This criterion was considered adequate because there were 18 categories into which the various behaviors could be scored. To ensure consistent agreement among the observers, 189 separate reliability checks were performed.

The observers rated a therapist's behavior according to the general category of whether the therapist intervened on an individual level (i.e., individual interventions toward a certain child with the specific purpose of increasing, decreasing, stopping, or maintaining behaviors a child exhibited), or on a group level (i.e., group interventions toward two or more children with the specific purpose of increasing, decreasing, stopping, or maintaining behaviors exhibited by two or more children). The observer then specified the therapist's behavior with respect to the following categories: directions, physical contact, praise, positive attention, holding, criticism, threats, negative attention, and time-out. (See Appendix A for instructions on administration of the scale and definition of leader behavioral categories.)

Strengths

- Provides highly reliable data.
- Provides data that indicate whether treatment was implemented.
- Permits comparison of a child's behavioral change over time with therapist interventions.

Weakness

Categories may not be relevant to the assessment of whether treatment was implemented; that is, other categories may be more appropriate to test whether treatment was implemented.

Inventory Assessment of Type of Treatment and Its Implementation by Therapist

Following each meeting observers filled out a scale indicating the type of treatment method that was employed. (See Appendix B for instructions on administration of the scale and definition of treatment methods.)

Strength

Provides an additional source of data on the implementation of treatment.

Weakness

Characteristically, reliability checks are not executed on these types of data as was the case in this study.

Self-Inventories Completed by Children

All children completed two types of self-inventories at the community center. The inventories were administered 8 weeks after the initial session of the program and 4 weeks before the program terminated. Approximately 5 months elapsed between the test periods. The first inventory, titled Child's Checklist, was designed to measure the average incidence of prosocial, nonsocial, and antisocial behaviors that a child thinks he or she exhibits during an average week. Behaviors listed on the checklist were analogous to the behavior contained within the behavioral time-sampling method. At the same time, a similar inventory, titled Therapist's Checklist, was administered to the children's group therapists. In addition, the children also completed a subclass of the Jesness inventory (1969) designed to measure self-reported tendencies toward manifest aggression. The manifest aggression scale consists of 31 items. Jesness contends that these items reflect an awareness of unpleasant feelings, especially of anger and frustration, a tendency to react readily with these emotions, and other obvious discomfort concerning the presence and control of these feelings. (See Appendix C for Child's Checklist.)

Strengths

- Measures perceptual attributes that behavioral measurements do not tap.

- Needs less financial cost, time, and energy; entails fewer organizational and administrative constraints.
- Enables the comparison of data provided in the study with other studies.

Weaknesses

- Low reliability between measures that purport to measure the same item.
- When tests are limited to pre- and posttests, power to assess change over time is reduced.
- Younger children may not interpret questions correctly, and in some instances, do not understand the instructions.

Inventories Completed by Other Significant Adults in Child's Life

This is analogous to the inventories filled out by children except that their inventories are completed by referral agent, parent, group leaders, or behavioral observers. Behaviors denoted on the checklist were similar to those listed on an observational scale used for the research and to those reported on a self-inventory completed by the children. (See Appendix D for Observer Checklist.)

Strengths

- Provides data from significant adults on how they perceive the effects of the program.
- Provides data on child's behavior outside the treatment context.

Weaknesses

- Low correlations between significant others' ratings of child's behavior.
- Lack of uniformity in filling out the inventory.

Interview Schedules

These introduce parents to the program and help secure necessary background data. They also provide an opportunity for answering questions parents have about programs. (See Appendix E for interview schedule.)

Strengths

- Provides additional sources of information.

- Enables more flexibility in securing information.
- Provides opportunity to clarify questions.
- Helps participant become familiar with treatment context.

Weaknesses

- Difficulty in analyzing data, that is, how it relates to empirical questions.
- Problems in controlling how consistently the interview is conducted.
- Costly in terms of money and time.

SUMMARY

This chapter emphasizes the importance of choosing outcome criteria for research and reviews basic considerations in choosing appropriate outcome measures. Following the choice of types of measures, adequate baseline rates must be secured. Another essential prerequisite of empirical research is the assessment of the reliability and validity of the means to secure data. A researcher must address certain questions regarding the data in order to evaluate a program. The means available to collect the data must be decided on by the strengths and weaknesses of the measure. As research and practice become more integrated, practitioners should include such considerations in their treatment plans, the outcome of which will improve services offered to clients.

APPENDIX A: INSTRUCTIONS FOR ADMINISTRATION OF THE CHECKLISTS

Observations are made at 10-sec intervals. Observe the child at the beginning of the 10-sec interval and record the first behavior exhibited onto the checklist. After all children are observed once, please mark the leader's behavior by observing him or her at the beginning of the 10-sec interval and by recording the first behavior exhibited onto the rating scale (Figure A.4.1). Repeat this procedure throughout the observational period. Circle the data box on the checklist when the group activity changes. Indicate what the previous activity was on the blank line at the end of the first data row, or what the new activity is on the line at the end of the second data row. Repeat this procedure as necessary.

The numbers 1, 2, and 3 stand, respectively, for the ratings of prosocial, nonsocial, and antisocial behaviors.

PROSOCIAL BEHAVIORS

Mark "1" if the child exhibits any of the following behaviors:

1. One child hands another child a material object, such as a basketball or hockey stick, which the latter child needs to continue participating in the group activity.

2. One child asks the group leader or another child to help someone in the activity.

3. Two children work on the same activity together. For example, one child shows the other how to or helps the other child overcome difficulties so that they may execute the activity.

4. One child helps another participate in the discussion of some topic by making a comment that elicits continued verbal behavior. Example: One child is talking about drugs and the other says "good point," "please continue," or "tell us more."

5. A child is engaged in the group activity.

6. A child asks the worker about the group activity.

7. A child engages in the decision-making process verbally or nonverbally: for example, nods his head, pats another child for engaging in the process, smiles, is listening or sitting, has eye contact with the worker or another child.

8. A child makes an appropriate comment.

NAME _____ DATE _____ OBSERVER _____ GROUP _____ ACTIVITY

1 2 3	1 2 3	1 2 3	1 2 3	1 2 3	1 2 3	1 2 3	1 2 3	1 2 3	1 2 3	1 2 3
1 2 3	1 2 3	1 2 3	1 2 3	1 2 3	1 2 3	1 2 3	1 2 3	1 2 3	1 2 3	1 2 3
1 2 3	1 2 3	1 2 3	1 2 3	1 2 3	1 2 3	1 2 3	1 2 3	1 2 3	1 2 3	1 2 3
1 2 3	1 2 3	1 2 3	1 2 3	1 2 3	1 2 3	1 2 3	1 2 3	1 2 3	1 2 3	1 2 3
1 2 3	1 2 3	1 2 3	1 2 3	1 2 3	1 2 3	1 2 3	1 2 3	1 2 3	1 2 3	1 2 3
1 2 3	1 2 3	1 2 3	1 2 3	1 2 3	1 2 3	1 2 3	1 2 3	1 2 3	1 2 3	1 2 3
1 2 3	1 2 3	1 2 3	1 2 3	1 2 3	1 2 3	1 2 3	1 2 3	1 2 3	1 2 3	1 2 3
1 2 3	1 2 3	1 2 3	1 2 3	1 2 3	1 2 3	1 2 3	1 2 3	1 2 3	1 2 3	1 2 3
1 2 3	1 2 3	1 2 3	1 2 3	1 2 3	1 2 3	1 2 3	1 2 3	1 2 3	1 2 3	1 2 3
1 2 3	1 2 3	1 2 3	1 2 3	1 2 3	1 2 3	1 2 3	1 2 3	1 2 3	1 2 3	1 2 3
1 2 3	1 2 3	1 2 3	1 2 3	1 2 3	1 2 3	1 2 3	1 2 3	1 2 3	1 2 3	1 2 3
D H	D H	D H	D H	D H	D H	D H	D H	D H	D H	D H
PC C	PC C	PC C	PC C	PC C	PC C	PC C	PC C	PC C	PC C	PC C
P T	P T	P T	P T	P T	P T	P T	P T	P T	P T	P T
PA NA	PA NA	PA NA	PA NA	PA NA	PA NA	PA NA	PA NA	PA NA	PA NA	PA NA
TO	TO	TO	TO	TO	TO	TO	TO	TO	TO	TO

Figure A.4.1 Rating scale.

86

9. A child tries to help someone, shares something with another child, stops other children from arguing or fighting, helps children be friends with one another, or tries to do something nice even though nobody expected it.

10. A child says nice things to another child, such as "I like you."

11. A child helps other group members straighten up their belongings, solve a problem, or fix something that was broken.

12. A child helps the group leader by paying attention, cooperating, or carrying out the leader's reasonable instructions.

NONSOCIAL BEHAVIOR

Mark "2" if the child you observe exhibits any of the following nonparticipating behaviors:

1. The child looks out the window or stares into space.
2. The child plays with some object but does not disturb other children.
3. The child does not engage in appropriate tasks for the interactional situation: for example, the children are playing basketball, but he sits in the corner.
4. The child lays his or her head on the table or furniture.
5. The child pulls at his or her hair or clothing.
6. The child cleans or digs in the desk or table without disturbing another pupil.
7. The child draws on the desk or table.
8. The child plays with a wallet, purse, or book.
9. The child sucks his or her thumb or other objects.
10. The child bites his or her nails.
11. The child engages in motor activities that do not disturb others: for example, takes off his or her shoes, rocks in a chair, moves a chair in place, or sits out of position.

ANTISOCIAL BEHAVIOR

Mark "3" if the child you observed exhibits any of the following behaviors:

1. *Verbalizations.* The child talks to another child and, thus, disrupts the other child's participation in the group activity; the child talks to

another child and, thus, disrupts someone else who is trying to participate in the group activity; the child speaks without directing the conversation toward anyone; the child engages in name calling, crying,
screaming, laughing loudly, coughing loudly, singing disruptively, or
whistling disruptively.

2. *Gross motor behaviors.* If the children are seated around the table,
the child is out of his or her seat without the group worker's permission,
running, jumping, skipping, standing up, hopping, moving a chair, or
walking around, which disrupts the group activities.

3. *Object interference.* A child plays with some object that interferes
with another child's participating in the group: taps a pencil or other
object, claps, taps feet, rattles or tears paper, throws books on table, or
slams things on furniture.

4. *Physical contacts.* Contact is initiated by one child toward another
who is participating in the group activity. This contact disrupts the latter
child's participation. The contact may include hitting, kicking, shoving,
pinching, slapping, striking with an object, throwing an object that hits
another person, poking with an object, biting, pulling hair, touching,
patting, or disturbing another child's property.

5. *Distracting behaviors.* A child engages in physical movement that
attracts another child's attention and causes that child to stop participation in the group activity. The first child may turn his or her head or
body to look at another child, show an object to another child, rock in
a chair, sit out of position, or rummage in furniture.

TYPE OF INTERVENTION

If the group worker is not intervening at the time you observe him, just
leave these letters blank. If the group worker has intervened, specify
whether he intervened on a group level (G) or on an individual level (I).

1. Please mark "I" if the group worker exhibited any of the following individual interventions toward one certain child with the specific
purpose of increasing, decreasing, stopping, or maintaining behaviors
the child exhibits: physical contact, praise, facial expression, attention,
holding, suggestion, criticism, threats, negative attention, time-out.

2. Please mark "G" if the worker exhibited any of the following
group interventions toward two or more children with the specific purpose of increasing, decreasing, stopping, or maintaining behaviors

exhibited by two or more children: physical contact, praise, facial expression, attention, suggestion, criticism, threats, negative attention, time-out.

WORKER'S BEHAVIOR

Please mark the appropriate letter that corresponds to the worker's behavior that you observed.

Positive Reinforcement

Directions (comments that request group members to exhibit a specific behavior).

1. Therapist asks children to clean up materials.
2. Therapist suggests alternate activity for the group: for example, by saying "Let's go to the gym," or "Let's start on our models."

Physical contact (positive contact between the group leader and the child).

1. Embraces the child while the child is in an activity.
2. Pats the child while the child is in an activity.
3. Holds the child's arm or hand while the child is in an activity.

Praise (comments that indicate approval, commendation, or achievement).

1. Says "That was good" to a child who is participating.
2. Says "You are doing it right" to a child who is participating.
3. Says "You are studying well" to a child who is participating.
4. Says "I like you" to a child who is participating.
5. Says "You made me happy" to a child who is participating.

Note: Facial expressions of the worker are considered a positive intervention if the group leader smiles or nods to the child while the child is participating in an activity.

Positive attention is also considered a positive intervention if the group leader directs it toward a certain child while the child is participating in an activity.

Punishing Interventions

Holding (the group leader's physical grasping of the child).

1. Forcibly holding the child.
2. Putting the child in the hall.
3. Grabbing, hitting, spanking, slapping, or shaking the child.

Criticism (from the group leader).

1. Yelling.
2. Scolding.
3. Raising voice and using such statements as, "Don't do that!" "Be quiet!" "Sit in your place!" "That's wrong!" "Stop talking!" "Did I call on you?" "Are you wasting time?" "Don't laugh!" "You know what you are supposed to do!"

Note: Threats (the group leader's statement of undesired consequences to occur at a later time). Examples: "If you aren't quiet, we won't go to the gym." "If you don't stop fighting, we won't take the ride on the bus." "No ice cream for you guys until you clean up!"

Negative attention (the group leader frowns or grimaces at the child).

Time-out refers to specific disciplinary procedures wherein the child is removed from the activity, thus depriving the child from obtaining reinforcement or participating in the group activity.

TREATMENT METHOD

This inventory will be filled out at the end of each group meeting. It will be the last data sheet in the packet.

Check the blank that best describes the treatment method the leader used during most of the meeting: _____ social learning _____ traditional _____ group-centered _____ none

If the leader used other treatment methods in addition to the one mentioned above, but not for most of the meeting, please check the blank that corresponds to the treatment methods utilized: _____ social learning _____ traditional _____ group-centered _____ none

Note: If one child initiates an antisocial behavior and that behavior is emulated by another child when the latter's observational period occurs, the behavior of the latter child is coded as antisocial.

If a child leaves the group because of anger or frustration, you do not record data (such as "3") for that child while he is out of the room.

COMMENCEMENT OF DATA COLLECTION

Begin 5 min before the official starting time for the group meeting. If the leader is present, star the first box on your data sheet. If the leader is not present, star the appropriate data box when he joins the group. This same procedure is to be used whenever the leader departs from the meeting (use a triangle to denote return).

GOING FROM ACTIVITY TO ACTIVITY

No data will be taken while a group is in transit, either within the building or outside the building. An empty box on the data sheet will designate that the child was not present at that moment; nevertheless, a 10-sec period should elapse before the next child is observed. This procedure should be followed throughout the meeting. If certain children are absent from the meeting, 10-sec intervals should elapse for every child that is absent before the next child is observed. This procedure also should be followed throughout the meeting.

GROUP SPLITTING

The observer will take data even if some of the children leave the group. The observer should continue to record for that portion of the group that has the leader present, regardless of the physical context (i.e., club room, gym). This procedure also should be followed in contexts other than the treatment center. Skip the appropriate time intervals for children who are not present. A blank data box indicates that the child has left the group. Leave his data boxes blank until he returns, then begin securing data again at the appropriate time interval.

IDENTIFICATION OF CHILDREN

1. At the first meeting, you and the children will be introduced to one another. Try to identify the child by certain outstanding characteristics so that you can record behavior.
2. After the meeting, check with the worker so that you can match the child's characteristics with the child's name.

3. Your observations should begin with the first child mentioned on the checklist.
4. Mark the behaviors only according to the way they are defined.

AMBIGUOUS BEHAVIORS

You must record each observed behavior for a child as "1," "2," or "3." However, if certain types of coding responses are questionable or in doubt, seek clarification after the meeting from the project directors.

APPENDIX B: OBSERVER'S REPORT

Date:
Group:
Leader:
Observer:

Indicate the basic leadership style used (1, 2, or 3):

1. The leader seldom, if ever, structured group activities, friendship relationships, and task relationships. The leader permitted members to select their own activities and develop their own friendship, task, and interpersonal relationships with one another.

2. The leader structured group activities, friendship relationships, and task relationships by helping members to set specific group goals with specific ensuing rewards for the group as a whole or for individual members. Usually all members were expected to share equally in the rewards, if any, of the group's goal attainment endeavors.

3. The leader structured group activities, friendship relationships, and task relationships by helping both the individual members and the group as a whole to set goals. Without delineating specific rewards, selected individual members were expected to engage in certain relationships, thus benefiting from them, and the group as a whole sometimes was expected to benefit from certain group-oriented interventions by the leader.

APPENDIX C: CHILD'S CHECKLIST

Name:

Group:

Date:

Directions: The research staff asks that you answer the following questions voluntarily. We think you will enjoy this. It is not a test like reading or arithmetic. There is no grade or mark. When we ask you about things, the only right answer is exactly what you honestly tell us. Each of you may give a different answer and all of you will still be right. For example, if we ask, "How many ice cream cones did you eat yesterday?" each of you could say a different number and all of you will be giving the right answer.

Your answers will be seen only by the research staff. No one else will ever see your answers. That includes the group leader, supervisory staff, your parents, your friends, or anyone else. Be completely honest in your answers.

OK, let's go! Please tell us the number of times that you think you did these things during the past week. Don't include those that were done accidentally.

1. _____ How many times did you say nice things, such as "I like you," to someone?

2. _____ How many times did you help your friends by paying attention to them, cooperating with them, or staying with them until you both finished what you started out to do?

3. _____ How many times did you help adults by paying attention to them, cooperating with them, staying with them until you both finished what you started out to do, or by carrying out reasonable requests or instructions?

4. _____ How many times did you try to help someone, share something of yours, stop others from arguing or fighting, help other boys or girls to be friends with one another, or try to do something nice even though nobody expected it?

5. _____ How many times did you bother adults by being restless, moving about, tapping an object, having a temper tantrum, or not carrying out reasonable requests or instructions?

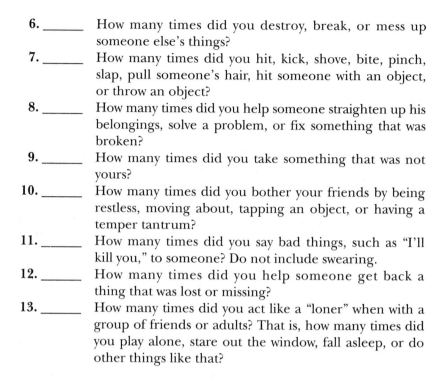

6. _____ How many times did you destroy, break, or mess up someone else's things?

7. _____ How many times did you hit, kick, shove, bite, pinch, slap, pull someone's hair, hit someone with an object, or throw an object?

8. _____ How many times did you help someone straighten up his belongings, solve a problem, or fix something that was broken?

9. _____ How many times did you take something that was not yours?

10. _____ How many times did you bother your friends by being restless, moving about, tapping an object, or having a temper tantrum?

11. _____ How many times did you say bad things, such as "I'll kill you," to someone? Do not include swearing.

12. _____ How many times did you help someone get back a thing that was lost or missing?

13. _____ How many times did you act like a "loner" when with a group of friends or adults? That is, how many times did you play alone, stare out the window, fall asleep, or do other things like that?

Thank you for answering these questions.

APPENDIX D: OBSERVER'S CHECKLIST

Child:

Group:

Date:

Observer:

Directions: Please answer the following questions for the child listed above. Your answers will be seen *only* by the research staff and will not be communicated to supervisory staff, parents, or anyone else other than research staff.

Please tell us the number of times you think the child did these things during the past week. Don't include those that were done accidentally.

1. _____ How many times did he say nice things, such as "I like you," to someone?

2. _____ How many times did he help friends by paying attention to them, cooperating with them, or staying with them until they both finished what they started out to do?

3. _____ How many times did he help adults by paying attention to them, cooperating with them, staying with them until they both finished what they started out to do, or by carrying out reasonable requests or instructions?

4. _____ How many times did he try to help someone, share something of his, stop others from arguing or fighting, help other boys or girls to be friends with one another, or try to do something nice even though nobody expected it?

5. _____ How many times did he bother adults by being restless, moving about, tapping an object, having a temper tantrum, or not carrying out reasonable requests or instructions?

6. _____ How many times did he destroy, break, or mess up someone else's things?

7. _____ How many times did he hit, kick, shove, bite, pinch, slap, pull someone's hair, hit someone with an object, or throw an object?

8. _____ How many times did he help someone straighten up his belongings, solve a problem, or fix something that was broken?

9. _____ How many times did he take something that was not his?

10. _____ How many times did he bother his friends by being restless, moving about, tapping an object, or having a temper tantrum?

11. _____ How many times did he say bad things, such as "I'll kill you," to someone? Do not include swearing.

12. _____ How many times did he help someone get back a thing that was lost or missing?

13. _____ How many times did he act like a "loner" when with a group of friends or adults? That is, how many times did he play alone, stare out the window, fall asleep and do other things like that?

Thank you for answering these questions.

APPENDIX E: INTAKE INTERVIEW SCHEDULE

I. PURPOSE OF THE PROGRAM

Our purpose is to help children who are having difficulty in relations with adults and/or children. We would like to enroll your child in one of the friendship groups that the center provides. These groups engage in different activities that may improve how your child gets along with children and adults. In the past, these groups have helped children with various types of social and behavioral problems.

II. OVERVIEW OF THIS INTERVIEW

A. I will go into more detail regarding the program.

B. I will ask you a variety of questions that will help us determine whether your child can be included in the program. (Any and all information will be confidential.)

C. We will discuss the financing of your child's activity at the community center.

D. We will discuss government requirements, since our program is financed through a federal research grant.

E. We will try to determine periods when your child has free time in order to help us find a convenient group for him.

F. If you would like, we will tour the facilities of the center.

III. FURTHER EXPLANATION OF THE PROGRAM

A. The group will be a regular friendship or activity group at the community center.

1. These groups usually engage in a variety of activities, such as basketball, swimming, handball, and participation in community projects.

2. Most groups will have from 8 to 12 members.

B. The groups generally meet for 2 hours a week, usually during a weekday after school or the weekend. The groups will meet for about 15 weeks.

C. The meetings will usually be held in _____. If your child is accepted for the program, he will receive a letter or telephone call from a staff member to notify him of the time and place for the first meeting. Meetings will begin around _____.

D. Group leaders will be either regular community center group leaders (usually college students interested in working with children) or graduate students at a graduate school of social work. All group leaders

    1. have had previous experience in working with children's groups

    2. have undergone special training for this program

    3. will be under the supervision of a professional staff member

IV. SCHEDULING

Which of the following times could your child attend a club meeting? Indicate by placing an X in the appropriate box.

	Sun	Mon	Tue	Wed	Thur	Fri	Sat
1 PM							
2 PM							
3 PM							
4 PM							
5 PM							
6 PM							
7 PM							
8 PM							
9 PM							

V. BACKGROUND DATA

Now we would like to ask a number of routine questions for the program. As with all other information you give me, your answers will be confidential.

Please answer the following questions.

A. Information concerning father

1. Age:
2. Religion:
3. Occupation:
4. Gross yearly income (check one):

   None
   $1–$3,000
   $3,001–$6,000
   $6,001–$9,000
   $9,001–$12,000
   $12,001–$15,000
   $15,001–$18,000
   $18,001–$21,000
   $21,001–$24,000
   $24,001 or above

5. Last year of school completed:

B. Information concerning mother

1. Age:
2. Religion:
3. Occupation:
4. Gross yearly income (check one):

   None
   $1–$3,000
   $3,001–$6,000
   $6,001–$9,000
   $9,001–$12,000
   $12,001–$15,000
   $15,001–$18,000
   $18,001–$21,000
   $21,001–$24,000
   $24,001 or above

5. Last year of school completed:

C. Information concerning the child

1. Current medical information:

Please list any type of physical handicaps, medical information, or any other information that the program staff should know about.

2. Does the child's physical condition limit the child in any way with reference to participation in center activities?

_____ Yes
_____ No

If yes, please describe.

3. What is your child's average school grade?

_____

4. How much does your child like his present school?

_____ Likes very much
_____ Likes somewhat
_____ Neither likes nor dislikes
_____ Dislikes somewhat
_____ Dislikes very much

5. Does your child have any particular learning difficulties?

_____ Yes
_____ No

If yes, please describe and indicate whether the child has been referred for special help.

6. Is your child a foster child or adopted child?

_____ Yes
_____ No

7. Are there other children in the family?

_____ Yes
_____ No

If yes, list their names, sex, and ages.

8. Do any of the sisters or brothers (if applicable) have any particular learning difficulties?

_____ Yes
_____ No

If yes, please list child's name and indicate whether the child has been referred for special help.

9. Do any of the sisters or brothers (if any) have any particular behavioral difficulties?

_____ Yes
_____ No

If yes, please list child's name and indicate whether the child has been referred for special help.

VI. DEVELOPMENTAL HISTORY

A. Behavioral difficulties

1. At what age did his/her difficulties first start?
2. Since they first started, have his/her difficulties (Check one):

_____ Become worse?
_____ Become better?
_____ Remained about the same?

3. Were there any very outstanding events that occurred before the onset of his/her difficulties?

_____ Yes
_____ No

If yes, describe the events and how long before the onset.

4. Have there been any outstanding events that further con-
tributed to these difficulties since they first started?

_____ Yes
_____ No

If yes, describe the events.

5. Whenever the difficulty occurs are there other children or
adults who seem to make it worse?

_____ Yes
_____ No

If yes, please describe.

B. Pick three of the child's most serious difficulties (if there are three)
and please answer the following questions concerning them.

1. Difficulty 1.
   a. Briefly describe the difficulty.

   b. About how many times per week does it occur?

   c. About how long does each incident last?

   d. Describe what happens *just before* the difficulty occurs.

   e. Describe what happens *just after* the difficulty occurs.

2. Difficulty 2.
   a. Briefly describe the difficulty.

    b. About how many times per week does it occur?

    c. About how long does each incident last?

    d. Describe what happens *just before* the difficulty occurs.

    e. Describe what happens *just after* the difficulty occurs.

3. Difficulty 3.
    a. Briefly describe the difficulty.

    b. About how many times per week does it occur?

    c. About how long does each incident last?

    d. Describe what happens *just before* the difficulty occurs?

    e. Describe what happens *just after* the difficulty occurs.

VII. BEHAVIORAL CHECKLIST

Now you can help us by filling out this list regarding your child's behavior during the past three weeks. We ask you to estimate how many times the child has done each of the things noted on the checklist. At the end of the checklist there are a few other questions. If you need any help with them, I'll be glad to assist you. (Interviewer: If both parents are present, have each one fill out a checklist individually.)

VIII. NAME AND STATUS OF INTERVIEWEE

Write the name of the interviewee(s) and relationship to child (e.g., father, mother, aunt, uncle).

REFERENCES

Bijou, S. W., Peterson, R. F., Harris, F. R., Allen, K. E., & Johnston, M. W. (1969). Methodology for experimental studies of young children in natural settings. *Psychological Record, 19,* 177–210.

Bloom, M., & Fischer, J. (1982) *Evaluating practice: Guidelines for the accountable professional.* Englewood Cliffs, NJ: Prentice Hall.

Caplinger, T. E., Feldman, R. A., & Wodarski, J. S. (August, 1979). *Agents of social control: Prosocial and antisocial peer groups.* Paper presented at the ninth World Congress of Sociology, Upsala, Sweden.

Conger, A. J., & Coie, D. J. (1975). Who's crazy in Manhattan: A reexamination of treatment of psychological disorder among urban children. *Journal of Consulting and Clinical Psychology, 43,* 179–182.

Corcoran, K., & Fischer, J. (1987). *Measures for clinical practice.* New York: The Free Press.

Empey, L. T., & Erickson, M. L. (1972). *The Provo experiment.* Lexington, MA: D.C. Heath.

Empey, L. T., & Lubeck, S. G. (1971). *The Silverlake experiment.* Chicago: Aldine.

Feldman, R. A., Caplinger, T. E., & Wodarski, J. S. (1983). *The St. Louis conundrum: The effective treatment of antisocial youths.* Englewood Cliffs, NJ: Prentice Hall.

Garfield, S. L., & Bergin, A. E. (Eds.) (1978). *Handbook of psychotherapy and behavioral change.* New York: Wiley.

Graycar, A. (1979). Political issues in research and evaluation. *Evaluation Quarterly, 3,* 460–471.

Jesness, C. F. (1969). *The Jesness inventory manual.* Palo Alto, CA: Consulting Psychologist Press.

Johnson, O. G. (Ed.) (1976). *Tests and measurements in child development: Handbook II.* San Francisco: Jossey-Bass.

Lindsey, E. W., Wodarski, J. S., & Streever, K. L. (1986). Assessing social agency functions: A model. *Journal of Sociology and Social Welfare, 13,* 385–399.

Luborsky, L., Mintz, J., & Christoph, P. (1979). Are psychotherapeutic changes predictable? Comparison of a Chicago counseling center project with a Penn psychotherapy project. *Journal of Consulting and Clinical Psychology, 47,* 469–473.

Nelson, R. O., Lipinski, D. P., & Black, J. L. (1975). The effects of expectancy on the reactivity of self-recording. *Behavior Therapy, 6,* 337–349.

Reynolds, P. (Ed.). (1975). *Advances in psychological assessment.* (Vol. 3). San Francisco: Jossey-Bass.

Robinson, J. P., & Shaven, P. R. (1973). *Measures of social psychological attitudes.* Ann Arbor, MI: Institute for Social Research.

Rossi, R. J., & McLaughlin, D. H. (1979). Establishing evaluation objectives. *Evaluation Quarterly, 3,* 331–346.

Sarri, R. C., & Selo, E. (1974). Evaluation process and outcome in juvenile corrections: Musings on a grim tale. In P. O. Davidson, F. W. Clark, & L. A. Hamerlynck (Eds.), *Evaluation of behavioral programs in community, residential, and school settings.* Champaign, IL: Research Press.

Segal, S. P. (1972). Research on the outcome of social work therapeutic interventions: A review of the literature. *Journal of Health and Social Behavior, 13,* 3–17.

Shireman, C. H., Mann, K. B., Larsen, C., & Young, T. (1972). Findings from experiments in treatment in the correctional institution. *Social Service Review, 46,* 38–59.

Thomas, E. J. (Ed.). (1974). Behavior modification procedure: A sourcebook. Chicago: Aldine.

Wodarski, J. S. (1977). The consistency of antisocial children's behavior across different behavioral contexts as compared to prosocial children: An empirical investigation. *Journal of Experimental Psychiatry and Behavior Therapy, 8,* 275–280.

Wodarski, J. S. (1981). Group work with antisocial children. In S. P. Schinke (Ed.), *Community application of behavioral methods: A sourcebook for social workers.* Chicago: Aldine.

Wodarski, J. S., & Bagarozzi, D. (1979). *Behavioral social work: An introduction.* New York: Human Sciences Press.

Wodarski, J. S., & Pedi, S. J. (1977). The comparison of antisocial and prosocial children on multicriterion measures at a community center: A three-year study. *Social Work, 22,* 290–296.

Wodarski, J. S., Feldman, R. A., & Pedi, S. J. (1975a). Labeling by self and others: The comparison of behavior among antisocial and prosocial children in an open community agency. *Criminal Justice and Behavior, 2,* 258–275.

Wodarski, J. S., Feldman, R., & Pedi, S. J. (1975b). The comparison of antisocial and prosocial in multicriterion measures at summer camp. *Journal of Abnormal Child Psychology, 7,* 255–273.

Wodarski, J. S., Feldman, R. A., & Pedi, S. J. (1976a). Integrating antisocial children into prosocial groups at summer camp: A three-year study. *Social Service Review, 50,* 256–272.

Wodarski, J. S., Feldman, R. A., & Pedi, S. J. (1976b). The comparison of antisocial and prosocial children on multicriterion measures at summer camp. *Journal of Abnormal Child Psychology, 50,* 256–272.

Wodarski, J. S., Hudson, W., & Buckholdt, D. R. (1976). Issues in evaluative research: Implications for social work. *Journal of Sociology and Social Welfare, 4,* 81–113.

CHAPTER 5

Designs for Daily Practice Evaluation

T he use of a research design in empirical practice is justified by the need to know: Did my interventions make a difference for this client? In technical terms, this means obtaining data to indicate whether interventions were effective while controlling for as many confounding factors as possible that might influence therapeutic outcome. The major aim is to keep all conditions constant except those in which the practitioner is interested. Until recently, designs that controlled for confounding factors and that could be used within daily agency operations without causing substantial disruptions were not available.

In this chapter, time-series designs are reviewed with examples of how they can be used in practice. Chapter 6 reviews traditional designs, their relationship to time-series designs, and their role in the evaluation of practice.

It has frequently been assumed that the only way therapeutic services can be evaluated is through the employment of classical experimental designs; those in which participants are assigned randomly to one or more experimental or control groups. However, such designs may not be the most appropriate for the initial evaluation of services.

They may be costly in money, energy, and administrative time (Bloom & Fischer, 1982; Wodarski & Buckholdt, 1975). Initial use of classical designs in practice research violates one of the basic tenets of research—execute the requisite pilot studies before large evaluations are undertaken. Moreover, the criterion of random assignment of subjects in traditional designs is usually hard to meet in the evaluation of services provided. Single-case studies and time-series designs overcame many of these difficulties. These approaches can be easily implemented in social work; they are economical in terms of money and energy required to implement them, and they are uncomplicated in administrative execution. Above all, single-case studies and time-series designs provide data that will enable workers to determine if their interventions have had an effect on client behaviors and provide the foundation data for the decision to engage in sophisticated designs involving control groups, the major aim of which is to present conclusive data on the effectiveness of services.

In the traditional experimental design, clients are grouped into experimental and control groups, although this process is diametrically opposed to a basic practice assumption that every individual is unique and needs to be considered in his or her own Gestalt. The single-case study, on the other hand, may alleviate many of the measurement problems discussed. In this approach, clients serve as their own control and their change is evaluated against data provided by themselves during a baseline period preceding the application of treatment.

The single-case study methodology also alleviates the moral and legal aspects of placing clients in a no-treatment control group. It is too early to predict the effects of various legal decisions on the use of a traditional no-treatment control group in practice evaluation research. However, the use of this methodology may be challenged in the future on two legal bases: denial of the right to treatment and denial of equal protection to the client. For more information, see Tripodi (1994).

The time-series designs described in the classic clinical research literature provide practitioners with tools they can utilize in their everyday practice to evaluate the effect of their practice interventions on clients (Bloom & Block, 1977; Gottman & Leiblum, 1974.) These designs, which include the ABAB, multiple baseline, and the AB, can be implemented easily in social work. The time-series designs are economical in money, energy, administrative execution, and personnel required to implement them. Thus, their accessibility to practitioners for the evaluation of their practice interventions is significant.

THE ABAB DESIGN

The classical single-case study of the time-series format is the ABAB design, which consists of four basic phases in which behaviors are observed for a specific time period. In the first phase, the client is exposed to a baseline period. During this period, the worker does not rationally plan interventions that are likely to influence the display of target behaviors. After the client's observed incidence of target behavior reaches a stabilized or "natural" level, the behavior-change strategy is introduced, and in phase two, the client's behavior is monitored until it is once again stabilized. A behavior is considered stabilized when the average of its measurements do not vary more than 10% for 3 to 5 days. After the behaviors stabilize, a baseline condition is reintroduced in the third phase. This condition is termed the reversal period. The procedure enables the practitioner evaluating the changes to determine whether the influence attempt was responsible for the various changes in behavior; it clearly reduces the number of confounding factors that could account for the behavior changes. Immediately after it becomes evident that the strategy has been effective in reducing the target behavior, the treatment procedures are applied once again in the fourth phase. In many instances, a follow-up phase has been added to the ABAB design, thus providing the opportunity to determine how lasting the changes were.

The data presented in Table 5.1 provide an example of the ABAB design used to evaluate group work service provided to one 5th grade antisocial child in one facet of the St. Louis study (Wodarski, Feldman, & Pedi, 1976).

Table 5.1 Average Percentage of Prosocial, Nonsocial, and Antisocial Behavior for One Child, According to Four Experimental Conditions

	Experimental condition			
Type of behavior	Baseline[a]	Reinforcement	Reversal	Reinforcement
Prosocial	66.00	92.00	80.00	93.00
Nonsocial	16.50	4.75	1.50	7.00
Antisocial	17.50	3.25	18.50	0.00
	100.00	100.00	100.00	100.00

[a] The first baseline condition extended for four meetings, the first reinforcement condition for six meetings, the reversal for two meetings, and the last reinforcement condition for two meetings.

Percentage frequencies of prosocial, nonsocial, and antisocial behavior were graphed for the entire group of children who met for 2-h sessions over a period of 14 weeks at a community center. An ABAB design was implemented because it met the structured program requirements of the agency and provided for the systematic evaluation of treatment efficacy.

The group workers were trained in several behavior modification techniques. Specifically, they were taught to utilize positive reinforcement and group contingencies to increase the incidence of prosocial behavior and to use mild punishments and extinction to decrease the incidence of antisocial behavior (Feldman, Caplinger, & Wodarski, 1983). Initial training consisted of a 3-hour seminar during which behavior modification techniques were presented and discussed. In the latter part of the seminar, role playing was used to demonstrate the application of these techniques. The group worker held weekly conferences with a supervisor to discuss implementation of the technique. In addition, consultations were held periodically with various behavior modification specialists. Reinforcers, such as candy, money, free play time, and special field trips, were used along with other inducements more readily available at the community center, such as access to the gym or pool. Sequentially, the experimental group underwent the first baseline condition for 4 weeks, the first reinforcement condition for 6 weeks, the reversal condition for 2 weeks, and the experimental reinforcement condition for 2 additional weeks. For more rigorous experimental evaluation, it might have been useful to expand the duration of the last reversal and experimental reinforcement conditions. It was necessary to modify the program to fit within the agency's prestructured calendar, however. Such modifications are basically inimical to an individualized treatment program and should be avoided if possible.

A unique nonparticipant observation technique was devised to measure the frequency of prosocial, nonsocial, and antisocial behavior exhibited by the children. This procedure seldom has been implemented in relatively open settings, such as community centers.

A trained observer was placed in the group 3 weeks before the baseline period so that members could adapt to the observer's presence before gathering data. The observer was instructed to remain as unobtrusive as possible to avoid virtually all social interaction with the members. On introduction, the children were informed that observers would not interfere in any way with the group, that all information to be obtained by them would be kept confidential and would be reviewed only by the research team, and that they could help the observers do their job by ignoring them.

A checklist titled Behavioral Observational Scale for Children and Therapist Interacting in a Group, which yielded highly reliable data, was used to tabulate the respective incidence of prosocial, nonsocial, and antisocial behaviors observed (Wodarski & Feldman, 1976). Checklist reliability was established through simultaneous ratings of behavior recorded on videotapes illustrating the small-group behavior of similar children. The tapes included numerous illustrations of anti-social behavior. Observers also were trained with videotapes. The training sessions were completed when each observer could reliably agree on behavioral coding with one of the investigators and with other observers at a level of 0.90 or above, utilizing the rating categories later described. An agreement criterion of 0.90 or above was required. Observations were made in a fixed order every 10 sec for 1 of the 10 children, then for another child, and so on, until all the children had been observed. The procedure was repeated for the duration of each group meeting. In each 10-sec time frame, the first behavioral act observed for a child was rated as prosocial, nonsocial, or antisocial. To ensure consistent agreement among observers, individual reliability checks were performed for their ratings at six separate points during the program. A more comprehensive description of the procedure for ascertaining observers' reliability.

BEHAVIORAL CATEGORIES

Definitions

Antisocial Behavior

Antisocial behavior was defined as any behavior exhibited by a group member that disrupts, hurts, or annoys other members, or that otherwise prevents members from participating in the group's tasks or activities. These might include gross motor behaviors, physical contacts, verbalizations, object interference, or other such behaviors. No effort was made to differentiate qualitatively the extent to which each particular behavior could be classified as antisocial. Instead, the importance of the recording scheme adheres, in its capacity to tabulate systematically obvious antisocial behaviors according to a time-sampling format and, consequently, to calculate relatively accurate frequencies of antisocial, prosocial, and nonsocial behaviors per unit time for each child. More-over, in conjunction with the data presented below, the format permits an approximation of the proportion of total behaviors observed for each child that is antisocial, prosocial, and nonsocial in nature.

Prosocial Behavior

Prosocial behavior was defined as any behavior exhibited by a group member that helps that group complete a task or behavior that other-wise exemplifies constructive participation in the group's activities. Illustrative prosocial behaviors include instances in which a given child helps another, demonstrates skills, provides others with materials or objects necessary for participation, asks the group leader to help some-one who is experiencing difficulty, requests others to engage in the group's activities, positively reinforces others' task participation and similar actions.

Nonsocial Behavior

All behavior cannot be categorized solely as prosocial or antisocial. In many instances, children temporarily withdraw from group activity without either helping or disrupting others. In the present study, non-social behavior was defined as any behavior exhibited by a group mem-ber that is not directly related to the group's ongoing activity. Such behavior is neither directed toward helping the group move toward completion of a task nor directed toward disrupting, hurting, or annoy-ing others participating in the group's activities. Relevant illustrations include staring out of a window or into space, laying one's head on a piece of furniture, and playing or remaining alone while others are engaged in a group activity.

Results

Prosocial Behavior

The data presented in Figure 5.1 indicate that the average incidence of prosocial behavior exhibited by the group members increased from 70% during baseline to an average of 88% at the first introduction of reinforcement contingencies. During the reversal period, the incidence of prosocial behavior dropped to an average of 81% and to a low of 70% at the end of that period. In contrast, prosocial behavior rose to its highest point—an average of 94%—when the contingencies were introduced. The differences between the baseline and reinforcement

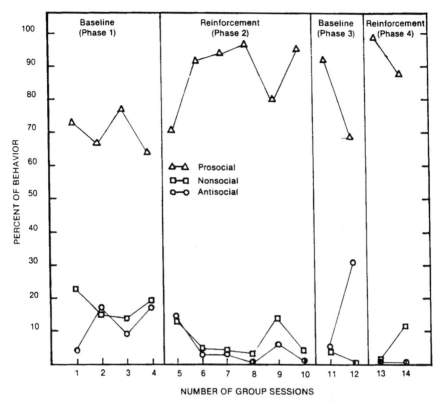

Figure 5.1   Average percentage of prosocial, nonsocial, and antisocial behavior exhibited by 10 children, according to number of group sessions.

conditions are significant $(F = 20.88;$ df $= 1,56;$ $p < 0.05)$. The statistical evaluation procedures are expounded in Chapter 7.

Nonsocial Behavior

With the first introduction of reinforcement contingencies, nonsocial behavior was reduced from an average of 18% to 7%. During the next reversal period, it continued to fall to an average of 2%. When contingencies were reintroduced, the incidence rose to an average of 7%. It is evident that nonsocial behavior was reduced considerably after the first baseline period but was not appreciably reduced thereafter. Although the incidence of nonsocial behavior increased again to 7%, the variation from 2% to 7% was not statistically significant; therefore, it may well represent a fluctuation within normal limits. Unfortunately, relatively little empirical data exist regarding normative rates of nonsocial behavior for children's groups. Such data would be very useful for child care workers and, accordingly, represents a useful subject for future field research.

Antisocial Behavior

Antisocial behavior was reduced from an average of 12% during the first baseline period to an average of 5% during the first introduction of contingencies. At reversal, it rose to an average of 18%, and in the last two periods, an average of 0% of antisocial behavior was recorded. The differences between the baseline and reinforcement conditions are statistically significant ($F = 11.20$; df $= 1,56$; $p < 0.05$). The data regarding antisocial behavior reflect only the frequency of acts observed; qualitative features of the behavior were not measured. Many of the antisocial behaviors that occurred at low frequencies, such as jumping out of a window, and hitting others, were highly disruptive for children, whereas other behaviors were of lesser consequence. These data, along with less systematic data obtained from postexperimental conferences with the group worker and clinicians who informally observed the group, suggest that the treatment just described brought about a significant reduction in virtually all types of antisocial behavior demonstrated by the children. This is all the more striking because the program was conducted within the context of an open and fluid community setting. Postprogram discussions with the group leader and other personnel within the agency suggested that the program also yielded a number of other positive results, including stronger friendship relations, greater peer cooperation, and more effective accomplishment of group objectives. Data from multicriteria measures has indicated a positive evaluation of the intervention.

Interventive Methods

Space limitations preclude the full presentation of requisite graphs, statistical tests, and discussions for each child. Instead, the average incidence of prosocial, nonsocial, and antisocial behaviors exhibited by all 10 group members are depicted in Figure 5.1. For illustrative purposes only, data are presented in Table 5.1 for a child whose behavioral profile was considered representative of the group members. Before examination of these data, a brief summary of the child's behavioral characteristics and subsequent treatment contingencies is presented.

A Case Illustration

Stan is a 10-year-old boy in the 5th grade of a school system considered one of the most progressive in the St. Louis metropolitan area. His parents are relatively affluent. Stan appears to be of normal height, weight, intelligence, and health for his age. Stan's behaviors during the baseline and reversal periods included pushing peers and throwing furniture at them, running in the halls, disrupting other groups by name calling, loud noises, and nonparticipation in group activities. Diagnosis revealed that the foregoing antisocial behaviors were reinforced by positive reinforcement from peer attention, particularly from his pal, Bill. This included supportive laughter, joining Stan in such behavior, and physically reinforcing him with pats on the back and smiling. Additionally, it was apparent that the group worker's reprimands to Stan tended to reinforce such behavior rather than diminish it, particularly by reaffirming Stan's position of preeminence within the peer group.

Contingencies of behavioral change were implemented after baseline. The worker began by engaging the group in an activity that the members found particularly enjoyable. This practice is common to virtually all effective group therapies and, regardless of any theoretical basis, tends to enhance the worker's attractiveness and capabilities as a therapeutic agent. However, as in previous instances, Stan and Bill attempted to disrupt the activity. Because the majority of members wished to engage in the activity, the group worker reinforced them for constructive participation with smiles and praise (positive reinforcers) and ignored the behaviors of Stan and Bill (extinction). Shortly thereafter, the disruptions of Stan and Bill ceased and they began to participate constructively in group activities. However, extinction represents a viable change strategy only as long as the target members' disruptive behaviors do not entail significant stress or harm for their peers. In this case, as nonthreatening disruptive behaviors diminished, the group worker reinforced the members' prosocial behavior through smiles, verbal praise, and other reinforcing acts. In instances in which disruptive behaviors entail greater stress, other techniques of behavioral change, such as time-out, punishment, stimulus control, and positive reinforcement of prosocial behaviors should be implemented to facilitate the attainment of group tasks (Wodarski & Feit, 1994).

To enhance the members' efforts to build cooperative relationships and plan and complete increasingly difficult tasks, the group worker paired the children with one another in subsequent sessions and structured further group contingencies. Specifically, the members were told that each person would earn 20 cents if the group could plan an activity in which everyone could participate. They were also informed that each member would receive an additional 20 cents if everyone participated in the chosen activity. In almost all instances of contingency construction and instruction, the members agreed with this regimen. Such contingencies helped Stan to plan and to participate more effectively and consistently in group activities. The group contingency increased peer pressure on Stan and others to participate in the chosen activity. Each group member's reinforcement was contingent on the participation of both himself and others. Additionally, as they earned social reinforcements from the worker and from their peers, the members were more readily accepted by one another and felt correspondingly more comfortable in the group. To avert satiation of monetary reinforcements, other group contingencies and reinforcers were introduced at periodic intervals. For example, the group was asked to engage in a given activity without any one member disrupting the others after which the members could have a special party, go swimming, or enjoy refreshments. As members' prosocial behavior increased, all forms of reinforcement and behavioral contingencies, including group contingencies, were gradually phased out, thus making the treatment environment more comparable with other peer groups in the open community.

Data provided in Table 5.1 on Stan's prosocial, nonsocial, and antisocial behaviors correspond with data in Figure 5.1. Data show an increase in prosocial behavior and a decrease in antisocial behavior during reinforcement periods. Nonsocial behavior showed a steady decline until the last reinforcement period. The group data presented in Figure 5.1 and individual data presented in Table 5.1 show nicely how practice interventions can be evaluated through the use of the ABAB design. The conclusion of the agency program schedule limited the ability to secure follow-up data. Such data would have permitted a strong evaluation of intervention effects. Another design which can be used in instances where it is not possible to engage another baseline condition is the AB design. Actually, it is the first half of the ABAB design. The AB design involves securing a baseline and introducing treatment after the behavior to be altered is stabilized. This is a minimum prerequisite to demonstrate the intervention's effect on treatment goals. However, such an evaluation is not as strong as the evaluation offered by the ABAB since the AB design does not control for as many biasing factors.

THE MULTIPLE BASELINE DESIGN

In many practice situations, the ABAB design may not be feasible due to the types of behaviors being modified or for various ethical reasons. The primary reason for utilizing an alternate design is that in the ABAB design the modified behavior usually will not reverse itself because it is maintained now by natural reinforcements existing in the client's environment. Also, in certain instances, reversals would be too damaging to the client or significant others in his life. For example, when fighting is brought under control in a home, when marital partners decrease the frequency of their interpersonal altercations, or when abusive parents develop better child-discipline skills, it would not be feasible to do a reversal on this behavior since physical harm has been inflicted on others in the past.

A design that may be utilized in lieu of the ABAB design is the multiple baseline design wherein a series of behaviors for modification are operationalized. Predictions are made on how the various techniques will affect different behaviors. Each behavior is then modified according to a time schedule. Usually one or two behaviors are modified at a time. For example, the worker might want to decrease such behaviors as yelling, fighting, throwing objects, and straying from the group, and increase prosocial behaviors, such as task participation and appropriate verbal comments. The worker in this instance might choose first to ignore the yelling and use positive reinforcement to increase appropriate verbal comments. Once the yelling decreases and the appropriate verbal comments increase, the worker would sequentially modify the second, third, and fourth behaviors. In Table 5.2, an outline is provided on how such a process operates. The technique being employed becomes more efficacious every time the behaviors change in the directions predicted for the child; that is the scientific concept of replication rules out other factors that neglect the responsibilities for the change.

Table 5.2 illustrates the application of a multiple baseline design by practitioners who evaluated the use of task-centered casework to improve mother-child communications.

Purpose of the Intervention

The client is a divorced 26-year-old woman primarily supported by public welfare. She has three children, ages 5, 3, and 1. The client stated that she was having difficulty understanding the speech of her 3-year-

Table 5.2   Example of Multiple Baseline Design

Behavior		Time period at which modification plan is instituted[c]
Antisocial[a]	Prosocial[b]	
Not sitting with group	Task participation	1
Yelling	Appropriate speech	2
Fighting	Helping behavior	3
Throwing objects	Cleaning up	4

[a] Extinction used to decrease.
[b] Positive reinforcement used to increase.
[c] Length of time periods, not specified, depends on how rigorous one wants to be in showing the effects of the modification plan. A period usually lasts until the behavior stabilizes at a variance of less than 10% point variability for 3 to 5 days.

old son, who was being treated for lead poisoning at a pediatric hospital, a 62-bed, long-term care facility for children up to 18 years old. The speech department at the hospital tested his skills and found them to be slightly above average for his age level. Therefore, the authors, in consultation with the speech department and the mother, decided to teach various language skills to the mother with the aim being to increase the son's verbal skills and the mother's understanding of her son's verbalizations.

Theoretical Rationale for Intervention

Task-centered casework was chosen because it is a structured intervention that details the role of the therapist and client in specific terms. The client stated that she had problems understanding the child and was not familiar with the stages of a child's verbal development. The authors felt that a structured interaction between the mother and child based on specific verbal-skills training would increase the mother's understanding of the child's speech and help the child acquire requisite verbal skills. Unfortunately, many lower-income individuals do not have adequate models, resources, or knowledge of how to teach their children verbal skills. With task-centered casework, both the mother and the child learned within a structured task situation.

The client's difficulties fit one of the seven target typologies Reid and Epstein (1972) discuss: difficulty in role performance. Reid and Epstein state that clients with perceived problems in role performance are aware of a gap between how they execute their roles and how they would like to execute their roles. The mother could not understand how her son's verbal abilities were above average when she could not always understand him. The verbal learning tasks were designed to enhance her execution of her parent role. Briefly, the three demonstration tasks for the mother were naming an object, describing the function of an object, and verbalizing commands clearly.

Previous Research

Task-centered casework is a theoretical system of short-term intervention that emerged in 1980 with the publication of *Task-Centered Casework* by Reid and Epstein. In 1977, Reid and Epstein published a follow-up book, *Task-Centered Practice*, and Reid has another book, *The Task-Centered System* (1980). Task-centered casework is unique in development because researchers and practitioners have worked together to specify its constructs and have tested an intervention variable. This process shows how research can be used to develop, to test, and to provide an empirical rationale for practice principles.

In 1975, Reid took a major step in placing task-centered casework on firm empirical grounds by operationalizing the variable of task performance in a five-step plan called task implementation sequence (TIS). TIS is a progressive treatment sequence that includes "enhancing commitment, planning task implementation, analyzing obstacles, modeling, rehearsal, guided practice, and summarizing," with the goal being to elicit specific client behaviors. The introduction of "operational tasks" was part of a beginning effort to specify the model's constructs and to place the paradigm on firmer scientific grounds by specifying the unit of attention—the task—in more measurable terms.

At the time of the study, a review of the literature produced only three research articles on task-centered casework (Reid, 1975; Rossi, 1977; Tolson, 1977). Two authors included task-centered casework in their discussions of short-term or structured approaches to practice (Goldberg, 1974; Goldmeier, 1976). The review further revealed that the concepts of task-centered casework had not been used in research outside the social work profession. Nevertheless, task-centered casework is part of a growing movement in intervention practices focused toward time-limited, structured, goal-specific, and empirically measurable interventions (Cormican, 1977; Garvin, 1974; Gurman & Razin, 1977).

In the study by Rossi (1977), a baseline treatment design, AB was used to evaluate effects of the worker's intervention on increasing verbalizations of a mute child. Tolson (1977) used a multiple baseline design to systematically evaluate the intervention across three targeted behaviors seen as creating communication problems for a couple. Tolson's study was also the only study that had communications behavior as its target task. Communication between parent and child was not investigated in any study.

Method

It was hypothesized that task-centered casework would increase a mother's communication skills with her child. The independent variable is task-centered casework. Conceptually defined, task-centered treatment is a short-term model of social work practice designed to alleviate specific problems of individuals and families (Reid & Epstein, 1972). The operational definition can be stated in a step-by-step progression: The client's problems are explored, a target problem is identified, a task is formulated, time limits are structured to attain casework goals, work on the task is carried out, and termination is effected (Reid & Epstein, 1972). As stated in *Webster's New World Dictionary* (Guralnik, 1975), communication means "to give or exchange information," and skills means "expertness that comes from training, practice, and so forth." Skills the child learns are the dependent variables, such as identifying objects, explaining the function of an object, and responding to verbalized commands.

When determining the target problem, the authors used the format in *Task-Centered Casework* (Reid & Epstein, 1972). The problem about which the client was concerned was explored first. More than any other problem, the mother discussed her communication difficulties with her 3-year-old child. This problem was defined in behavioral terms. In this case, the mother said that when he was excited and wanted to tell her something, she could not understand his verbalizations. The authors therefore classified the target problem in the typology of difficulty in role performance as difficulties in communicating with a child.

The Verbal Language Development Scale by Mecham (1971) was given to the mother to assess what she thought her child's verbal-skills level was. It was revealed that the mother did not think her child's verbal behaviors were appropriate for his age level. Her assessment was shared with the speech department to help determine the appropriate skills to teach the child. The speech department, the researchers, and the mother agreed that the tasks focused on should increase the child's ability to identify objects and to explain their functions, and should increase his responsiveness to verbal commands.

The overall design of the experiment is outlined in Table 5.3. For the first baseline session, the authors met with the mother in the play kitchen in the hospital's preschool nursery. The mother was instructed to make a dinner with her son for 10 min in the play kitchen, a setting familiar to the child. The authors observed and tape recorded the baseline frequency of the three verbal task skills. After this session, the mother was told that the first skill she would perform was object identification.

For the first intervention with the child, the mother was to make a dinner in the same play kitchen with her son's help. She was instructed that she would point out objects in the kitchen and state, "This is a pot [pitcher/fork/refrigerator]." In accordance with TIS, the authors first modeled the expected behaviors and then the mother rehearsed them with the authors, but without her son. When the mother learned the task, the authors repeated the original instructions. The mother then made a play dinner with her son for 10 min.

For the second intervention, the mother was instructed to describe the function of an object while making dinner with her son: for example, "The refrigerator keeps food cold," "The broom sweeps dirt," and "The pot cooks food." The authors modeled the task, the mother rehearsed it and carried it out.

For the third intervention, again the verbal skills she would be using with her son were explained. The mother was informed that the third task would be to verbalize two commands, such as "Get the broom from the closet and sweep up the dirt," or "Get the dolls from their bed and put them in high chairs." Expressing two commands at the same time gives the child an opportunity to use and develop a more complex cognitive skill: The child must remember one command while carrying out the other. The authors modeled the skill, the mother rehearsed it to an acceptable level, and the intervention was carried out.

After each session, the authors measured the frequency of each task by using a tape recorder. The authors required 100% agreement among themselves for reliability on criterion behavior.

At the conclusion of the three intervention sessions, the results of the study were summarized for the mother. She was encouraged to discuss any problems she had during the intervention or which she might have when using the skills in the future at home. Two follow-up sessions

Table 5.3 Multiple Baseline Design According to Phases

Communication problem	Day				
	1	4	8	14	19	109
Name	Baseline	Intervention			Follow-up 1	Follow-up II
Function	Baseline	Baseline	Intervention		Follow-up 1	Follow-up II
Command	Baseline	Baseline	Baseline	Intervention	Follow-up 1	Follow-up II

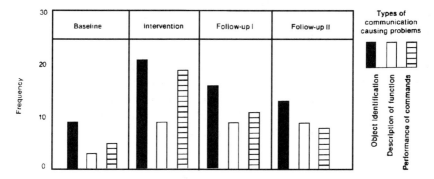

Figure 5.2   Frequency of communication problems during 10-min sessions according to the phase of multiple baseline design. Baseline data were secured on naming for one session, function for two sessions, and responsiveness to commands for three sessions. Follow-up data collection sessions were 5 and 109 days after treatment.

to measure the maintenance on all three levels were executed 5 days and again 3 months after the conclusion of the study.

Results

Baseline

Baseline frequencies of the respective behaviors were nine occurrences of object identification, three of description of function, and five of the performance of two commands (Figure 5.2).

Intervention

Task performance was greatest during each respective intervention. The data on task performance in Figure 5.2 show that for intervention 1, there was an increase in the occurrence of the targeted behavior from a frequency of 9 to 21; for intervention 2, from a frequency of 3 to 9; and for intervention 3, from a frequency of 5 to 19. For tasks 1 and 2, the intervention was at least double that of the baseline. For task 3, the intervention tripled the baseline rate.

Follow-up

Data in Figure 5.2 show that for verbalizing the function of an object, the child's follow-up scores were stable compared with the treatment phase. Both follow-up values equaled 9. A decrease, compared with the treatment-phase frequency of 21 occurred for naming an object in the first and second follow-ups (16 and 13, respectively), and for responsiveness to commands, with a treatment-phase frequency of 19, and follow-ups of 11 and 8, respectively. However, scores were still higher than baseline rates. The follow-up data on naming an object and on responsiveness to commands suggest that additional casework sessions might have been warranted. However, scores client felt this was not necessary.

SUMMARY

All the foregoing designs, the ABAB, AB, and multiple baselines, can be easily implemented in empirical practice. The actual design of any study depends on the context of the behavioral change situation in terms of behaviors to be altered, time and treatment considerations, and administrative concerns.

These pilot projects illustrate how practitioners can use research to evaluate practice and, thus, increase their confidence in their effectiveness. That is, one may observe the demonstrated significant impact on client behaviors. Empirical knowledge is essential for any profession. The ABAB, AB, and multiple baseline, time-series designs provide a clinical research methodology that can be easily implemented by practitioners and used to improve practice. Thus, the divisions between researchers and practitioners may be narrowed through the use of the discussed methodologies (Wodarski & Feldman, 1973; Wodarski, Hudson, & Buckholdt, 1976).

Within the foreseeable future, it is apparent that the designs discussed will be applied to evaluate various practice interventions on a larger scale. The outcome of such a process inevitably will be that the knowledge base of social work practice will become increasingly complex, and only then will it be able to reflect and cope effectively with the immensity of those problems social workers typically face every day.

REFERENCES

Bloom, M., & Block, S. R. (1977). Evaluating one's own effectiveness and efficiency. *Social Work, 22,* 130–136.

Bloom, M., & Fischer, J. (1982). *Evaluating practice: Guidelines for the accountable professional.* Englewood Cliffs, NJ: Prentice Hall.

Cormican, E. J. (1977). Task-centered model for work with the aged. *Social Casework, 58,* 490–494.

Feldman, R. A., Caplinger, T. E., & Wodarski, J. S. (1983). *The St. Louis conundrum: The effective treatment of antisocial youths.* Englewood Cliffs, NJ: Prentice Hall.

Garvin, C. D. (1974). Task-centered group work. *Social Service Review, 48,* 494–507.

Goldberg, G. (1974). Structural approach to practice: A new model. *Social Work, 19,* 150–155.

Goldmeier, J. (1976). Short-term models in long-term treatment. *Social Work, 21,* 350–355.

Gottman, J. M., & Leiblum, S. R. (1974). *How to do psychotherapy and how to evaluate it: A manual for beginners.* New York: Holt, Rinehart, & Winston.

Guralnik, D. G. (Ed.). (1975). *Webster's new world dictionary.* New York: Popular Library.

Gurman, A. S., & Razin, A. M. (Eds.). (1977). *Effective psychotherapy.* New York: Pergamon.

Mecham, M. J. (1971). *Verbal language development scale.* Circle Pines, MN: American Guidance Service.

Patterson, G. R. (1971). *Families: Application of social learning to family life.* Champaign, IL: Research Press.

Reid, W. J. (1975). A test of a task-centered approach. *Social Work, 20,* 3–9.

Reid, W. J., & Epstein, L. (1972). *Task-centered casework.* New York: Columbia University Press.

Reid, W. J., & Epstein, L. (Eds.). (1977). *Task-centered practice.* New York: Columbia University Press.

Reid, W. J. (1980). *The task-centered system.* New York: Columbia University Press.

Rossi, R. B. (1977). Helping a mute child. In W. J. Reid & L. Epstein (Eds.), *Task-centered practice* (pp. 147–156). New York: Columbia University Press.

Tolson, E. R. (1977). Alleviating marital communication problems. In W. J. Reid & L. Epstein (Eds.), *Task-centered practice.* New York: Columbia University Press.

Tripodi, T. (1994). *A primer on single-subject design for clinical workers.* Washington, D.C.: National Association of Social Workers.

Wodarski. J. S., & Bagarozzi. D. A. (1979). *Behavioral social work.* New York: Human Sciences Press.

Wodarski, J. S., & Buckholdt, D. R. (1975). Behavioral instruction in college classrooms: A review of methodological procedures. In J. M. Johnston (Ed.), *Behavior research and technology in higher education.* Springfield, IL: Charles C. Thomas.

Wodarski, J. S., & Feit, M. D. (1994). Applications of reward structures in social group work. *Social Work with Groups, 17,* 123–142.

Wodarski, J. S., & Feldman, R. A. (1973). The research practicum: A beginning formulation of process and educational objectives. *International Social Work, 16,* 42–48.

Wodarski, J. S., & Feldman, R. A. (1976). Behavioral observational scale for children and therapist interacting in a group. In O. G. Johnson (Ed.), *Tests and measurements in child development: Handbook II* (pp. 1168–1171). San Francisco: Jossey-Bass.

Wodarski, J. S., Feldman, R. A., & Pedi, S. J. (1976). Reduction of antisocial behavior in an open community setting through the use of behavior modification in groups. *Child Care Quarterly, 5,* 198–210.

Wodarski, J. S., Hudson, W., & Buckholdt, D. R. (1976). Issues in evaluative research: Implications for social work practice. *Journal of Sociology and Social Welfare, 4,* 81–113.

CHAPTER 6

Traditional Designs

APPROPRIATE APPLICATIONS

The last chapter reviewed time-series designs and their applications in clinical practice. In terms of administrative execution, time, personnel, and money, time-series designs are easy to implement. Their role in research is to provide beginning knowledge about practice techniques and theory; they provide preliminary data as to whether intervention should be evaluated more formally. Such knowledge provides the empirical rationale for practice. Other designs that control for confounding factors (provide a stronger assessment of therapeutic interventions that might affect those variables the practitioner is interested in) are necessary to refine the knowledge developed through time-series designs. The designs discussed in this chapter are pertinent to the internal and external validity of any experiment. *Internal validity* refers to how well the experiment controls for rival hypotheses; that is, factors other than worker interventions that can be responsible for therapeutic effects. *External validity* refers to how extensively the results can be generalized to other practice populations, contexts, and workers.

In constructing studies, one should, if at all possible, use random assignment of participants to experimental and control groups, and include a control group composed of individuals as similar as possible to experimental groups. Random assignment controls for the confounding factors described below that can influence a study, along with the variables of interest (Bernstein, 1975; Bernstein, Bohrnstedt, & Borgatta, 1975; Campbell & Stanley, 1967; Campbell, 1967, 1969). Control groups provide the natural expected changes through time. Confounding factors have been grouped according to their influence on a study's internal validity or external validity.

INTERNAL VALIDITY

Historical Effects

Without a control group, the practitioner cannot be certain if the effects on the outcome variables are due to the intervention or some other variable. That is, something else could have happened at the same time treatment was initiated that could account for the effect, such as the client receiving a raise, finishing an educational degree, or securing a divorce. When a control group is employed, however, such effects have the same probability of being present as in the experimental group. For this procedure to function adequately, the control group must be as similar as possible to the experimental group in all aspects (dimensions), such as race, age, sex, income, and so on, except for the operations involved in the provision of treatment. As the control differs on relevant dimensions, the ability to rule out confounding factors decreases.

Maturational Effects

If only one experimental group is used and is pre- and posttested without a control group, effects could be due to boredom, fatigue, participants getting older, or individuals getting better over time without treatment interventions. A control group isolates what is a normal rate of behavior change over time in outcome measures without therapeutic intervention. This rival hypothesis is particularly relevant for human service providers because research is accumulating that suggests that a substantial portion of clients with difficulties improve with the passage of time in the absence of therapeutic interventions (Bergin, 1980; Bergin & Garfield, 1971; Franks & Mays, 1980; Mays & Franks, 1980; Segal, 1972; Wodarski, 1987; 1989; Wodarski & Bagarozzi, 1979; Wodarski & Pedi, 1978; Wolfgang, Figlio, & Sellin, 1972).

Testing Procedures (Pretest Sensitization)

Pretest sensitization is especially important in studies in which attitude change is a major outcome variable. Administering a test may sensitize clients to what you are interested in, especially if the studies deal with sensitive social topics, such as racism, marital satisfaction, and sexism. Testing alone can cause changes in people if individuals begin to think about appropriate responses. If control groups are used, this confounding factor may be identified and its effects isolated. In spite of its importance, pretesting sensitization is not controlled in many social psychology studies on these kinds of topics, thereby confounding the data obtained (Wodarski, Hudson, & Buckholdt, 1976).

Measurement Procedures

Problems can be caused by changes in calibration of measurement due to fatigue of data collectors, in testing procedures, and in manner of explaining instructions. One must control for the sex, age, and race of the person giving the questionnaire, and, in relevant instances, time of year the questionnaire is administered. Moreover, one must ensure that interviewers ask questions consistently, dress appropriately, and present themselves similarly. If behavioral observers are used, they must be observing reliably the same behavior, and measurement procedures must be constant in pre- and posttests. Experimenter biases must be controlled for in the study. The researcher should not word questions in a way that could reveal the outcomes the interviewer seeks. Random assignment of different testers to experimental and control groups, videotaping administration of testing, audiotaping the instruction for the questionnaire if given in a group situation, and the execution of periodic reliability tests to assess how well the data collectors are executing their tasks all aid in controlling measurement difficulties (Goldstein, 1962; Rosenthal & Rosnow, 1969; Rosenthal, 1966, 1976; Shapiro, 1971).

Statistical Regression Effects

How participants are picked for a study influences the outcome. If the most deviant group of a population is picked for study, there will be some improvements through time. Deviant individuals will reduce the frequency of unusual behaviors through time due to regression toward the average, otherwise known as statistical regression. Random assignment controls for this factor in the control group give an accurate estimation of the regression effect.

Differential Selection of Subjects

If one conducts an experiment with a preformed group, it is impossible to tell what factors were involved in the group selection. There could likely be an interaction between the independent variable and group selection. If experimental and control groups are not formed in the same way, the ability to place confidence in the results of the study is substantially reduced.

Experimental Mortality

Individuals who complete treatment may be substantially different from those who do not (Wodarski, Filipczak, McCombs, Koustenis, & Rusilko, 1979; Howing, Wodarski, Kurtz, & Gaudin, 1993). Attrition rates must be similar in experimental and control groups and should be kept under 30% in both groups to reduce data confoundment.

The seven factors described above affect the internal validity of a study (McCombs, Filipczak, Friedman, & Wodarski, 1978). They may operate singularly or in conjunction with one another. It is possible that a study might have multiple rival hypotheses operating to compromise its internal validity.

EXTERNAL VALIDITY

If the study lacks adequate internal validity, the results are not clear of contamination and the data cannot be generalized to other populations. Thus, internal validity is prerequisite to external validity. Four major factors may affect external validity: interactional effects of selection biases and the experimental variable, effects of pretesting, reactive effects of experimental procedures, and multiple treatment interference.

Interactional Effects of Selection Biases and the Experimental Variable

If clients are not chosen for control groups in the same manner as for treatment groups, there is no way to isolate how the selection factors interact with treatment, and the effects may be attributed to the selection process.

Effects of Pretesting

If the effects of pretesting have not been isolated, it is impossible to separate the effects of testing from the effects of the independent variable.

Reactive Effects of Experimental Procedures

Where the study is conducted has an effect on how the results can be generalized. All organizations differ on a number of relevant variables. The study may need to include a cross-section of organizations to increase the potential of the data for generalizing to other situations.

Multiple Treatment Interference

The combination of different treatments (i.e., behavioral, problem solving, and task centered) confounds effects. When multiple treatments are used, the isolation of effects of each treatment on outcome variables is not possible without an adequate design to control for this factor.

CHARACTERISTICS OF CONTROL GROUPS

Much of the controversy in human services centers on whether services offered to clients significantly affect their lives. Control groups are necessary to determine if interventions were effective. Ideally, two control groups should be used in research conducted to evaluate services, a waiting-list control group and an active control group. An active control group provides a baseline rate of improvement or deterioration over time, to which the experimental intervention can be compared and evaluated. To provide an accurate comparison, this control group should contain all the essential features of the treatment group except for the variables under investigation. For example, if we are evaluating task-centered casework, the control group should be similar in worker expectations for change, testing procedures, and context and length of sessions. An active control group provides a refined analysis of the components of effective treatment. However, such a fine analysis may be too costly in time, energy, and administration. A waiting-list control group isolates the number of clients who improve through the passage of time without receiving documented professional help. Although the employment of an active control group is preferable, a waiting-list control group is the minimal prerequisite for the adequate evaluation of treatment effects. Both groups should be offered services immediately after the collection of requisite data.

COMMON EXPERIMENTAL DESIGNS

Classical Design

In the following example, the basic objective of the classical design is to evaluate family therapy provided in a family service agency. The assumption is made that the independent variable (the therapist's intervention) and the dependent variable (the measure of change or outcome variables) are well specified. One hundred cases are available for the study: 50 are randomly assigned to treatment, and 50 are randomly assigned to a waiting-list control group. Both groups are pretested and posttested on the same outcome variables. Random assignment of clients equalizes both groups on most of the variables that could confound a study, and the employment of pre- and posttest measures enables the assessment of the amount of change. The waiting-list control group provides the rate or level of change that could be expected in the clients over time. The major concern in such a design is that the testing mechanism itself may produce change in individuals. This concern may be more relevant for behavioral scientists, who do not work in human service agencies characterized by frequent employment of assessment batteries, to provide diagnostic information for choosing appropriate treatment interventions. In such agencies, testing effects would be minimal because clients are subjected to the procedure routinely. If a practitioner wishes to isolate the effects of the interaction of the assessment with the treatment, the Solomon four-group design, explained next, should be employed. Because this design doubles the number of experimental and control groups, the practitioner must consider the additional time, money, and administrative requisites involved.

Example of Classical Design

One hundred clients are randomly assigned:

1. Fifty clients assigned to experimental group: pretest, service, posttest.
2. Fifty clients assigned to waiting-list control group: pretest, no service, posttest.

Solomon Four-Group Design

The Solomon four-group design controls for pretest sensitization hypothesis, but it is costly because four groups are used instead of the traditional design of one experimental group and one control group. To isolate testing effects, one experimental group and one control group are pre- and posttested. The other experimental and control groups are posttested, but not pretested. Random assignment of participants is essential because the assumption is made that all pretest scores would be similar if all groups were tested. To isolate the effects of testing, these pretest scores are used in the calculation of the differences between experimental and control groups that were pretested and those that were not pretested. Testing effects are isolated by noting the difference between the two control groups: one receives a pre- and posttest and the other receives only the posttest. Through a similar process, this design also enables the isolation of testing and treatment interaction. The effects are isolated by comparing the differences between outcome variables in the two experimental groups, as illustrated below.

Example of the Solomon Four-Group Design

Two hundred clients were randomly assigned to four different groups:

1. Fifty clients: pretest, no service, posttest
2. Fifty clients: no pretest, no service, posttest
3. Fifty clients: pretest, service, posttest
4. Fifty clients: no pretest, service, posttest only

Multiple Groups Design

This design is utilized when the desire is to evaluate more than one treatment against others. In the future, studies will be executed that will evaluate the use of different interpersonal helping approaches, such as problem solving, task-centered casework, or behavioral casework. As in the classical design, participants are pooled and are randomly assigned to experimental and control groups. The design allows for each treatment to be compared to the others but also permits the comparison of results against a control group. To elaborate on the classical design, a family service agency has 200 cases on which to execute the design; 50 each are randomly assigned to problem-solving casework, task-centered casework, behavioral casework, and a waiting-list control group. The rationale for the employment of the design is to determine which of two or more treatments are most effective and will produce the greatest change in the shortest period of time.

Example of Multiple Groups Design

Two hundred clients were randomly assigned to different casework approaches:

1. Fifty clients: pretest, problem-solving casework, posttest
2. Fifty clients: pretest, task-centered casework, posttest
3. Fifty clients: pretest, behavioral casework, posttest
4. Fifty clients: pretest, waiting-list control group, posttest

Factorial Design

As knowledge about the phenomena social workers deal with increases in complexity, significant questions about effective treatment technologies and how they are combined with such things as worker attributes and context variables to produce more efficient use of person power will be needed. Factorial designs in which variables are combined to isolate such interactional effects will ease the development of this complex knowledge.

In an evaluation of a community-based treatment program for antisocial children, the following individual variables—treatment strategies, various types of group composition, and various degrees of worker training and combinations—were evaluated through a factorial sign to assess which variables had the greatest effect on the behaviors exhibited by antisocial children.

Methods

A 3 x 3 x 2 factorial design was utilized. The first factor consisted of group-treatment strategies: social learning, traditional group work, and group-centered. The second factor was group composition: antisocial, mixed, and prosocial. Each cell of the design was apportioned to

Table 6.1   Examples of Factorial Design

Treatment program	Group composition		
	Antisocial	Mixed	Prosocial
Behavior modification	2 MSW	2 MSW	2 MSW
	2 BSW	2 BSW	2 BSW
Traditional	2 MSW	2 MSW	2 MSW
	2 BSW	2 BSW	2 BSW
Group centered	2 MSW	2 MSW	2 MSW
	2 BSW	2 BSW	2 BSW

enable evaluation of the third factor, degree of worker training—bachelor's-level (BSW) or master's-level social workers (MSW). Such a design provides 18 combinations of the various variables that can be tested and whose effects can be isolated.

Participants

Thirty-six groups of children were utilized. Twelve groups consisted of antisocial subjects, 12 groups consisted of one antisocial subject and the remainder prosocial, and 12 groups consisted of prosocial children. The size of the groups varied from 8 to 12 members. Participants were males ranging in age from 9 to 16 years. Antisocial children were defined as subjects who exhibit a high incidence of behaviors that disrupt interactional situations in which they participate. Prosocial children were defined as subjects who exhibit a low frequency of these behaviors (Table 6.1).

Each cell of the design is composed of four groups of children. Two have an MSW leader and two groups have a BSW leader to isolate the training factor (Feldman, Caplinger, & Wodarski, 1983).

Counterbalanced Design

In many instances, a research practitioner wants to evaluate a number of services. However, assignment of clients to a treatment or control group is not possible. In such instances, a counterbalanced design may be employed to provide an adequate evaluation. In this design, all clients are exposed to all the treatments for the same limited time period. In this design, clients are entered into all treatments in a random order. The process provides for the replication of the experimental effects and experimental groups serve as their own controls.

In the following example, the counterbalanced strategy was utilized in gathering data to evaluate the effects of four reinforcement conditions—individual consequences, group-shared consequences, and two different proportions of individual and group-shared consequences—on (a) peer tutoring, (b) arithmetic performance, (c) studying, (d) non-studying, and (e) disruptive behavior. The study employed 60 experimental and 34 comparison children from three 5th-grade classes. To allow for clear specification of the effects of the four different reinforcement contingencies, a 4 x 4 counterbalanced design was employed using four experimental groups and two comparison groups. This design protected against rival hypotheses that could account for the changes in the dependent variables. The four experimental groups were secured by dividing each of two experimental classrooms into two groups of randomly chosen children.

A 4 x 4 counterbalanced design was chosen because the children could not be placed in a pool and then randomly assigned to one of the four experimental groups. By entering all children into all treatments the rival hypotheses of history, maturation, testing, instrumentation, regression, selection, and mortality that could be postulated to account for the data were controlled for. The design provided for the replication of the effects of the independent variables four times. The central idea is that if treatment effects are strong enough, they should occur each time the variable is introduced. This design also provided a way of dealing with the fact that the experimental groups started at different criterion levels on the dependent variables. It was realized that the design had confounding effects, but the replication feature provided a powerful test for the independent variables under the circumstances.

The above procedures were instigated when the original plan—utilization of all four of the 5th grades as experimental groups—had to be modified. This occurred because two of the teachers chose not to become involved in the experiment as experimental groups but volunteered only as controls. It was realized that these were not true control groups; because school had been in progress for 4 months, it was impossible to place all the students in a pool for random assignment into the traditional experimental and control groups. These comparison groups did not provide as much protection against the previously stated rival hypotheses that could be postulated to account for the changes in the dependent variables as randomized control groups, but it was believed better to conduct the experiment in this manner because the comparison groups provided a criterion against which the progress

Table 6.2   Example of Counterbalanced Design

Groups	Order of experimental treatments			
1	B	C	D	A
2	C	B	A	D
3	A	D	B	C
4	D	A	C	B
5 (Comparison)	Baseline	Baseline	Baseline	Baseline
6 (Comparison)	Pretest			Posttest

of the experimental groups could be judged. It was understood that such a comparison would have limitations and that these limitations would have to be considered in evaluating the data provided by the experiment.

Each of the four experimental groups was in each of four treatment conditions (A–D) for 14 days and went through the four reinforcement contingencies in a randomized order, illustrated here in Table 6.2. The limitation of the counterbalanced design is the difficulty of isolating differential treatment effects from multiple interaction of treatments with the passage of time.

SUMMARY

These last two chapters presented the various designs that can be used to develop and refine practice knowledge. Time-series designs discussed in Chapter 5 should be used initially to develop knowledge, and subsequent designs discussed in this chapter should be used to refine the knowledge. As research practitioners consider the use of the traditional designs discussed here, the following critical question must be addressed: Has a practice technique or theory been isolated that warrants the time, personnel, and money involved in implementing a traditional design?

REFERENCES

Bergin, A. E. (1980). Negative effects revisited: A rejoinder. *Professional Psychology, 11,* 101–105.

Bergin, A. E., & Garfield. S. L. (1971). *Handbook of psychotherapy and behavior change*. Toronto: Wiley.

Bernstein, I. N. (1975). Validity issues in evaluative research: An overview. *Sociological Methods and Research, 4,* 3–12.

Bernstein, I. N., Bohrnstedt, G. W., & Borgatta, E. F. (1975). External validity and evaluative research: A codification of problems. *Sociological Methods and Research, 4,* 101–128.

Campbell, D. T. (1967). From description to experimentation: Interpreting trends as quasi-experiments. In C. W. Harris (Ed.), *Problems in measuring change*. Madison, WI: University of Wisconsin Press.

Campbell, D. T. (1969). Reforms as experiments. *American Psychologist, 24,* 409–429.

Campbell, D. T., & Stanley, J. C. (1967). *Experimental and quasi-experimental designs for research*. Chicago: Rand McNally.

Feldman, R. A., Caplinger, T. E., & Wodarski, J. S. (1983). *The St. Louis conundrum: The effective treatment of antisocial youths*. Englewood Cliffs, NJ: Prentice Hall.

Franks, C. W., & Mays, D. T. (1980). Negative effects revisited: A reply. *Professional Psychology, 11,* 93–100.

Goldstein, A. P. (1962). *Therapist-patient expectancies in psychotherapy*. New York: Pergamon Press.

Howing, P. T., Wodarski, J. S., Kurtz, P. D., & Gaudin, J. M. (1993). *Maltreatment and the school-aged child: Developmental outcomes and system issues*. New York: Haworth Press.

Mays, D. T., & Franks, C. M. (1980). Getting worse: Psychotherapy or no treatment—The jury should still be out. *Professional Psychology, 11,* 78–92.

McCombs, D., Filipczak, J., Friedman, R. M., & Wodarski, L. S. (1978). Long-term follow-up of behavior modification with high-risk adolescents. *Criminal Justice and Behavior, 5,* 21–34.

Rosenthal, R. (1966). *Experimental effects in behavior research*. New York: Appleton.

Rosenthal, R. (1976). *Experimental effects in behavioral research* (rev. ed.). New York: Irvington.

Rosenthal, R., & Rosnow, R. L. (Eds.). (1969). *Artifact in behavioral research*. New York: Academic.

Segal, S. P. (1972). Research on the outcome of social work therapeutic intentions: A review of the literature. *Journal of Health and Social Behavior, 13,* 3–17.

Shapiro, A. K. (1971). Placebo effects in medicine, psychotherapy, and psychoanalysis. In A. E. Bergin & S. L. Garfield (Eds.), *Handbook of psychotherapy and behavior change*. New York: Wiley.

Wodarski, J. S. (1987). *Social work practice with children and adolescents*. Springfield, IL: Charles C Thomas.

Wodarski, J. S. (1989). *Preventive health services for adolescents*. Springfield, IL: Charles C Thomas.

Wodarski, J. S., & Bagarozzi, D. A. (1979). A review of the empirical status of traditional modes of interpersonal helping: Implications for social work practice. *Clinical Social Work Journal, 7,* 231–255.

Wodarski, J. S., Filipczak, J., McCombs, D., Koustenis, G., & Rusilko, S. (1979). Follow-up on behavioral intervention with troublesome adolescents. *Journal of Experimental Psychiatry and Behavior Therapy, 10,* 181–188.

Wodarski, J. S., & Pedi, S. J. (1978). The empirical evaluation of the effects of different group treatment strategies against a controlled treatment strategy on behavior exhibited by antisocial children, behavior of the therapist, and two self-ratings measuring antisocial behavior. *Journal of Clinical Psychology, 34,* 471–481.

Wodarski, J. S., Hudson, W., & Buckholdt, D. (1976). Issues in evaluative research: Implications for social work practice. *Journal of Sociology and Social Welfare, 4,* 81–113.

Wolfgang, M. E., Figlio, R. M., & Sellin, T. (1972). *Delinquency in a birth cohort.* Chicago: University of Chicago.

CHAPTER 7

Application of Statistical Techniques in the Evaluation of Practice

T his chapter examines the use of statistical procedures that enable us to evaluate the effectiveness of practice. The aim is not to provide a background in statistics.[1] It is assumed that the reader has a working knowledge of statistical methods. The intent here is to provide examples of the application of appropriate procedures in the evaluation of research for practice. The more sophisticated multivariate techniques are discussed in Chapter 8.

Statistical procedures are tools that help decide whether research results are meaningful or significant enough to apply in social work practice or theory. Two assumptions are made in regard to statistical

---

[1] For more on statistics, see: Bruning, J. L., & Kintz, B. L. (1977). *Computational handbook of statistics.* (2nd ed.). Dallas, TX: Scott, Foresman, and Company. Glass, G. V., & Hopkins, K. D. (1984). *Statistical methods in education and psychology* (2nd ed.). Englewood Cliffs, NJ: Prentice Hall. Harris, M. B. (1995). *Basic statistics for behavior science research.* New York: Allyn and Bacon. Loether, H. J., & McTavish, D. G. (1993). *Descriptive and inferential statistics: An introduction* (4th ed.). Boston: Allyn and Bacon. Wonnacott, T. H., & Wonnacott, R. J. (1990). *Introductory statistics.* New York: John Wiley & Sons.

procedures: (a) There is order to the universe, and through systematically studying the phenomena of interest, knowledge will be developed; and (b) only a limited number of events are related to each other. Simply stated, statistics help us to describe and put order into the phenomena dealt with in social work. The major aim of statistics is to find consistency in the data of interest.

DATA DESCRIPTION

Data can be categorized and depicted through tables, graphs, frequency distribution scales, and scatter diagrams. Such graphic forms usually elucidate the relationship between two variables, for example, different treatment conditions and frequency of certain types of behavior. These techniques are not statistical methods. Measures of central tendency permit us to make meaningful statements about data that have been depicted in the manner mentioned above. The central tendency is a characteristic of a distribution of scores or values that tells us where these scores or values tend to cluster. Three common measures of central tendency are the mean, median, and the mode. Means (averages), medians (the point at which 50% of the scores or values fall below and 50% above), and modes (the most frequently occurring scores or values) communicate quickly the focal points of the data. These descriptive procedures are frequently used in pilot research. For example, in a study that described the competencies mental health workers need in order to work with the rural aged, data were secured through interviews with 15 practitioners who worked in a variety of agencies. Once the data were secured, descriptive statistics were used to present the data as knowledge needed for practice. The information centered on agency operational procedures, psychological and sociological aspects of aging, physiological aspects of aging, treatment modalities, and administrative tasks.

Table 7.1 shows how the mean can be used to communicate quickly what competencies social workers felt were the most and least necessary for workers who provide services to the aged in rural areas. Descriptive statistics were employed also in the studies reviewed in Chapter 5. There they were used to summarize the considerable amount of data collected on the behavior of the subjects in the group in relationship to the various experimental conditions, as well as to depict the behavior of one child.

Table 7.1   Responses of Practitioners Regarding Necessary Competencies for Providing Mental Health Services to the Aged in Rural Areas

Respondent	Agency operational procedures	Psychological aspects of aging	Physiological and sociological aspects of aging	Treatment modalities	Administrative
1	3[a]	5	1	2	4
2	4	2	1	3	5
3	3	4	1	2	5
4	4	2	1	3	5
5	4	2	3	1	5
6	1	3	2	4	5
7	4	2	1	3	5
8	2	3	1	4	5
9	3	4	1	5	2
10	4	1	2	3	5
11	4	1	2	3	5
12	4	3	1	2	5
13	3	5	1	2	4
14	4	1	3	2	5
15	4	2	1	3	5
Mean	3.8	2.6	1.4	2.8	4.6

[a] Rated on a scale of 1 (most important) to 5 (least important).

Another valuable descriptive statistic that facilitates workers' practice endeavors is standard deviation. Standard deviation (SD) is used to describe the amount of variation in the data, that is, how the data group themselves around the average score. For instance, assume that in the intake process workers at a community mental health center used a 25-item scale to measure depression. After a large sample was secured, SD provided information by which to compare individual scores. It provides data on the percentage of individuals that score within one, two, and three standard deviations. Each of the 25 items has five possible responses; therefore, an individual can score anywhere from 0 to 125. A mean of 75 and an SD of 10 would indicate that 68.26% of scores would be between 65 and 85. Likewise, 95.44% of the scores would fall within two SDs, or between 55 and 95. Finally, 99.74% of all scores would fall between 45 and 105, or three standard deviations. In this case, standard deviation can help determine whether the individual needs treatment.

BASIC STATISTICAL FUNCTIONS

In addition to describing data, statistical operations can perform three other basic functions: They (a) can indicate how closely variables are associated with one another; (b) tell us whether significant differences exist between groups; and (c) may be used to indicate the amount of variation in one variable that is related to variation in another. Statistical operations range from simple analyses, such as measuring the association between two variables or testing the differences between groups, to complex operations involving determination of the association between many variables or development of a prediction equation from representative data.

Beginning knowledge generally is developed through the use of correlational statistics and statistics that determine whether significant changes have taken place in the phenomena of interest. Refinement of knowledge occurs with the use of statistics that delineate exact relationships between variables. Thus, the employment of progressively stringent statistical procedures could be considered a sequential process in the knowledge-building process.

STATISTICAL CORRELATIONS

In many areas of empirical practice, only beginning knowledge is available on which variables are associated with the phenomena of interest. Statistics that indicate association are correlational. They reveal how strongly variables are related to one another. Various assumptions have to be met concerning measures of the variables, and appropriate correlational techniques are then chosen, depending upon whether the data are nominal, ordinal, interval, or ratio level.

An example of the use of correlational techniques can be found in delinquency studies. For many years, social workers have provided services to delinquent children. Provision of these services has resulted in the accumulation of massive amounts of descriptive data. In this case, correlational statistics can be used to determine those characteristics that are associated with delinquency, such as failing grades, low family income, peers who exhibit deviant behaviors, and the child's negative self-image (Bramblett, Wodarski, & Thyer, 1991).

Likewise, social workers have been called upon lately to provide services to women who are abused by their spouses. Correlational data could help isolate the following factors related to wife abuse: the attraction of women lacking self-esteem to dominating men, dependency, isolation, strong attachment to children, husband's lack of self-esteem, feelings of inadequacy, hostility, feelings of powerlessness, and traditional views of sex roles. Ultimately, it may be possible to identify potential spouse abusers and develop programs geared toward prevention (Dwyer, Smokowski, Bricout, & Wodarski, 1995).

Since the inception of social work practice, the "trait" versus the "situational specific" hypotheses of behavior have been debated. Do situations affect behavior more than individual traits or vice versa? If measures of the same behavior occur in different contexts, this question could be answered by correlational statistics. For example, in a 3-year investigation, the behavior of 251 children labeled as antisocial was measured in an open community agency. A checklist was used to secure the incidences of prosocial, nonsocial, and antisocial behaviors at the community center where the children met for 2 hr to engage in group activities. Behavioral data provided by 22 weeks of observation were averaged over four time periods and revealed an average correlation among time periods of 0.43 with a range of 0.04 to 0.95. These data indicate that the behavior of the children was not consistent over different situations (Wodarski, 1977).

t TESTS

Following the adequate description of the data, the next logical step is for empirical social workers to evaluate through statistical procedures whether their client's social functioning significantly improved. Have the clients changed sufficiently to warrant confidence in the interventions? One means of determining this is to compare statistical results of services provided to one group with results obtained from a comparison group of similarly composed individuals. Many classic studies (Brown, 1968; Meyer, Borgatta, & Jones, 1965; Powers & Witmer, 1951; Reid & Shyne, 1969) have attempted to evaluate social work practice through such procedures. In these studies, clients are randomly assigned to experimental or control groups. Differences between pre- and posttests and subsequent changes are evaluated through the *t* test, whereby the amount of change in the experimental group is compared with the amount of change in the control group. The probability that such changes are the result of chance is calculated. If significant changes have occurred, the same procedure can be used to assess whether these changes are maintained after a sufficient follow-up period. For example, delinquent children who made impressive gains during a behavior modification program were followed up 5 years later. Their scores were compared with a control group to evaluate whether gains were maintained. In the study, the behavior of 40 of the original 60 adolescents was assessed on the basis of their employment and educational status, program participation, involvement in leisure time and community activities, self-esteem, aspirations and expectations, delinquent activity, relationships with family and friends, and their anticipated aversive consequences of engaging in criminal acts.

Analyses of self-report data collected from the participants indicated no substantial differences. Of the items directly related to the evaluation of the program, three favored the experimental participants: happier home environment, participation in fewer gang fights, and greater avoidance of trouble; and three favored the control participants: reading more, experiencing more guilt about engaging in antisocial activities, and having less tendency to engage in aggressive behaviors to secure reinforcers. The data have to be interpreted with caution because of the large number of variables studied (in making 119 comparisons, six significant differences would be expected by chance), and a tendency toward failure to yield consistent trends (the significant differences seem to cancel out various components of the conceptual model).

Data comparisons in Table 7.2 on the variables where significant differences occurred between experimental and control participants indicate no long-term maintenance of behavioral change (Wodarski, Filipczak, McCombs, Koustenis, & Rusilko, 1979).

ANALYSIS OF VARIANCE

When more than two groups of clients are studied, the appropriate evaluation procedure is the analysis of variance (ANOVA). The ANOVA, which is similar to the t test, enables the investigator to compare simultaneously more than two change scores. In the factorial design described in Chapter 6, in which two different treatments were evaluated against a control treatment, ANOVA was utilized to isolate the significant differences between the groups. This procedure also enabled the simultaneous evaluation of combinations of variables described in Chapter 6. ANOVA facilitated the assessment of treatment method,

Table 7.2   Mean, Standard Deviation, and *t* Values of Statistically Significant Differences Between the Experimental (E) and Control (C) Groups of Delinquent Children from Self-Reported Follow-Up Data 5 Years Later

	Group	Mean	Standard deviation	*t*
Hours per week in reading	E	2.43	1.57	2.38
for pleasure	C*	3.74	1.91	
Program evaluation by children	E*	3.50	0.51	2.63
	C	2.95	0.78	
Program evaluation by parents	E*	3.53	1.02	
	C	2.95	1.33	2.49
Evaluation of home as positive	E*	1.81	0.40	3.35
	C	1.33	0.49	
Recommend program to	E*	3.33	0.73	
a friend	C	2.63	1.07	2.45
Assistance from program staff	E*	1.95	0.22	2.35
	C	1.67	0.49	
Experiencing guilt after doing	E	1.86	0.36	3.60
something wrong[a]	C*	1.37	0.50	
Engaging in aggressive behavior	E	3.65	1.23	
to achieve goals	C*	4.47	1.72	2.14
Participation in gang fights	E*	1.00		2.15
	C	1.26	0.56	
Attempts to avoid trouble	E*	2.00	0.00	
	C	1.74	0.45	2.67

* Indicates whether the experimental or control group had the significantly favorable difference.
[a] Due to wording of the question concerning guilt, a higher value indicates less guilt.

group composition, and worker training and various combinations that produced significant outcomes (Feldman, Caplinger, & Wodarski, 1983).

ANALYSIS OF COVARIANCE

In many instances, research executed to evaluate human services employs groups that are significantly different at the outset in outcome variables. Groups often cannot be restructured for purposes of the study because of agency operating procedures. In such situations, clients cannot be assigned randomly to experimental and control groups to control for initial differences. Changes, therefore, in the experimental group cannot be evaluated against a comparison group without employing a statistical procedure that can correct for initial differences. The analysis of covariance procedure provides the opportunity to control for such initial differences, thus permitting a fairer evaluation.

When groups are compared and statistical control procedures, such as covariance, have been employed to correct for initial differences, the covariates must be considered carefully to ensure that important variables are controlled for; that is, variables that have certain conceptual associations with the dependent measures. The covariant should equate all the groups on a scale that measures, or is directly related to, the performance criteria employed in the investigation to evaluate the effects of the intervention. For example, if antisocial behavior is an outcome criterion, children can be measured during a baseline period and during treatment and follow-up. The baseline measure of antisocial behavior can be used as a covariate. In one study (Wodarski & Pedi, 1978), analysis of variance and covariance (ANCOVA) were used to evaluate two group-treatment strategies against a control-treatment strategy on the behaviors exhibited by antisocial children, behaviors of their therapists, and two self-rating scales. For the first year, 139 antisocial children were stratified according to age and then randomly placed into 14 groups. For the second year, 100 children were placed into 11 groups composed of antisocial children. Behavioral measurements of the children's and therapists' behaviors were secured at each weekly 2-hr meeting. For the data depicted in Table 7.3, analysis of covariance, performed by the NYBMUL computer program, was used to adjust for initial differences in baseline scores and to control for significant variables that could be postulated to account for the results, such as age, worker style, superior style, dropouts, and methodological factors of observer and tester style. This statistical technique provided for the evaluation of the experimental treatments through analysis of change scores between T1 and T2, with adjustments made for initial group differences at T1. Thus, this technique provided the opportunity to assess what changes took place in clients after treatment was introduced. The testing procedure consisted initially of evaluating general factors, such as treatment methods. When the F scores were significantly different, additional analyses specifically assessed which levels of the factors were significantly different; that is, the procedure evaluated each treatment against the others to determine exactly where the differ-

Table 7.3 Behavioral Data in Terms of Average Incidence of Prosocial, Nonsocial, and Antisocial Behavior for Baseline (B) and Treatment (A) According to Treatment Method and Year[a]

	Number		Behavior category												
			Prosocial				Nonsocial				Antisocial				
	1st Year	2nd Year	1st Year		2nd Year		1st Year		2nd Year		1st Year		2nd Year		
Treatment method			B	A	B	A	B	A	B	A	B	A	B	A	
Behavior modification	59	32	0.91	0.91	0.90	0.94	0.05	0.04	0.02	0.01	0.04	0.05	0.07	0.05	
Traditional	42	21	0.90	0.90	0.96	0.97	0.06	0.03	0.04	0.02	0.04	0.07	0.00	0.01	
Controlled treatment	36	37	0.90	0.94	0.94	0.95	0.05	0.03	0.02	0.02	0.05	0.04	0.05	0.03	

[a] Baseline consisted of an average of six meetings, and the treatment period consisted of an average of 22 meetings. The controlled-treatment groups served as a baseline for the entire study. Additional regular analysis of variance tests in which the data were analyzed according to three time periods after treatment, consisting of the mean of six consecutive meetings each, yielded no significant differences for treatment. Similarly, the use of subjects who had a 5% higher incidence of antisocial behavior during baseline for both the analysis of covariance and regular analysis of variance yielded no significant difference.

ences lay. Consequently, to secure these data, the appropriate 1 degree of freedom comparisons were executed to isolate which levels of the factor contrasted against each other were significantly different (Finn, 1969).

REGRESSION ANALYSIS

The essence of research is the isolation of those variables that are related to the phenomena being studied. If this is possible, then the subsequent ability to influence the phenomena is increased. Regression analysis enables researchers to determine how certain variables are related to one another in their prediction of a phenomenon; it permits isolation of those variables that are significantly related to the phenomena of interest, and enables the specification of the magnitude of the various relationships. For example, in predicting the behavior of 251 antisocial children at a community center, six predictors were employed: self-inventories filled out by referral agents, parents, children, leaders, and observers, and a subclass of the Jesness inventory (1969) filled out by the children and designed to measure self-reported tendency toward manifest aggression. The Manifest Aggression Scale consists of 31 items. Jesness contends that these items reflect an awareness of unpleasant feelings, especially anger and frustration, a tendency to react readily with these emotions and other obvious discomfort concerning the presence and control of these feelings. Data presented in Table 7.4 indicate that for both years of the study, the checklist filled

Table 7.4 Amount of Variance Explained by the Various Predictors in Baseline Antisocial Behavior at the Community Center According to Each Year of the Study

Independent variables	Percent of variance		Change in proportion of variance	
	1st Year	2nd Year	1st Year	2nd Year
Observer checklist	0.3213	0.2513	0.3213	0.2513
Leader checklist	0.3735	0.3505	0.0522	0.0992
Child checklist	0.3915	n.s.	0.0180	n.s.

Note: n.s., not significant. Only variables that predict a significant amount of the variance are included in the table.

out by the behavioral observer explained the greatest amount of variance in the incidence of antisocial behavior exhibited by the children at the community center during baseline. The amounts of variance explained for the first and second years were, respectively, 0.3213 and 0.2513. The checklist filled out by the leader of the children's group yielded the next greatest amount of variance explained, 0.0522 and 0.0992, respectively. For the first year, the child's checklist yielded a significant amount of variance explained: 0.0180. This finding did not hold true for the second year (Wodarski, 1978).

In the future, regression analysis will help social work isolate variables relevant to child abuse, family violence, and marital discord. Such knowledge will be crucial in developing the preventive approach in social work. For example, regression analysis can isolate those children who are at risk during the divorce process by age, sex of the child, length of marital discord, time of divorce in relation to the developmental cycle, number of siblings, race, children's perception of the divorce process, and family income. Ultimately, the procedures will facilitate the planning of appropriate interventions.

MULTIVARIATE ANALYSIS

As knowledge is developed in social work practice, more sophisticated statistical procedures will be employed to develop the next levels of learning. Generally grouped under multivariate procedures, these statistical techniques consider simultaneously the effects of many variables on a phenomenon. Probably the most familiar to social work clinicians is factor analysis, used to isolate attributes that a self-inventory purports to measure. Other statistical techniques that will be utilized in the future include path analysis, canonical correlations, and multiple regression analyses. For example, path analysis might be used to test various theories of delinquent behavior. This procedure can isolate the factors involved in causation of a phenomenon and test how they relate to each other through a time sequence. This will enable the determination of the relationship between the factors of income, family interaction patterns, achievement at school, peer reinforcement patterns, and subsequent delinquent behavior. Multivariate procedures are covered in Chapter 8.

SUMMARY

It is most important for social workers to remember that statistics are tools to be used to enhance practice. The concept of statistical significance determines whether the associations, differences, or relationships between variables are meaningful or strictly caused by chance. Statistics enable empirical social workers to determine whether variables isolated through research are relevant in helping clients. As practitioners begin to incorporate these skills in their repertoires, the future will witness a more sophisticated application of statistical procedures, and, thus, the development of a more elaborate knowledge base. On the basis of this knowledge, the social worker will derive the complex interventions necessary to help clients. Appendix A attached to Chapter 8 contains an analysis of the various competencies that arise from computer-assisted programs that can facilitate students' statistical knowledge.

REFERENCES

Bramblett, R., Wodarski, J. S., & Thyer, B. A. (1991). Social work practice with antisocial children: A review of current issues. *Journal of Applied Social Sciences, 15,* 169–182.

Brown, C. E. (Ed.). (1968). *The multiproblem dilemma.* Metuchen, NJ: The Scarecrow Press.

Dwyer, D. C., Smokowski, P. R., Bricout, J., & Wodarski, J. S. (1995). Domestic violence research: Theoretical and practice implications for social work. *Clinical Social Work, 2,* 185–198.

Feldman, R. A., Caplinger, T. E., & Wodarski, J. S. (1983). *The St. Louis conundrum: The effective treatment of antisocial youths.* Englewood Cliffs, NJ: Prentice Hall.

Finn, J. D. (1969). *NYBMUL.* Buffalo, NY: Computer Center Press.

Jesness, C. F. (1969). *The Jesness inventory manual.* Palo Alto, CA: Consulting Psychologist Press.

Meyer, H. J., Borgatta, E. F., & Jones, W. C. (1965). *Girls at Vocational High: An experiment in social work intervention.* New York: Russell Sage Foundation.

Powers, E., & Witmer, H. (1951). *An experiment in the prevention of delinquency: The Cambridge-Somerville youth study.* New York: Columbia University Press.

Reid, J. W., & Shyne, A. W. (1969). *Brief and extended casework.* New York: Columbia University Press.

Wodarski, J. S. (1977) A comparison of behavioral consistency of antisocial and prosocial children in different contexts. *Journal of Behavior Therapy and Experimental Psychiatry, 8,* 275–280.

Wodarski, J. S. (1978). The prediction of antisocial behavior: An application of regression analysis. *Corrective Psychiatry and Journal of Social Therapy, 24,* 102–110.

Wodarski, J. S., Filipczak, J., McCombs, D., Koustenis, G., & Rusilko, S. (1979). Follow-up on behavioral intervention with troublesome adolescents. *Journal of Experimental Psychiatry and Behavior Therapy, 10,* 181–188.

Wodarski, J. S., & Pedi, S. J. (1978). The empirical evaluation of the effects of different group-treatment strategies against a controlled-treatment strategy on behavior exhibited by antisocial children, behavior of the therapist, and two self-ratings measuring antisocial behavior. *Journal of Clinical Psychology, 34,* 471–481.

CHAPTER 8

Advanced Statistical Techniques in Social Work Research

Eileen M. Lysaught and John S. Wodarski

This chapter provides an overview of advanced statistical methods that can be applied effectively in social work. These evaluative tools can be used to isolate or find correlations between variables that may be influencing treatment. The data obtained can be used to create or improve intervention strategies. For example, if a clinician were to develop a program to discourage smoking among adolescents, a preintervention questionnaire could be administered to gather and analyze information on factors that describe these individuals, such as income, peer-group, socioeconomic status, and school performance, using advanced statistical methods. This information could serve a dual purpose: first to assist in the assessment of the population and then to help in the design of an effective intervention. Several evaluative methods can determine the nature, strength, and direction of the relationship between variables. These tools help researchers develop questions for further study and help clinicians in their practice. The procedures to be discussed include multivariate analysis, multidiscriminate analysis, path analysis, factor analysis, canonical correlations, and structural equations.

MULTIVARIATE ANALYSIS

To describe multivariate analysis, it is first important to provide a brief description of a simplified version of this process, known as analysis of variance—or ANOVA. ANOVA can be used for "assessing differences in means for two or more samples that are suspected of arising from different populations" (Amick & Walbery, 1975). In ANOVA, comparisons are made between data sets to observe any correlation between variables or determine if variables function independent of one another.

An illustration of ANOVA can be found in a social psychology experiment conducted by Harrison and McClintock. The investigators wanted to predict the cooperativeness of dyads playing prisoner-dilemma games by collecting information on their behavioral patterns (Amick & Walbery, 1975). Four experimental conditions described prior experiences of the two individuals in the dyad. The hypothesis was that the varying experimental conditions would produce a range of ability to cooperate as a dyad. An ANOVA was then used to describe variables that related to their ability to cooperate as a dyad.

Multivariate analysis (MANOVA) extends the ANOVA to several dependent variables. Unlike ANOVA, MANOVA determines whether statistically significant differences exist between two or more groups, based on the group members' scores on the set of dependent variables rather than on one single variable (Amick & Walbery, 1975). The MANOVA, therefore, is a much more powerful evaluative tool.

In social work practice, this type of procedure could be very useful. For example, an agency wishes to study the attitudinal biases of the staff. Three groups could be divided on length of time working: less than one year, more than one year, and longer than two years. Several dependent variables could be tested using written questionnaires to describe attitudes toward different types of clients. Dependent variables to be measured included perceived gender differences in attitude toward minority clients, perceptions of age, and religious affiliation. Using a MANOVA, data could be collected and analyzed to observe any potential professional biases, promote agency awareness, and facilitate any necessary changes in policy or staff.

Studies have also been conducted using MANOVA to describe factors related to healthy bonding between mother and child. Attachment theory describes the personality of the "good enough" mother, who provides a child with the basis of a healthy self-identity through nurturing, acceptance, and balanced discipline. Research has given clinicians direction in the treatment of abusive mothers by developing potential goals to be achieved in therapy. For example, these mothers can be taught parenting skills that are conducive to healthy childhood development as shown by previously collected data.

For more on MANOVA and other statistical tools, see Stevens (1992) and Winer (1991).

DISCRIMINATE ANALYSIS

Discriminate analysis is a technique especially designed to classify variables. This is achieved when values of continuous variables are used to construct categories of a nominal variable. An example of this process can be viewed in Table 8.1. This table demonstrates how four independent variables can be represented with labels and evaluated using regression analysis. Loether and McTavish (1974) reported on a study in which respondents were asked to give their personal opinions of the general standing of 88 occupations on a 5-point scale ranging from excellent to poor. These numbers were then placed on a comparison scale ranging from a score of 20 to a score of 100. By using an accompanying personality inventory scale, the data were then formulated to predict which types of people would rate which jobs as either excellent or poor (Loether & McTavish, 1974). This tool could be very effective if, for example, a counselor were attempting to strategize what type of instructional classroom setting would be most appropriate for an acting-out versus a more passive student. While other factors certainly would need to be taken into account, multidiscriminate analysis could help in the process of developing a plan appropriate to a child's needs.

PATH ANALYSIS

Although ANOVA and MANOVA are statistical tools designed to describe correlations in dependent variables, path analysis (PA) demonstrates the complexity of relationships through the use of models.

Table 8.1   A Model of Variable Label in Multidiscriminate Analysis

Marital status	Dummy variables
1 Currently married	1 Currently married (1 = Yes) (0 = No)
2 Never married	2 Never married (1 = Yes) (0 = No)
3 Widowed	3 Widowed (1 = Yes) (0 = No)
4 Separated	4 Separated (1 = Yes) (0 = No)
5 Divorced	

From H. Loether & D. McTavish (1974). *Descriptive and inferential statistics: An introduction* (p. 337). Boston: Allyn and Bacon. Reprinted with permission.

Graphs represent hypothesized effects and direction of factors within an experiment. Additionally, PA allows for an intervention to be diagrammed so that the potential impact of various factors within treatment can be predicted. A basic assumption of PA is that relationships between variables exist so "a set of independent variables influences a set of dependent variables and not vice-versa" (Amick & Walbery, 1975). However, models can also incorporate the possibility of reciprocal or feedback relationships between and among variables. Therefore, path diagrams can use relationship factors to gather information on the direct and indirect influences of variables.

Path analysis is a relevant tool for therapists who wish to generate practice-oriented theories to describe certain characteristics of human behavior. PA can compare a model of direct and indirect relationships that are presumed to be between several variables and observed data in a study in order to examine the fit of the model to the data. If the fit is close, the model is retained and used or further tested. If the fit is not close, a new model may be devised or, more likely, the old one will be modified to fit the data better (Loether & McTavish, 1974). Using PA, practitioners are better able to relate theory and practice, because this technique allows for strength and direction of variables to be observed in treatment.

An example of path analysis can be found in Figure 8.1 which is a diagram of an experiment that studied the impact of several intervention measures used to treat antisocial boys. This type of graph is useful for two reasons: First, the actual interventions are documented, and second, the predicted or actual impact on youth behavior is recorded. This data can be analyzed to observe which factors were most effective in treating the client population and, if applicable, generalized to other intervention settings.

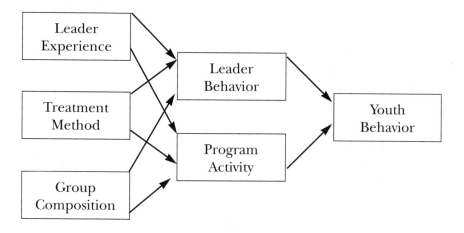

Figure 8.1   An example of a hypothesized path mode.

From A. R. Feldman, E. T. Caplinger, & J. S. Wodarski (1983). *The St. Louis Conundrum: The effective treatment of antisocial youths* (p. 219). Englewood Cliffs, NJ. Prentice Hall.

FACTOR ANALYSIS

Another powerful analytical technique, known as factor analysis (FA), is able to analyze the intercorrelations within a set of variables. Specifically, this method is used to determine the number and nature of the underlying variables called factors among a larger set of measures. FA can locate the common factors within a group of measures and, therefore, minimizes the data to be analyzed. By regrouping the information, a more organized and focused data evaluation can be accomplished. Best of all, this type of procedure allows for the observance of patterns in data, which can be used in future research or intervention strategies.

A model of how FA can group and organize data is found in Table 8.2. Although this technique is mainly used to load together scores and numerical data, other types of measures (scales, questionnaire items, and self-monitoring tasks) can be grouped. This is a pragmatic way to manipulate data in social work, considering how at times several types of objective standards may be incorporated into treatment to record client progress.

Table 8.2 An Example of the Regrouping of Data in Factorial Analysis

Item

Satisfaction with field agency
Satisfaction with field instructor
Satisfaction with field learning

	Item mean	Factor loading
Factor 1: School-Agency Liaison		
My contact with my field liaison has been satisfactory to meet my learning needs.	4.10	.918
If there are problems at my field placement, I am comfortable consulting with my field liaison.	4.01	.873
When I have problems in my placement, I go to my field liaison.	3.05	.838
I am aware of the possible roles of my field liaison.	4.68	.708
Communication between the school of social work and my agency is adequate.	3.99	.663
Factor 2: Professional Role		
I have the same responsibilities as the professional staff at my agency.	5.44	8.59
I am included in all agency activities that professional staff are expected to attend.	5.54	.825
I have the same privileges as the professional staff at my agency.	5.23	.779
I have been able to meet the expectations of my field placement.	6.13	.636
I agree with my agency's policies.	5.00	.457
Factor 3: Relevant Learning		
I enjoy working with the type of client I serve at my agency.	5.94	.840
My field work assignments this year have been relevant to my learning goals.	5.64	.751
I was able to actively participate in designing my learning experience.	5.54	.616
Factor 4: Supervision		
My field instructor enjoys his or her role as "teacher."	5.79	.770
I have been encouraged to express different ideas in my practicum setting.	5.30	.654

(continued)

Table 8.2   *(continued)*

Item	Item mean	Factor loading
Factor 5: Practicality		
My agency provides adequate physical facilities (i.e., desk, office, supplies) for students.	5.11	.727
My courses this year have been relevant to my field experience.	4.75	.536
Factor 6: Evaluation Anxiety		
There is conflict between the agency and the school's policies concerning expectations for students in the field.*	4.39	.716
Having a "pass/fail" system reduces my anxiety concerning my field placement.	5.74	.668

Source: *Fortune* 1985.

*Scoring is reversed (higher = less perceived conflict). On all other items, higher scores indicate more quality.

From Reid, J. W., & Smitz, D. A. (1989). *Research in social work* (2nd ed., pp. 280–281). New York: Columbia University Press.

STRUCTURAL EQUATIONS

Often in social work, practitioners find themselves attempting to measure behaviors or cognitions that do not easily lend themselves to being objectively monitored. Structural equations can be utilized in this situation by incorporating related concepts that are more easily evaluated to represent changes or improvements in the variable to be studied (Sorbom, 1979).

Structural equations could be helpful in trying to measure the degree of motivation of high-school students applying to enter baccalaureate programs. School performance, school attendance, preparation for entrance exams, individual career interests, and ability to use problem-solving skills could be used as indicators of varying levels of motivation. However, since any quantitative tool may possess some degree of error, several descriptive variables are needed to represent the "immeasurable" measure. The practicality of structural equations in daily therapeutic practice is apparent. The reality of measuring the

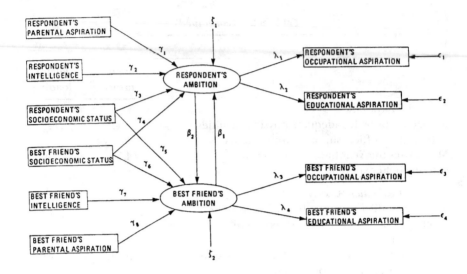

Figure 8.2   A model of how structural equations are mapped.

From *Advances in factorial analysis and structural equations*, K. G. Jolreskog & D. Slohom. (1979). *Advances in factor analysis and structural models.* Cambridge: Abt Books.

progress of clients using subjective terminology—degrees of anger, levels of frustration, or anxiety—this requires a method of objectifying vague concepts not easily defined or monitored. In the future, with counselors being held more accountable for their work, structural equation analysis can be used to diminish the level of subjectivity that has not allowed for strict analysis of data in the past. A model of a structural equation analysis is located in Figure 8.2, which demonstrates how peers, socio-economic status, and intelligence interrelate with ambition.

CANONICAL CORRELATION

Another analytical tool, canonical correlation (CC), is used to investigate the relationship between two sets of variables when each set consists of at least two variables. This procedure can investigate the following questions (Thompson, 1984):

1. To what extent can one set of two or more variables be predicted or explained by another set of two or more variables?

2. What contributions does a single variable add to the explanatory power of the set of variables to which the variable belongs?
3. To what extent does a single variable contribute to predicting or explaining the composite of the variables in the variable set to which the variable does not belong?
4. What different dynamics are involved in the ability of one variable set to explain in different ways for different portions of the other variable set?

The mathematical side to this method is extremely complicated. However, canonical correlations are useful since they provide information on the relationships between different data sets and the individual variables within sets of data. Unfortunately, any practical use of this procedure requires a large number of subjects to ensure validity. Canonical correlations offer one added advantage in that a researcher can choose what degree of relationships between variables is considered a priority to investigate. One study that used this type of analysis comes from Tatsuoka who attempted to establish a relationship between personality traits and academic achievement among high school students. Through the administration of both personality inventories and a series of achievement tests, data was obtained on what type of personality "profile" tended to be associated with patterns of academic achievement. Canonical correlations would be effective in gathering data on multicultural counseling techniques to observe if culturally oriented interventions are more helpful to clients involved in the therapeutic process.

SUMMARY

So what is the future of analytical strategies in the field of social work practice? Currently, there are advanced computer software programs for the social sciences, such as SPSS, as well as a small number of tutorial packages created to train persons studying in the field of social sciences. However, in the use of statistical analyses it is important to remember shortcomings in these procedures. Specifically, critical reasoning and hypotheses derived from a sound theoretical base should be used to guide the research design as well as the analysis of data. Additionally, the number of participants in a study should be large enough to warrant findings as reliable. Most importantly, the data must be collected, analyzed, and disseminated in a manner that is relevant for social work practitioners. Although social workers may not be in a position to use the analyses described in this chapter, it is still imperative that they develop a basic understanding of these tools so they may become informed consumers of the research. It is hoped that as more practitioners are able to review literature and test this data in practice, their work will challenge researchers to develop more effective theories for assessment and intervention in social work practice.

ACKNOWLEDGMENTS

Special thanks to Scott Sweetland from the Center for Educational Resources and Technologies at the State University of New York at Buffalo for his help in interpreting the software programs and organizing the information presented.

APPENDIX 8.1

A Discussion of the Applicability of Computer-Assisted Learning Programs and Statistical Packages for MSW Students, PhD Students, and Practitioners

The goal of this review is to analyze the usefulness of various tutorials and computer software programs in order to offer recommendations for MSW or PhD students who may need help when working with statistics during their course of study. The method by which software was collected and organized involved researching software companies, writing to universities for information on specific research projects on tutorials, compiling data from the Lockwood Memorial Library at the State University of New York at Buffalo, and seeking out experts in computer technology at the Center for Educational Resources and Technologies at the State University of New York at Buffalo. Four programs are discussed as potential resources for students: Microcase—a tutorial for statistics, ASP—a tutorial for students, SYSTAT—a statistics package, and Understanding Biostatistics—a computer-based tutorial.

Each program was run through to observe the advantages and disadvantages in functioning so that recommendations could be made to students who may consider using such software. To critique the effectiveness of these software packages, certain factors were examined: the technological requirements of each program, the capabilities of the software, the applicability for students, and the difficulties that arise when trying to run these programs. In general, one needs an IBM compatible computer, a hard drive with a minimum of 500k memory, and a video graphics card to run any of these four programs. Each individual software program has specific guidelines for its use, which will be discussed as each program is reviewed.

The software tutorial package found to best match the needs of students was the Microcase program, officially titled, Social Statistics using Microcase by William Fox, which includes two disks (5.26 and 3.25), a workbook, and an accompanying text to guide the learning experience. Generally, the program was easy to install, relatively easy to use, and well organized; meaning the user could follow the material without excessive difficulty. The specific equipment requirements for Microcase are an IBM computer or a fully compatible clone that operates under MS or PC DOS 3.2 or higher, at least 612k of memory, a graphics card, and, if printing is desired, a dot matrix printer. Basically, this program can be described as the equivalent of an introductory class in statistics.

Microcase is truly pragmatic as a tool for novice students in statistics. This is a powerful program that can analyze data without requiring the user to learn complex commands. The integration of a workbook and a manual with the software allows the student to feel competent since questions about the program can be easily answered. There is one major drawback to using Microcase: To use the program effectively, each step of the program must be followed in order to comprehend the system. Unfortunately, some students may only want to skim through a text as opposed to learning an entire book on statistics. Additionally, if students attempted to seek out an answer to a specific question, this would be difficult, considering the lessons are written in a progressive fashion from simple concepts to highly advanced measures in statistics. It also would require a considerable amount of time to learn the program since the accompanying manual is about 325 pages and the workbook has assigned tasks for every lesson in the tutorial. Microcase, however, could definitely function as a resource for students who can manage the time to learn the system.

The second application, ASP Tutorial and Student Guide, was produced by DC software. This program contains software, a manual, and a pamphlet that describes how to install and load the system. The tutorial is designed to provide a systematic introduction to statistics for students in the fields of business, economics, and the social sciences. The system requires an IBM PC or compatible computer with a fixed disk, at least 512k memory, installation on a hard disk or on the hard drive, use with a VA monitor as well as an HP laser jet printer and lastly, and IBM compatibility for all graphics. The accompanying manual contains a 10-chapter outline that delineates the capabilities and concepts of ASP. This flexible program offers many options that are applicable to students, including various statistical analysis options, hypothesis testing, analysis of variance, regressions, factor analysis, times-series designs, and linear equations.

The major fault with this system lies in attempting to install the program into the hard drive. The instructions are at times vague and can leave a user feeling quite frustrated, especially a person with a limited computer background. The list of instructions is long, confusing to work with, and may not coincide with the IBM-compatible system being used. In fact, the average student may have difficulty loading the program in either the school computer lab or their own personal system since it requires an expansive memory base. On the whole, the process of installation to overview the program can be wrought with frustration and leave the user believing a textbook would be much easier to work with.

SYSTAT software is a DOS SYSTAT 5.0 program capable of running such statistical procedures as descriptive statistics; t tests; ANOVA; and nonlinear, linear, and multilinear regressions. The hardware needed to run this highly advanced program is very specific: 640k memory RAM, MSI PC DOS 3.0, and at least a 20 MB hard disk. While not a tutorial, this remains a possible resource for students because it can analyze between 125 and 250 variables, depending on the statistical procedure used. There are two major types of packages in SYSTAT, SYSTAT for Windows and MAC SYSTAT 5.2. Although easy to install, the feasibility of such a powerful program is unlikely for students who are trying to grasp the basic concepts in statistics. Realistically, this software would be better suited to those who are exclusively conducting research, due to the fact that this program is far more advanced than the average student would need.

REFERENCES

Amick, D. J., & Walbery, H. J. (1975). *Introductory multivariate analysis: For educational, psychological, and social research*. Berkley, California: McCutchen Publishing Corporation.

Blackford, B. G. (1992). ASP: *A statistical package for business, economics, and the social sciences [computer software]*. Grand Blanc, MI: DC Software.

Cody, P., & Just, S. *Understanding biostatistics: A computer-based tutorial [computer software]*.

Feldmen, A. R., Caplinger, E. T., & Wodarski, J. S. (1983). *The St. Louis conundrum: The effective treatment of antisocial youths*. Englewood Cliffs, NJ: Prentice Hall.

Fox, W. (1992). *Social statistics using microcase* [computer software]. Bellevue, WA: Microcase Corporation.

Health Sciences Consortium. (1990). Health Sciences Library, Media Resources Center, South Campus, University at Buffalo, NY, 14214.

Kim, J. (1978). *Introduction to factor analysis; What it is and how to do it*. Beverly Hills: Sage Publications.

Jolreskog, K. G., & Slohom, D.(1979). *Advances in factor analysis and structural equation models*. Cambridge: Abt Books.

Loethner, J. H., & McTavish, D. G. (1974). *Descriptive and inferential statistics: An introduction* (4th ed.). Boston: Allyn and Bacon.

Maxwell, A. E. (1977). *Multivariate analysis in behavioral research*. London: Chapman and Hall.

Reid, J. W., & Smith, D. A. (1989). *Research in social work* (2nd ed.). New York: Columbia University Press.

Sorbom, J. (1979). *Advances in factor analysis and structural equation models*. Massachusetts: Abt Books.

SYSTAT. (1993). Evanston, IL. [computer software]. SYSTAT.

Tatsuoka, M. (1971). *Multivariate analysis: Techniques for educational and psychological research*. New York: John Wiley and Sons.

Thompson, B. (1984). *Canonical correlation analysis: Uses and interpretations*. Beverly Hills: Sage Publications.

Wilson, D. (1975) *Canonical correlations and the relations between sets of variables*. Madison, WI: University of Wisconsin.

Wodarski, J. S. (1981). *The role of research in clinical practice: A practical approach for the human services*. Baltimore, MD: University Park Press.

CHAPTER   9

Preparing for Research

The previous chapters have provided the conceptual and methodological tools necessary for research. This chapter addresses practical aspects of planning and implementing research in social service agencies. The items discussed stem from the author's research experiences in implementing and evaluating groups in schools, family service agencies, correctional institutions, community mental health programs and agencies serving youths.

Most topics in this chapter become increasingly complex as empirical knowledge is used in implementing sophisticated classical experimental designs discussed in Chapter 6. The use of time-series designs reviewed in Chapter 5 simplifies research implementation.

THE ASSESSMENT OF AGENCY CHARACTERISTICS

The most important prerequisite in planning any research is that the empirical practitioner spends sufficient time within the agency to evaluate its operations and to gain an accurate understanding of what research questions can be logically addressed within that context (Katz, 1966). The amount of time required for this initial step is roughly proportionate to a number of key sociological variables, including agency size, number and variety of services provided, and fluidity of the agency's internal structure and its immediate social environment.

166

During this period, the practitioner should determine the research interests of administrators and other practitioners in the agency so that the investigative interests of all concerned parties will approach maximum compatibility, especially for those who will work closely with the practitioner. A study formulated this way is likely to earn essential support from the administration and line staff, as well as remain consonant with the interests of any involved funding agencies and the social worker's own empirical concerns. Most successful studies meet the agency's goals, the funding agency's objectives, and the practitioner's own interests. In effect, then, if other individuals are to be involved in the research, the initial stages of the research must be devoted to mutually validated research objectives.

In the formulation of one funded study, for example, the goals of the funding agency, the host agency, a large community agency offering substantial group work services, and the researchers were met in several ways. The host agency had a history of serving children with social, emotional, and educational difficulties in its various children's and youth programs. Practitioners and administrators within the agency believed that the agency's programs were helping clients, but they wished to develop a systematic evaluation of their program's effects. At the same time, the funding agency was interested in evaluating the efficacy of established community-based treatment programs for children with behavioral problems and in assessing which factors, or combination of factors, lead to the greatest amount of positive change in their behaviors. Through communications between the administrator and the research practitioner, it was possible to design a study that examined questions such as the following:

1. What effects do children with behavioral difficulties have upon other children within the agency as a result of their interactions in club and activity groups?
2. Is it best to help children with behavioral difficulties in groups composed solely of children with similar problems or within groups composed primarily of children with few or no significant behavioral difficulties?
3. What type of worker training constitutes the best preparation for working with such children?
4. Which of three social group work methods (social learning, traditional, or group centered) is most effective in facilitating positive behavioral changes among the children?

These questions were the primary ones in which the practitioners and administrators were interested. Moreover, these questions were thoroughly compatible with other questions of interest to the empirical practitioner and the funding agency. Among these were: What modeling effects do children with behavioral difficulties have upon other children within the agency? What types of group composition are best for facilitating prosocial modeling effects among children with behavioral difficulties? How well do certain variables, such as group size and self-rated scores on antisocial behavior, predict actual incidence of antisocial behavior? These questions indicate that all major parties were basically interested in similar research questions, although they placed different emphases upon certain conceptual and theoretical frameworks and upon the intended applied results of the research.

In the initial appraisal, it is essential that the empirical practitioner consider whether the agency has sufficient resources to meet the demands of the research design and whether sufficient control can be exercised over variables that might confound the study. For example, even though advances in computer analysis allow for the ex post facto control of many variables, the empirical practitioner should strive to manipulate all relevant variables through the random assignment of subjects, when the classical experimental design is being used to evaluate practice. If the agency cannot meet these requirements, the empirical practitioner should determine whether different questions can be answered within the context, if a different research design can be used, or, as a last resort, whether another research site must be chosen.

Likewise, empirical practitioners must evaluate the extent to which agency personnel will be involved in the study and must secure the agency personnel's commitment before the study's inception. This procedure is essential in any research project, but is particularly necessary if the study is to place significant demands upon staff time. In the planning stages, it is often difficult to estimate the amount of time that will be required of agency practitioners and other staff. In order to secure their informed and sincere commitment, the empirical practitioner should outline, as fully as possible, whatever time commitments the study will entail. The practitioner should indicate also that there may be additional time requirements as the study evolves but, preferably, that such decisions will be made in conjunction with the pertinent staff. Although most activities just mentioned are essential for the successful execution of an empirical research study, these activities are especially crucial because they occur early in the research process and, as a result, serve to define the various opportunities and constraints that will determine the project's long-term success. The amount of time spent dealing with these issues depends upon the complexity of the research study. For example, a single-case study design is easier to implement than a classical experimental procedure in staff time, administrative coordination, and financial resources.

COORDINATION OF THE RESEARCH

If the agency staff and the principal empirical practitioner meet early enough to define their various goals and responsibilities, coordination of the research should be relatively uncomplicated. Should the project involve more than one researcher, the various responsibilities of the entire staff should be defined clearly and promptly. In conjunction, there should be explicit statements regarding to whom the research practitioner is accountable if the research is taking place in an agency where the research practitioner is not employed. The ideal relationship for large research studies exists when all researchers involved in the study are accountable to the principal researcher who, in turn, is responsible to the chief executive of the agency for administration and coordination but not for research design or evaluation. Confusion and ambiguity regarding accountability can produce ill feelings that may deter the research. The process of defining accountability and responsibility must be handled delicately because, in some instances, agency executives may wish the researchers who are employed to be integrated into the agency to such an extent that they lose their autonomy. By maintaining sufficient autonomy the researchers can opt for requisite alterations in agency policies, should they be essential for the research.

In the previous example, the agency had closed its membership because of over-enrollment. The research staff believed that 150 referred children, many of whom were referred from conventional treatment agencies, however, should acquire agency membership in order to minimize differentiation and possible stigmatization from regular members. Consultation with the executive staff resulted in the granting of agency memberships to these children. Similarly, mutual discussions resulted in the modification of traditional agency policies prohibiting services for groups with enrollments of fewer than 10 children. The reason for this revision was that the traditional restriction would severely limit implementation and analysis of the research design. If a study's findings are to be properly applied to other agencies, the research practitioner must evaluate also the extent to which each proposed change will influence the ability of the practitioner to generalize the findings in one direction or another. Once a study begins, continued communication and feedback with executives and other staff are essential and are well worth the added expenditures of the empirical researcher's time.

INTERPRETATION OF THE RESEARCH TO THE AGENCY STAFF

Most research investigations involve a substantial proportion of agency personnel whose commitment to the research is essential for its completion. To secure the necessary commitment, research practitioners should be able to discuss major aspects of the research, emphasizing the essential nature of staff cooperation for the execution and completion of the project. In social work agencies, naturally, an emphasis upon service aspects of the study may be more appealing to staff than would an emphasis on its research attributes. Preferably, however, professional staff should realize that the two activities need not be at all mutually exclusive and, indeed, usually should proceed in conjunction with one another. In the aforementioned project, the agency's metropolitan area lacked facilities for the treatment of antisocial children. In their presentation to agency personnel, the researchers stressed the importance of providing services that were unavailable elsewhere within the community. They also indicated that the agency executives, board directors, and lay board who sanctioned the research considered it beneficial to the agency; therefore, they wished to enlist general staff cooperation. Such a procedure sanctions the research and contributes to greater acceptance and participation by staff. Empirical researchers must present the main features of the research in a way that expectations of the other practitioners are held constant. A major by-product of such an approach is the early prevention of distortions that could bias the results of a study in an unpredictable direction. Much research data suggest that inducing certain expectations in social workers can produce substantial behavior change among clients (Goldfried & Davison, 1994; Goldstein, 1962; Rosenthal, 1969; Shapiro & Morris, 1978). Once the research begins, its goal must not be unduly enigmatic. It is essential that the researchers provide general feedback to participants; however, this feedback must be such that it does not bias the study. In addition, there must always be encouragement for the role agency members play throughout the duration of the study.

COLLABORATION WITH OTHER AGENCIES

This project involved the development of working relationships with 25 agencies who were to refer children with behavioral difficulties to the community center. In order to facilitate the referral process, the agency staff clearly specified the types of children to be served and the referral processes. The goals and purposes of the study had to be clearly explained to the referral agencies because they constituted the very first contact the clients and their parents had with the project. This procedure ensures that the project's aims are not misconstrued or otherwise distorted. Since the study dealt in large part with children who experienced difficulties in school, family, work, or peer group situations, the referral agencies had to be tactful in interpreting the program to the parents.

Many parents were unable to accept the professional judgment of teachers, counselors, therapists, or other social workers, which implied that their children experienced behavioral difficulty. Even with the best of preparation, some parents arrived for the intake interview with misconceptions about the program's goals. If lines of communication between the referral agencies and the empirical researchers had not been open, these misconceptions could not have been corrected and adequate preparation for the program would not have been possible. Likewise, once a program is initiated, communication channels must remain open between the referral agencies and staff to handle concerns realistically and constructively.

Some of the referral agencies contacted for the described project did not refer children to it. It is possible that these referral agencies chose not to do so because they did not believe that a predominately recreational agency could provide a treatment program for antisocial children, thus prejudging responses to one of the basic hypotheses even before it could be tested. Perhaps also, some referral agencies were overly concerned about the possibility that the host agency could deal effectively and less expensively with children who had not particularly benefitted from these referral agencies' own services. In any case, such concerns point to the relative importance of proper interpretation of the research to collaborative agencies, as well as to the host agency staff. It is indeed possible that some referral personnel experienced difficulty in viewing the host agency as an environment for treatment because it is a community-oriented agency that actually does not view its primary function as rehabilitation or treatment. It primarily provides recreational, educational, cultural, or leisure-time services for prosocial clientele; that is, clientele who do not or rarely engage in illegal or deviant behavior. Researchers' and my formal observations indicated that many social work practitioners believed that the type of children we, in the community agency intended to serve, could not be helped by any program. Consequently, these practitioners had given up on providing service to these children. Agencies may have been reluctant to refer children with whom they were unsuccessful, either to protect the rehabilitation image of their own agencies or, perhaps, in an effort to "protect" their clients from further change efforts. Although our interpretation of the research stressed its service elements, many agencies may have perceived the program as having a greater emphasis upon research than service, since its support was derived from a federal agency oriented toward research.

ATTITUDES ABOUT RESEARCH

It is often necessary for researchers to defend or explain questions regarding the research. In these instances, the empirical practitioner serves also as an educator. "What can be gained from the study?" can best be handled by indicating that the practitioner's and researcher's ultimate goals are actually quite similar: to help clients function adequately. In describing the program it was pointed out that two key aims were to provide an essential service lacking in the community and to delineate and evaluate explicitly the procedures in providing such a service so that, if effective, the relevant activities could be readily codified and communicated to other practitioners. Many times the question was asked: Why must random assignments be utilized? Consequently, it was necessary to clarify the research process for practitioners by explicating the rationale underlying randomization. One of the misconceptions constantly confronted was the mistaken belief that research was extremely easy to do, at least in comparison with the pressures faced by practitioners on the line. In these instances, it was necessary to share with others the various kinds of tasks and pressures that empirical practitioners experience.

CHOICE OF TERMS

Because some words have different connotations to practitioners and researchers, successful execution of the research study sometimes depends on the choice of terms used to communicate various features of the study. These can include semantic labels, such as control group, randomness, antisocial child, or behavior modification. When introducing such labels, empirical practitioners should be certain that there is a clear understanding of their terms so that workers do not assign incorrect or unintended meanings to these terms. The same procedures should be used in the interpretation of a research project to lay boards and citizens of the general community. A misinterpretation occurred, for example, when a treatment method labeled "behavior modification" was presented to the staff of the community center. Workers immediately responded with certain perceptions that indicated they viewed such treatment to include the "shocking" of children and similar punitive measures. Clear explication of the method used was necessary for the workers to understand its goals and implementation. For instance, it was explained that group leaders using behavior modification were taught primarily to avoid punitive measures and, instead, to set rewards for certain behaviors or decrease others by not attending to them.

CONSISTENCY OF SUPERVISION

When researchers evaluate the effects of certain types of treatment programs, they must ensure that agency supervisors are consistent in their supervision of the workers who apply treatment. Consistency of supervision can be achieved by conducting intensive training sessions for each method and by frequent and uniform monitoring of supervisory activity. Forms can be developed to serve as uniform guides and records for supervisory sessions devoted to each method. In the previously mentioned study, nonparticipating observers were placed in groups to secure data regarding the extent to which group leaders applied the various treatments. Videotapes of certain meetings provided an additional check on the quality of method application. If the method is applied correctly, tapes can be an instructional aid for other leaders and supervisors. The importance of impartial supervision for all methods must be stressed to prevent the creation of undue bias.

To enlist practitioners' support and also safeguard clients' welfare, guidelines must be set for the termination or alteration of unduly troublesome clients or groups. In one study, supervisors were concerned about whether they could change treatment methods or leaders if their groups were not developing as necessary. To avoid this consideration would have been tantamount to violation of a cardinal professional dictum—the provision of maximum feasible service for clients. Moreover, it would have been injurious to crucial collaborative relationships with the professionals. To deal with this concern, a procedure was developed for evaluating specific goals and progress, or lack of it, for the members of each group. Elaboration of this procedure entailed a joint conference between the clinical research team and the practitioners. Specific items, such as severity of behavior exhibited, the incidence of such behavior, and progress toward the attainment of treatment goals were discussed, and mutual decisions were made concerning whether changes were necessary. The best way to resolve conflicts that arise among practitioners is through discussions aimed at resolution and consensus.

Researchers also may have to deal with executives' and practitioners' concerns over evaluation by independent observers. This can be done by indicating the exact practices under investigation and the particular criteria for evaluation, and, perhaps, by citing practices and procedures that will not be considered, and stressing that evaluations will be used primarily to improve services to clients. Additionally, it may be helpful to indicate that evaluations will remain anonymous, will be reported as data groups, and will be reported after a delay.

IMPLEMENTATION OF METHODOLOGICAL PROCEDURES

Baseline Periods

In the aforementioned project, a no-treatment baseline period was integral to the research design. Utilization of this research procedure is gaining widespread acceptance even though it entails withholding a particular mode of treatment for a limited period of time. The application of baseline periods has proven to be particularly valuable in assessing the differential effects of one or more treatments immediately pursuant to the baseline. Practitioners particularly need support during the period of a study when no treatment interventions are employed. Frequently they may believe that excessive disruptive behavior occurs within the agency or, as in our case, that clients are being too antisocial, are not staying together in their groups, or are not engaging in constructive planning of activities. Our agency dealt with this concern by supplying the rationale for baseline procedures—that they provide an index against which each method can be evaluated—and setting specific baseline criteria for interventions. The criteria allowed interventions when the physical or psychological safety of one of the group members was in danger or when the group's unity was seriously at risk. It was also most helpful to point out that this period is analogous to a typical diagnostic period postulated by many group work theorists (Churchill, 1965), in which the worker does not intervene so that the treatment needs of the clients can be accurately diagnosed without contamination from his or her own efforts. This discussion showed how the research process and clinical procedure were similar.

Monitoring the Execution of the Study

Communication and monitoring structures must be parsimonious yet accessible throughout a study to ensure its successful execution. No matter how clearly one specifies communication structures, their undue enlargement presages a tendency for messages to be improperly received and interpreted. Although the staff of the project described above was composed of 5 researchers and 10 practitioners, it was most practical to channel the majority of communications through one research practitioner and two other practitioners, thus limiting the many permutations and variations of potential communication channels among the staff. This mode of centralization is especially helpful when the requisite communications tend to be relatively uniform, repetitive, and nonurgent. However, to facilitate the processing of urgent or idiosyncratic communications, efforts should be made to assign permanent liaison or coordinative responsibilities to one or more staff members, even if they are primarily clerical staff.

Any study also must have safeguards against artifacts to which the results can be falsely attributed. Because this study depended on bringing 150 children into the agency, it was necessary to obtain data on absences to ensure continuous attendance by the participants. Likewise, it was deemed essential to engage in first-hand observations of members' behavior within the groups. Periodic checks on supervisors' sessions and leaders' meetings with their groups were needed. Also, it was necessary to conduct extensive reliability sessions with observers to ensure consistent data collection and data analysis. Monitoring procedures are most readily executed when they are unobtrusive, guarantee anonymity and confidentiality, and are based upon the informed consent of subjects. To our pleasant surprise, monitoring procedures were readily accepted by all participants in the research, including the children, once the above considerations were addressed. Observers were trained to remain relatively inconspicuous; safeguards were devised to ensure the confidentiality of data; and, most important, the approval of participants was solicited and granted before inception of the monitoring procedure.

Follow-up

Critical to the evaluation of any program of interpersonal change is how lasting are the changes after treatment concludes. Follow-up data are necessary to determine what requisite maintenance procedures should be included in the treatment process (Filipczak & Wodarski, 1979; Howing, Wodarski, Kurtz, & Gaudin, 1993; Wodarski, 1980; Wodarski, Filipczak, McCombs, Koustenis, & Rusilko, 1979). To help the follow-up investigations, the research practitioner should keep the permanent address records on the participants, and should apply consistent measures in pre- and posttests and at follow-up.

STRUCTURAL COMPONENTS
FOR EVALUATION

One-Way Mirrors

Few agencies have considered the key organizational requirements for the evaluation of social work services. Most agencies are poorly structured for the delivery or evaluation of practice. This problem limits the information on how services are being implemented, which prohibits the evaluation and feedback workers need to become competent and provide effective service. For example, few agencies provide observation areas with one-way mirrors where workers can observe each other and isolate effective techniques for working with a child or his family unit. Viewing areas enable the unobtrusive gathering of samples of a child's behavior and make easy the recording of interactions between parents and child. Observation areas can facilitate training programs where parents learn to change interactional patterns with their child and can provide means by which parents can view and model therapist behaviors exhibited during work with the child. These features also may enable workers to secure necessary data for the systematic evaluation of therapeutic services. This feedback enables workers to sharpen their practice skills.

Videotapes

Another technological advance of considerable help in evaluating the services provided to clients is the videotape, which can document many verbal and nonverbal interactions. The videotape can provide an effective and reliable medium to evaluate therapeutic services. Many benefits are accrued by using videotape to evaluate social work practice. Videotaping provides a medium through which client-worker interactions can be more accurately recorded, by capturing more verbal details, such as association and clustering of words, duration of utterances, number of interruptions, questions, summary and interpretative statements, length of silent periods, and such nonverbal details as posture, gestures, eye contact, and touching, than a worker can amass through traditional recording methods. Likewise, with proper analysis, the videotape can sharpen practice skills and lead to an understanding of how behaviors exhibited by clients and workers influence their mutual interaction. Also, videotapes may be used as training vehicles for new and established workers, as educational devices for the community at large and other agencies in staff screening procedures, as documentation of important decisions made by executives, as a permanent record for current and future research activities, and in many other valuable capacities.

Preparing to Videotape. An agency should determine how videotaping improves service to client and if service is indeed better. In assessing the quality of client-worker interactions, the criterion can be stated in the following questions: Are worker practice behaviors changing in aspects of relationship formation and employment of change techniques? Are client behaviors changing in desired directions more readily by employing videotaping? Is the agency saving the worker's time through decreasing the amount of time spent on traditional audio recording, thus providing more time for the worker to interact with the client?

Once the agency secures its equipment, it should either hire a consultant or employ someone on the staff who can operate the machinery. A person on the staff capable of operating the equipment will provide the agency more access to the equipment. Likewise, having one person responsible for the operation of the tape will prevent mishandling, which in turn will decrease the probability of the malfunctioning of any parts of the system. Additionally, if agency personnel feel comfortable with the operator, resistance to being taped may be reduced.

Preferably, the agency should set up organizational procedures for taping and viewing of various social work practices. In the author's experience with videotapes in one agency, there was no specified place for viewing the tapes. Thus, every time a viewing was desired, someone would have to reserve an area and the equipment beforehand. The less energy required to view the tapes the more viewing will take place. Therefore, it is suggested that an agency provide a specific area where the tapes can be easily viewed; such an area might be designated the "practice skills center."

The optimal length of tapes chosen for review is approximately 20 min. Periods longer than that may overwhelm practitioners because of the large amount of information. In the initial stages of viewing, practitioners must discuss the criteria upon which the tapes will be reviewed. After viewing a few, they can decide to tape entire meetings or certain portions. Likewise, other aspects of taping, such as whether the camera should focus only on the worker or the client, or both, or what portion of the body should be taped, can be reviewed.

Staff Concerns Regarding Observation

Staff will have concerns about the use of videotapes in evaluating their practice. Most of these concerns can be handled by indicating the types of procedures that will be evaluated and assuring them that the videotapes will not be used to criticize any one worker or portray one in a negative light, but will be implemented only to improve services provided to clients. One technique for reducing anxiety over being taped is to have all workers and supervisors participate. However, how the person produces the tape and how the various supervisors utilize it for improving practice skills will be dependent on developing mutual relationships among persons using the tapes. These collegial relationships should be characterized by mutual trust, sharing, respect, encouragement, and acceptance, with the goal of improving services provided to clients. The review of tapes by the workers must be handled in the highest professional manner possible. Criticism offered professionally can lead to improved practice; degrading criticism will not enable one to tap the potential of taping to improve practice. Finally, procedures are best executed when they are unobtrusive and guarantee anonymity and confidentiality.

In the author's study, the researchers were pleasantly surprised that taping procedures were readily accepted by the participants. Specific factors that may have led to its ready acceptance in our situation include the agency executive's support of the use of taping to improve practice, the encouragement offered by the individuals implementing the taping procedure, and the professional manner of those executing the process. Since these factors may not be present in other agencies, professionals who want to use videotapes may have to be prepared to offer rationales as to its benefits and answer questions such as: Could taping be detrimental to the formation of the relationship between client and worker? Will client improvement be affected? Can the tapes be used to discredit my practice?

Potential Benefits to Agencies Through Videotaping

1. Improvement of social work practice may be accomplished through videotaping. Recent research indicates that after viewing videotapes, therapists are more willing to accept their deficiencies and to concentrate on improving them, are more receptive to new techniques, and are more aware of their verbal and nonverbal presence. Likewise, clients who view themselves on tape can increase their participation in the social services being provided and increase their self-awareness in verbal and nonverbal areas (Berger, 1970).

2. Videotapes provide a medium through which the quality of the social services being offered to clients can be monitored.

3. Videotapes provide a permanent record for research that can be used by the agency to improve practice and contribute to the knowledge of social work practice.

4. Records of important decisions made by the agency administration are readily available. If controversy develops regarding the decisions, a permanent record is available to provide the rationale for the decision and clarify discrepancies.

5. Various tapes can be made to efficiently demonstrate regular practice skills necessary for training social workers. This saves time for the practitioner who normally must explain these regular skills to each new worker.

6. Videotapes can take the place of audio recordings, freeing the worker to spend more time in helping the client.

SUMMARY

Research in an open setting requires that the empirical practitioner become well acquainted with the resources of the agency to determine the feasibility of the research design. In many instances, agency resources do not meet the requirements of a research design. In such cases, the research questions to be asked must be reconceptualized or another location sought for the study and/or research design.

All parts and phases of a research study are interrelated, and each depends on the successful implementation of the others. However, experiences associated with the writer's own research in typical social work agencies suggests that the following considerations are especially important for the successful execution of relevant clinical research studies: assessment of agency characteristics with resultant negotiations and contractual clarifications; the development of relationships—appropriate and operational, collaborative and coordinative—internal and external to the agency; the creation and sustenance of positive attitudes toward research; the selection and utilization of proper semantic terminology; the assurance of equal treatment for all relevant parties, including supervisors; and the implementation of crucial methodological procedures, such as baseline periods and the gathering of data through videotapes and one-way mirrors. An initial understanding of such considerations is necessary for practitioners, administrators, and empirical practitioners who would engage in joint investigative endeavors. Equally important to the success of research is the emphasis to the agency staff on the service aspects of the project.

REFERENCES

Berger, M. M. (Ed.). (1970). *Videotape techniques in psychiatric training and treatment.* New York: Brunner/Mazel Publisher.

Churchill, S. R. (1965). Social group work: A diagnostic tool in child guidance. *American Journal of Orthopsychiatry, 35,* 581–588.

Filipczak, J., & Wodarski, J. S. (1979). Behavioral intervention in public schools: Implementing and evaluating a model. *Corrective and Social Psychiatry, 25,* 104–116.

Goldfried, M. R., & Davison, G. C. (1994). *Clinical behavior therapy*. New York: Harper Colophon Books.

Goldstein, A. P. (1962). *Therapist-patient expectations in psychotherapy*. New York: Pergamon Press.

Howing, P. T., Wodarski, J. S., Kurtz, P. D., & Gaudin, J. M. (1993). *Maltreatment and the school-aged child: Developmental outcomes and system issues*. New York: Haworth Press.

Katz, D. (1966). Field studies. In L. Festinger & D. Katz (Eds.), *Research methods in behavioral science*. New York: Holt, Rinehart, & Winston.

Rosenthal, R. (1969). Interpersonal expectations: Effects of the experimenter's hypothesis. In R. Rosenthal & R. L. Rosnow (Eds.), *Artifact in behavioral research* (pp. 181–277). New York: Academic Press.

Shapiro, A. K., & Morris, L. A. (1978). Placebo effects in medical and psychological therapies. In S. L. Garfield & A. E. Bergin (Eds.), *Handbook of psychotherapy and behavior change* (pp. 369–410). New York: Wiley.

Wodarski, J. S. (1980). Procedures for the maintenance and generalization of achieved behavioral change. *Journal of Sociology and Social Welfare, 7*, 298–311.

Wodarski, J. S., Filipczak, J., McCombs, D., Koustenis, G., & Rusilko, S. (1979). Follow-up on behavioral intervention with troublesome adolescents. *Journal of Experimental Psychiatry and Behavior Therapy, 10*, 181–188.

CHAPTER 10

Competency-Based Agency Practice

Previous chapters showed the increasing demand for account-ability in the delivery of social services. Many social work theorists, researchers, and practitioners have called for the establishment of social work services on a more rational basis and the empirical evaluation of services to assess whether clients' needs are being met. The call for definite criteria of change, delineation of change methods, and evaluation of the effects of the change methods should increase the quality of social services provided. With limited exceptions, however, there have been few efforts to conceptualize and to formulate characteristics of effective agency practices (Alexander & Siman, 1973; Bergin, 1971; Briar, 1968, 1973; Briar & Miller, 1971; Eysenck, 1965, 1966; Fischer, 1973a, 1973b, 1975; Marks, 1972; Meyer, Borgatta, & Jones, 1965; Mullen & Dumpson, 1972; Newman & Turem, 1974; Reid & Shyne, 1969; Stuart, 1971; Wodarski & Bagarozzi, 1979a, 1979b; Wodarski, Feit, & Green, 1995; Younghusband, 1973). Hence, the central aim of this chapter is to discuss basic requisites for the establishment of competency-based agency practice.

The human services profession has operated in both "fat" and "lean" times in the past 30 years. The 1960s brought plentiful funds, expenditures, and support. The 1970s heralded the beginnings of the "lean" years with increased reports of casework having no effect on those it purported to help (Fischer, 1978; Wodarski & Bagarozzi, 1979a). With the 1980s came the Reagan administration's tight budgeting and subsequent demands for accountability. The 1990s have reinforced these themes through managed care systems (Johnstone et al., 1995). A review of the data reveals increased emphasis on the need for empirical support of the effectiveness of human service practice and education (Clark & Arkava, 1979; Jarrett & Clark, 1978; Jarrett, Kilpatrick, & Pollane, 1977; Kolevzon, 1977; Larsen & Hepworth, 1978; Newman & Turem, 1974; Parsons, Reid, & Green, 1993; Shepard & Wahle, 1981; Wodarski, 1979a, 1981).

Competency-based or performance-based education (CBE) is being instituted more frequently in departments of social services across the nation in response to the demand for accountability (Camasso & Jagannathan, 1994; Menefee & Thompson, 1994; Reid, Parsons, & Green, 1989). Proclaimed as both systematic savior and manipulative malarkey, it appears that CBE is nevertheless a growing force in the development of social services.

CBE focuses on:

1. Writings that offer definitions and explanations of CBE.
2. Literature that attempts to define competencies needed for practice at various organizational levels.
3. Studies and descriptions of existing CBE programs in human services education.
4. Literature that covers curriculum training and designs.

Definitions of CBE differ as widely as opinions concerning its value. There are, however, several ideal aspects of CBE that remain constant:

1. The objectives and goals (competencies) that workers are expected to master are stated in specific behavioral skill performance terms and provided in advance (Clark, 1976; Hohn & Meinke, 1978; Kennedy, 1976; Smith, 1974).
2. Criterion referenced assessment is utilized (Armitage & Clark, 1975; Schwartz & Baer, 1991).
3. Small, sequential units of instruction are employed (Gross, 1981; Shepard & Wahle, 1981).
4. An increasingly heuristic approach to learning is utilized, with the instructor taking on the role of facilitator and learning advisor (Jarrett et al., 1977).

5. Simulation techniques, such as role play, video feedback, and modeling exercises, are applied (Kelly, 1994).
6. Evaluations of competency achievement level are provided at desig-nated intervals.
7. Competency is demonstrated through multiple means and evaluated with several measures.

Criticisms of the approach include concern about "loaded" training; that is, emphasis on skill acquisition to the detriment of adequate theoretical background (Hohn & Meinke, 1978; Wahle & Shepard, 1981), self-paced learning moving so slowly that workers find themselves unable to complete program requirements (Edwards, 1973), problems in financing curriculum revision and protests from workers, humanist aversion to behavioral emphasis, and accountability (Smith, 1974). Moreover, data from one competency program indicate extensive costs, time commitment, and lack of agreement on competencies (Wodarski, 1983).

Perhaps the most compelling concern highlighted in the literature is specified competency. Extensive lists of required competencies are rare and not necessarily supported with empirical evidence that those skills are required for effective social service practice. The questions raised include: Who designates which skills must be mastered and at what performance level? At which occupational level should skills be acquired? Should skills change as roles change, or should they remain constant throughout? What are the continuities between different worker levels for posited competencies?

One suggestion that appears frequently in the literature is the curriculum planning challenge of differentiating among the objectives for each level of job specification and defining the appropriate relationship among them (Bernotavicz, 1994; Block, 1972; Levy, 1972; McNair & Stewart, 1971; Main, 1971; Meinert, 1978; Rothman & Vililante, 1974). This point has been argued time and again, without any agreement being reached. The result has been a profession held in check, duplication of curricula, and unclear directions for future development.

Inherent in the problem of defining which skills workers should acquire is the current controversy surrounding the various levels of occupational difference. Should the bachelor's-level program focus on skills attainment relevant to employment, or should it provide the prelude to increased worker complexities? Should the master's in social work lead to specialization or to general theory and skill learning (Roberts, 1973; Wodarski, 1986)? Lack of consensus on this issue is reflected in the dearth of literature stating specific skills needed at the various educational levels.

Priorities for future research include comparative evaluations between CBE programs, teaching/learning approaches, follow-up studies to indicate retentive value of programs and concurrence with actual practice skills used, greater consensus on skills needed, intensified concern for external and internal evaluation validity, interdisciplinary exchange about weaknesses and strengths of existing programs, and evaluation of CBE for appropriate learning areas compared with other approaches. Perhaps the most pressing need is the development of adequate measurement instruments and methodologies for evaluating current programs. As Main has said, "It is vitally important that we require of ourselves full descriptive analysis of new methods and approaches to education, with evaluation of what we believe to have been sound and effective or ineffective" (Main, 1971, p. 37).

The literature indicates demand for accountability in the delivery of social services. The call for definite criteria of change, delineation of change methods, and evaluation of the effects of the change methods will increase the quality of social services provided. With limited exceptions, however, there have been few efforts to conceptualize and formulate the aspects of human services practice common to many practice situations. Moreover, virtually all such endeavors have been rather limited, because they have shown a pronounced tendency to conceptualize human services practice through specific techniques, practice in certain agencies or fields, and so forth (Wodarski, 1985).

Initially, this chapter presents the means of securing practitioner agreement for developing a competency-based agency practice. Prerequisite to development of competency-based agency practice is the evaluation of current practices. Staff generally tend to be apprehensive of impending evaluations. Most concerns, however, can be handled by specifying the types of procedures that will be evaluated. The discussion centers, therefore, on the concrete items that can be evaluated, such as execution of written contracts, recording practice contracts (within 72 hours of each session), goal-setting forms, dictation specifying overall treatment plan, follow-up procedure, termination notes, and, if necessary, letters to referring professionals, first at the initiation of services regarding treatment plans and diagnosis, and then at the end of the intervention concerning plans for follow-up services.

The chapter focuses next on practice competencies that can be evaluated: interpersonal skills, theoretical knowledge, and practice skills, and procedures for testing these competencies. The mechanisms that can be utilized for evaluation of services are reviewed. The competencies that can be established for practice in a residential treatment center for children are elaborated in Table 10.1. Finally, issues in the implementation of competency-based practice are briefly reviewed: for example, cost-benefit factors in securing necessary evaluation data, mechanisms for resolving which competencies should be assessed, and the most feasible means of training competent social workers.

SECURING PRACTITIONERS' AGREEMENT

One of the most critical aspects of developing a competency-based practice is to secure a professional agreement regarding the evaluation. Many practitioners have concerns about being evaluated. These concerns can be alleviated by providing rationales for the evaluation, having both workers and supervisors participate in the process and in choosing items for evaluation, indicating the types of procedures that will be evaluated, and deciding mechanisms for the evaluation.

Professionals who must evaluate should be prepared to provide rationale as to its benefits and to answer such questions as: Could evaluation be detrimental to the formation of the relationship between client and worker? Will as much improvement take place in the client as would occur if evaluation were omitted? Can the data be used to discredit my practice? (Feldman & Wodarski, 1974; Wodarski & Feldman, 1974). Staff members must be assured that the evaluation will not be used to criticize any worker or portray anyone in a negative light, but will be implemented to provide the worker necessary feedback on practice behavior with the ultimate goal to improve services provided to clients.

One technique for reducing the amount of anxiety over being evaluated is to have all workers, including supervisors, participate in the evaluation. Additionally, workers should participate in the choice of criteria used in the evaluation of performances (e.g., the amount of client improvement or change on agreed outcome measures) and the means of evaluation (video and/or audio taping, behavioral observation, interview schedules, and self-inventories). What will be evaluated and how it will be evaluated must be clearly outlined prior to the initiation of evaluation. Keep in mind, too, that evaluation procedures are most readily executed when they are unobtrusive and guarantee anonymity and confidentiality.

Table 10.1 Competencies, Criteria, and Data for Assessing Worker Behavior in a Residential Treatment Center for Children

Competency	Criteria	Data
A clearly defined targeted population	Specify client population in terms of number of children accommodated, age, sex, behavior problems	Policy statement, descriptive survey
A clearly defined theoretical model validated through research; that is, behavioral group work and token economy	A policy statement reflecting the competency, staff development programs geared toward theory, testing the staff's knowledge of theory and practice techniques, behavioral observations of practice	Inspection of treatment plans (case records to see if the plan follows from theory) observation of staff behavior
Training program for staff to orient them toward practice model and philosophy used in the agency	Number and types of staff development activities within the agency, money allocated in the budget for staff development, initial orientation to agency in terms of the model of practice	Budget, training manual, the number of training sessions held, a record of participation in staff development programs
Clearly defined job description; that is, tasks to be performed by different levels of workers	Specify level of training for each task, type and years of experience, skills needed for job	Job requirements, how often they are updated
An individualized treatment plan with criteria for measuring change for each child	Are there individualized treatment goals and a specified treatment program for meeting these goals? They should include a time frame, behavioral	Case records, behavioral observations

(continued)

Table 10.1 (Continued)

Competency	Criteria	Data
	objectives, and specified activity, or all those involved in treatment and outcome specifications	
Direct family involvement with child in treatment	A specified number of family sessions, a family assessment, a family treatment program	Treatment plan, case records of staff time in terms of who they see and what they do
A contingent environment individualized for each child	Is staff behavior in accordance with theoretical model? For example, are reinforcers given for desired behavior?	Treatment plan, behavioral observations, videotaping of therapeutic environment
Encouragement of community contact and public education	Number and types of activities residents participate in outside of the residential center; number and types of activities community members participate in within the residential treatment center; number and types of activities geared toward public education brochures, speakers for community groups, etc.	A list of the activities participated in, in comparison to an ideal standard rationale for such activities
Provision of adequate schooling	Are all children attending an accredited school or one with accreditation pending within or outside the institution?	Case records
Assessment of overall treatment success	There is a prespecified proportion of children who meet the outcome	Policy statement containing this proportion. Case records of the

	criteria in order for the program to be considered successful	proportion of clients with successful outcomes against those not successful
Valid discharge criteria	Individualized reasons for discharging the child to the previous home, a new home; that is, a foster home, a different community agency, etc.; this should be based on the child's progress and the family's progress	Case records
Post-discharge follow-up	Has the achieved outcome been maintained for a specified time interval (i.e., monthly, for 6 months, at 1 year, and at 2 years)?	Follow-up studies to see if behavior is maintained
The coordination of services among agencies involved with the child and the family	A centralized program for all children's services. In lieu of this, residential treatment centers can have a staff liaison person to establish and facilitate communication among agencies. This person should act as a resource person for therapists who could then continue treatment with the family	Job descriptions
Return the child to the community as quickly as possible	As behavior moves toward the desired goals, the child's environment should be expanded to include increasingly longer home visits, progressing from partial residency to full residency. Therapist, family, and child should be involved in this planning	Case records, record of movement toward community placement; that is, number and the length of home visits

Specific factors that may lead to the ready acceptance of evaluation in an agency include the agency's executive support of evaluation to improve practice, the encouragement offered by individuals implementing the evaluation, the professional manner employed by those executing the process, and inclusion of the executive's requisite job performance in the evaluation.

The review of competency by workers must be handled in the highest professional manner possible. Positive criticism offered professionally can lead to improved practice; criticism offered degradingly will not.

How the evaluation process is executed and how various professionals treat the information for improving practice skills is dependent upon developing mutual relationships among individuals using the data. These collegial relationships should be characterized by mutual trust, sharing, respect, encouragement, and acceptance, with the goal of improving services provided to clients.

PROCEDURES THAT CAN BE EVALUATED

Numerous concrete items can easily be assessed regardless of the practice context. Contracts executed between client and workers can be checked for the inclusion of the following: purpose of the interaction, targeted problems and areas of difficulties to be worked on, various goals and objectives that might be accomplished, client and therapist duties, delineation of administrative procedures or constraints, techniques that will be used, duration of contracts and criteria for decisions for termination, and renegotiation procedures (Wodarski, 1980a; Wodarski & Bagarozzi, 1979b).

Agencies can use goal-setting forms that specify the type of client difficulty, plans for therapy, short- and long-term goals, plans for termination, and follow-up procedures (Cytrynbaum, Ginath, Birdwell, & Brandt, 1979). Such documentation should facilitate the evaluation of progress made toward treatment goals. Additionally, a summary form could be used to specify the overall treatment plan, including termination and follow-up procedures.

Other means of evaluation might include checking to see if practice notes summarizing the major events of the client's last visit are recorded within a time frame, such as 72 hr after each session, and determining if the following actions are executed and placed in the client's record within a reasonable time (1 week): letter to referring professional (if necessary) regarding treatment plans and diagnosis; summary termination notes including follow-up procedures; and, if necessary, a letter to the referring professional or family doctor about the termination of services. In all instances, the energy and time necessary to execute the forms should be kept to a minimum (Rinn & Vernon, 1975).

PRACTICE COMPETENCIES

Three areas of competency should be assessed: interpersonal skills, theoretical knowledge, and practice skills.

Interpersonal Skills

Mechanisms must be provided for assessing three critical interpersonal skills—empathy, unconditional positive regard, and genuineness—characteristics that empirical research shows are necessary ingredients for therapeutic change regardless of the approach being utilized by the social worker. *Empathy* is generally defined as the worker's ability to understand the world according to each client's unique perspective. Workers who are empathic can accurately feel and experience the world as the client does. *Unconditional positive regard* is defined as the ability to provide clients with a nonthreatening, safe, and secure atmosphere in which to express themselves. *Genuineness* is usually defined as the therapist's ability to establish genuine and nonexploitive relationships between himself or herself and the client. Recent research shows that attending behaviors, accurate reflection, and summary of feelings may be other relevant characteristics pertinent to inducing therapeutic change (Wodarski, 1979). These therapist traits can be readily measured within current agency practice because good measurement devices are available and are easily administered quickly and inexpensively, causing minimal disruption of the agency's regular operations (Carkhuff, 1977).

Few social work training programs have been evaluated for their effectiveness or relevance to development of the social worker's interpersonal practice skills; however, three empirically based programs are available: microcounseling, human resource training, and interpersonal process recall (Carkhuff, 1971; Ivey, Normington, Miller, Morrill, & Haase, 1968; Kagen, 1984; Stein & Lambert, 1995). The evaluation data on educational programs indicate deterioration in these essential skills (Wodarski, Pippin, & Daniels, 1988; Wodarski et al., 1995). Most participants are merely asked to indicate satisfaction with the training program or are given paper and pencil tests to measure learning or practice skills. Only recently have evaluations been developed that require demonstration of critical interpersonal skills. One procedure is the use of a test where trainees role-play how they would respond to certain practice situations that involve their use of interpersonal skills. Here trainees can be evaluated on observable criteria, and since students perform the interpersonal skills in the role plays, such evaluations more clearly typify practice situations.

Although role plays are not the same as actual situations, it is assumed that they more nearly simulate the real world than do paper and pencil tests. The problems incurred in developing role-play tests are the identification of the critical situations practitioners believe to be difficult and representative of requisite practice situations, and the development of criteria for judging effectiveness of worker performance in those areas (Rose, Cayner, & Edleson, 1977).

Simulated role-play tests have been used to prepare practitioners to work with delinquents, highly anxious women, the older people, clients of public welfare agencies, and inpatients of psychiatric wards. In studies comparing workers who received no interpersonal skills training and workers who received such training, the tests were sufficiently sensitive to favor the training (Goldsmith & McFall, 1975; Schinke & Rose, 1976). The training consisted of simulation exercises in which clinicians practiced clinical skills as interview skills of attending, accurate reflection, and summarization of feelings. Thus, the simulation model may be joined with competency scales and objective multiple-choice items to assess the competencies of beginning practitioners. The simulation model has potential for standardization of test stimuli, which would provide greater reliability. Using such procedures should enable finer discrimination between practitioners who are competent and those who are not.

A prototype of simulation technology that can be used to assess competencies is presented by Rose and colleagues (1977) in their article, "Measuring interpersonal competence." The evaluation mechanisms involve a step-by-step description of a role-play designed to evaluate the effectiveness of training programs, wherein the aims are: to improve interpersonal skills practice competencies in feeling empathy, identifying feelings, expressing opinions, showing persistence, seeking clarification, and giving clarification; and to implement treatment procedures using appropriate timing and appropriate verbal affect, latency, volume, and fluency.

Three steps in the development of the assessment instrument are outlined below:

1. *Situational analysis* involves identifying situations most social workers must effectively cope with in order to be considered competent. Among ways to conduct situational analyses are the two used in the study by Rose et al. (1977): self-report of the practitioners and records of the observers who monitored practice situations. Professionals and students were asked to list practice situations that posed problems and rate them on a 10-point scale on the relevancy of the items to their practice endeavors and the relative anxiety these items elicited. Items rated above the mean on both scales were included in the list used for training. The final list had 27 actual problem situations, such as dealing with attempted suicide, helping a client prepare for an employment interview, and discussing abortion.

2. *Response enumeration* is the process by which practitioners identify relevant responses to each situation. Responses were obtained by asking social workers to respond in writing to the 27 situations as if they were encountering them. For example, in a family therapy session where the general goal was to limit a father's domination of conversation, the intermediate goals consisted of (a) identifying the father's feelings of concern, (b) expressing the opinion that other family members should have equal time to speak, and (c) being persistent with the father despite anger from him. Later the same participants were asked to act out their responses. The assumption was made that these two processes would produce the greatest number of responses, because they provided greater reality and simulated more closely the actual practice situations (Rose et al., 1977).

3. In the *response evaluation,* once a number of ways of handling critical practice situations were identified, professional social workers rated each set of responses on a 4-point scale by its relative effectiveness in dealing with given situations.

The data provided by practitioners suggested that each situation called for a unique combination of responses. For each situation, an overall score indicating the participant's competence was determined on the basis of his or her success in meeting each subcriteria, such as empathy; expressing opinions; persistence; giving and seeking clarification; appropriate timing; use of an interpersonal skill; and verbal statements with appropriate affect, latency, volume, and fluency.

Weighing items in the above test depended on how the professional judges assessed the contribution of a response to a general competency. Of the 27 situations, the six selected for the test were the most anxiety producing and those in which participants in earlier experiments showed least competence in their responses: dealing with critical marks, dealing with hostile statements and unacceptable requests, taking a stand unpopular with a professional group, dealing with interpersonal conflict, and introducing ways of practice. The remaining situations were used for practice exercises in training. Before and after a training program, the test was administered to each participant individually in the presence of two testers. The responses were audiotaped. Rose et al. (1977) concluded that the experiences with a behavioral role-play test for evaluating training in interpersonal skills provide preliminary evidence that such a test is not only reliable and effective, but sensitive to changes in trainee performance. Although practice skills tests are difficult and time consuming to develop, they have the potential for broad use in evaluating the effects of professional programs. One limitation of this study is reliance on expert consensus rather than on researched findings that are consistent throughout the social work literature. Data are limited, and more development is required before researchers can be confident of the instrument's validity.

One difficulty is that role-play examines only how well participants act out critical situations under simulation. It would be desirable to check validity of role-playing with real situations. The role-play method, however, is assumed better than paper-pencil tests and other self-report measurements because actual behavioral observations are evaluated against specific criteria (Rose et al., 1977). More research is needed to develop and validate additional categories of relevant interpersonal skills.

Practice Skills

To determine practice skill levels, the workers might be asked to review a tape of a client interview or to read a contrived case, to make a diagnosis, to design a corresponding intervention plan, and to specify how they would evaluate the success of the plan to the satisfaction of practitioners who have demonstrated their competencies.

Inventories, such as the Barrett-Lennard, which measure the quality of the relationship between client and worker from the client's perspective, can be administered to clients to obtain consumer assessments of worker endeavors (Barrett-Lennard, 1962). This consumer aspect of the evaluation process is seldom addressed, but nevertheless, is necessary for a comprehensive evaluation (Wodarski, Filipczak, McCombs, Kousteins, & Rusilko, 1979).

There are skills-assessment scales available that contain lists of practice-performance requirements for social workers responding to live or simulated cases. These scales have been primarily devised to assess student performance in fieldwork; the potential of these scales for use in assessment of agency practice has not been tapped. Future research should be aimed at the evaluation of these scales for assessing competency of social workers already in practice or preparing for practice.

Early evaluation efforts in simulation technology for the assessment of initial practice skills include the Tulane Assessment Scale for caseworkers, developed by Harris Goldstein, and the Benjamin Rose Institute Interrupted Case Test. The Tulane Scale uses a filmed case and responses to questions at certain points during the film. Critics point to lack of objective criteria to measure correct responses and norms based on consensus of experts who view practice from the same theoretical framework. The Benjamin Rose test uses instead a printed vignette format. For both methods, further research is needed to establish acceptable levels of reliability and validity. There is debate on how experts are chosen and how much agreement exists among them. A simulated test may standardize the representation of practice and appears to offer greater reliability than a real practice situation. However, when used more than once, students can learn correct responses from others who have previously taken the test. To solve this problem, a series of tests should be devised (Arkava & Brennen, 1976; Clark & Arkava, 1979).

Theoretical Knowledge

To assess the worker's theoretical accuracy, an objective exam or assessment battery can be given, for example, on task-centered casework, family therapy, and behavioral social work. Once workers achieve acceptable criterion levels on these assessment batteries, they can then move on to implementing interventions based on the theoretical framework.

Thus, for adequate assessment of practice skills before the practitioner begins work with clients, sufficient theoretical knowledge and the necessary practice skills should be demonstrated through appropriate testing techniques. Before beginning an intervention with a client, the worker should review a tape of the client or read a contrived case; should make a diagnosis, design a corresponding intervention plan with specified outcomes and related means to measure said outcomes; and should specify how the success of the plan will be evaluated. These should be accomplished to the satisfaction of experienced practitioners.

GENERAL MEANS AVAILABLE TO ASSESS COMPETENCIES

The term "competency" indicates an ability to demonstrate empirically that an individual possesses a certain skill. Depending upon the specified skill, evaluation can be conducted through means of (a) videotapes of practitioners' behavior; (b) inventories designed to measure specific academic and practice skills; (c) behavioral observations using time-sampling procedures; and (d) structured and unstructured interviews with supervisors, clients, and seasoned agency practitioners. In all feasible instances, multicriteria measurements should be utilized to provide assessment of the multidimensions of learning.

In-Course Training Evaluation

Paper and pencil tests can be developed for each course in an undergraduate, graduate, continuing education curriculum, or agency inservice training workshop to assess the acquisition of the practitioner's academic knowledge. Computers can now easily score and provide previously unavailable feedback to learners. Moreover, computers can provide a longitudinal record of the acquired skills. This can be accomplished by pretesting and posttesting skills to determine whether the curriculum materials have accomplished their objectives. For example, the practitioners may be asked to do a community analysis by determining natural helping networks that exist and how they can be used to enhance the mental health of community residents.

Practice Observation

As part of the training procedures, practitioners can be evaluated on relevant practice skills through audio and video tapes and behavioral observations (Wodarski, Bricout, & Smokowski, in press). Videotaping client-worker interactions is the most rewarding for capturing the richness of clinical phenomena. Compared with traditional recording methods, videotapes capture more verbal details: association and cluster-ing of words, duration of utterances, number of interruptions, questions, summary and interpretative statements, and length of silent periods; and non-verbal details: posture, gestures, eye contact, and touching. Thus with proper analysis, tapes can sharpen practice skills by providing feed-back to practitioners, can lead to an understanding of how client and worker behaviors influence their interaction, can illustrate how worker behaviors effect behavioral changes in clients, and can provide checks on the observational procedures (Wodarski, 1975b). Moreover, record-ing behaviors of competent practitioners can reduce the length of time necessary to train those who are less experienced.

Behavioral observations are expensive in cost of observers, time involved in delineation of what behaviors should be observed and how, and the use of technical equipment necessary for accurate observation. However, they also capture the richness of practice phenomena and provide highly reliable data. Execution is facilitated when agencies have one-way mirrors and videotape equipment.

Interviews and Attitude Testing

At designated times, interviews should be conducted with clients, super-visors, and agency executive personnel to assess the adequacy of the training experience. Such procedures should facilitate any modifica-tions that may be necessary in the training program. Scales measuring values, interpersonal integration, mutual concern, motivation to help others, self-concept, anxiety, and the like can be administered before the trainees begin their education and at the conclusion to document the acquisition of competencies for practice.

Research has shown that interview schedules and self-inventories filled out by workers and/or clients are the least reliable of the evaluation methods. Therefore, they should always be checked with other measure-ment modes to ensure that the data they are providing are consistent and reliable (Wodarski, 1975a) (see Chapters 4 and 7 for means of evaluation).

Follow-up

Several months following completion of training, participating practi-tioners should be contacted to determine which skills they are using were acquired in their education. Also, observers can be sent to their agencies to note which procedures are being used and how. Such procedures would provide rarely available data on the adequacies of training for professional careers and would help ensure that relevant training experiences are provided in the future.

USE OF EVALUATION DATA
TO IMPROVE PRACTICE

Adequate baseline data on practice competencies will provide the information needed to facilitate the development of a competency-based practice. Following collection of baseline data, steps may be taken to develop a competency-based practice. Supervision should be provided in such a manner that it will help the worker alter dysfunctional therapeutic behavior. Such a process should include: (a) pinpointing the worker's behaviors that need to be altered, (b) measuring the frequency of such behaviors, (c) developing a program to alter the worker's behavior, and (d) providing the worker with feedback on targeted behaviors.

Videotaping client and worker interactions should facilitate isolation of those behaviors that need to be altered, and likewise provide the opportunity for supervisors to reinforce the worker's favorable practice behavior.

Table 10.1 illustrates 14 micro- and macro-level competencies along with the criteria for evaluation and pertinent data that might be used in the assessment of a residential treatment program for children. For example, a macro-level competency would be the agency's implementation of a training program for new staff to introduce the theoretical practice model being employed. Criteria to evaluate this competency would be: number of staff-development activities, money allocated to such activities, and initial orientation procedures. Data for competency-based agency practice would include the assessment of the competency budget, training manuals, the number of training sessions, and record of staff participation in such activities.

ISSUES INVOLVED IN THE IMPLEMENTATION
OF COMPETENCY-BASED PRACTICE

One cannot deny the cost involved in implementing a competency-based agency practice. Videotaping behavior, behavioral observation, and even administration of interview schedules and self-inventories are costly. However, the cost should be offset by the benefits clients derive from effective practice, by the support for effectiveness in malpractice suits, and by the increased ability of social service providers to document the relevance of their services to funding sources.

One of the major issues in implementing a competency-based practice model is securing agreement on the criteria that will be used to assess treatment outcomes. These criteria are usually tied to theories of human behavior. Such theories and how they relate to practice effectiveness have to be evaluated. Perhaps the one criteria that can be used universally concerning the effectiveness of a theory and practice behaviors derived is whether the theory produces desired outcome in client behaviors (Fischer, 1971, 1978; Wodarski, 1980b; Wodarski & Feldman, 1973).

Determining the most comprehensive and feasible means of training competent social workers is dependent on the agency in which the social worker is located. Schools of social work can train individuals in highly specialized treatment approaches. On the other hand, agencies will have to ensure that workers are competent by pre- and posttesting of skills and by developing and utilizing training packages that facilitate the acquisition of necessary skills for practice in particular agencies. For example, in practice with parents who abuse their children, workers could be trained to assess marital interaction, child-management practices, social satisfaction, and vocational satisfaction, and, according to the assessment, to implement the appropriate intervention strategies. Only when such training procedures are employed can social workers claim that they are ready to begin the complex task of implementing behavior change strategies with clients.

SUMMARY

Despite the recent attention to competency-based practice, well-developed and evaluative training programs for social workers are unavailable. The specification of competencies for training of social workers with delineation of entrance and exit skills represents a critical, yet relatively unexplored area in facilitating the acquisition of practice skills needed by social workers. This specification ensures that clients secure the services necessary to improve their functioning.

REFERENCES

Alexander, L. B., & Siman, A. (1973). Fischer's study of studies. *Social Work, 18,* 104–106.

Arkava, M. L., & Brennen, E. C. (1975). Toward a competency examination for the baccalaureate social worker. *Journal of Education for Social Work, 11,* 22–29.

Arkava, M. L., & Brennen, E. C. (1976). *Competency based education for social work: Evaluation and curriculum issues.* New York: Council on Social Work Education.

Armitage, A., & Clark, F. W. (1975). Design issues in the performance-based curriculum. *Journal of Education for Social Work, 11,* 22–29.

Barrett-Lennard, G. T. (1962). Dimensions of therapist response as causal factors in therapeutic change. *Psychological Monographs, 76,* (43, Whole No. 562).

Bergin, A. E. (1971). The evaluation of therapeutic outcomes. In A. E. Bergin & S. L. Garfield (Eds.), *Handbook of psychotherapy and behavior change.* New York: Wiley.

Bernotavicz, F. (1994). A new paradigm for competency-based training. *Journal of Continuing Social Work Education, 6,* 3–9.

Block, A. M. (1972). The dilemma of social work education: Restructuring the curriculum. *Journal of Education for Social Work, 8,* 18–23.

Briar, S. (1968). The casework predicament. *Social Work, 13,* 5–11.

Briar, S. (1973). The age of accountability. *Social Work, 18,* 2.

Briar, S., & Miller, H. (1971). *Problems and issues in social casework.* New York: Columbia University Press.

Camasso, M. J., & Jagannathan, R. (1994). The detection of AFDC payment errors through MIS and quality-control data integration: An application in the State of New Jersey, *Administration in Social Work, 18,* 45–68.

Carkhuff, R. R. (1971). The development of human resources. New York: Holt, Rinehart, & Winston.

Carkhuff, R. R. (1977). The functional professional therapeutic agent. In A. S. Gurman & A. M. Razin (Eds.), *Effective psychotherapy.* New York: Pergamon Press.

Clark, F. (1976). Characteristics of competency-based curriculum. In M. Arkava & C. Brennan (Eds.), *Competency-based education for social work.* New York: Council on Social Work Education.

Clark, F., & Arkava, M. (Eds.). (1979). *The pursuit of competence in social work.* San Francisco: Jossey-Bass.

Cytrynbaum, S., Ginath, Y., Birdwell, J., & Brandt, L. (1979). Goal attainment scaling: A critical review. *Evaluation Quarterly, 3,* 5–40.

Duehn, W., & Mayadas, N. S. (1977). Entrance and exit requirements of professional social work education. *Journal of Education for Social Work, 13,* 22–29.

Durlak, J. A. (1979). Comparative effectiveness of paraprofessional and professional helpers. *Psychological Bulletin, 86,* 80–92.

Edwards, C. H. (1973). Competency-based teacher education: A critique. *Contemporary Education, 44,* 188–191.

Eysenck, H. J. (1965). The effects of psychotherapy. *International Journal of Psychiatry, 1,* 97–178.

Eysenck, H. J. (1966). *The effects of psychotherapy.* New York: International Science Press.

Feldman, R. S., & Wodarski, J. S. (1974). Bureaucratic constraints and methodological adaptations in community-based research. *American Journal of Community Psychology, 2,* 211–224.

Fischer, J. (1971). A framework for the analysis and comparison of clinical theories of induced change. *Social Service Review, 45,* 440–454.

Fischer, J. (1973a). Has mighty casework struck out? *Social Work, 18,* 107–110.

Fischer, J. (1973b). Is casework effective? A review. *Social Work, 18,* 5–20.

Fischer, J. (1975). Training for effective therapeutic practice. *Psychotherapy: Theory Research and Practice, 12,* 118–123.

Fischer, J. (1978). *Effective casework practice.* New York: McGraw-Hill.

Goldsmith. B., & McFall, R. (1975). Development and evaluation of personal skill training program for psychiatric inpatients. *Journal of Abnormal Psychology, 84,* 51–58.

Gross, G. M. (1981). Instructional design: Bridge to competence. *Journal of Education for Social Work, 17,* 66–73.

Hohn, R. L., & Meinke, D. L. (1978). Competency-based education and educational psychology. *Contemporary Education, 19,* 211–244.

Ivey, A. E., Normington, C. J., Miller, C. D., Morrill, W. H., & Haase, R. F. (1968). Microcounseling and attending behavior: An approach to prepracticum counselor training. *Journal of Counseling Psychology Monographs, 15,* 1–12.

Jarrett, H. H. (1979). Operationalizing educational outcomes in the curriculum (pp. 93-108). In B. L. Baer & R. C. Federico (Eds.), *Educating the baccalaureate social workers: A curriculum development resource guide.* Cambridge, MA: Ballinger Publishing Company.

Jarrett, H. H., & Clark, F. W. (1978, Winter). Variety in competency-based education: A program comparison. *Alternative Higher Education: The Journal of Nontraditional Studies, 3,* 101–113.

Jarrett, H. H., Kilpatrick, A. C., & Pollane, L. P. (1977, February) *Operationalizing competency-based B.S.W. field experience.* Paper presented at the Annual Program Meeting of the Council on Social Work Education, Phoenix, AZ.

Johnstone, B., Frank, R. G., Belar, C., Berk, S., Bieliauskas, L. A., Bigler, E. D., Caplan, B., Elliott, T. R., Glueckauf, R. L., Kaplan, R. M., Kreutzer, J. S., Mateer, C. A., Patterson, D., Puente, A. E., Richards, J. S., Rosenthal, M., Sherer, M., Shewchuck, R., Siegel, L. J., & Sweet, J. J. (1995). Psychology in health care: Future directions. *Professional Psychology: Research and Practice, 26,* 341–365.

Kagen, N. (1984). Interpersonal process recall: Basic methods and recent research. In D. Larson (Ed.), *Teaching psychological skills: Models for giving psychology away* (pp. 229-244). Monterey, CA: Brooks/Cole.

Kelly, M. J. (1994). Training applications of expert systems. *Journal of Continuing Social Work Education, 6,* 15–19.

Kennedy, D. A. (1976). Some impressions of competency-based training programs. *Counselor Education and Supervision, 15,* 244–250.

Kolevzon, M. S. (1977). Negative findings revisited: Implications for social work practice and education. *Clinical Social Work Journal, 5,* 210–218.

Larsen, J., & Hepworth, D. H. (1978). Skill development through competency-based education. *Journal of Education for Social Work, 14,* 73–81.

Levy, C. S. (1972). A framework for planning and evaluating social work education. *Journal of Education for Social Work, 8,* 40–47.

Main, M. W. (1971). Restructuring social work education: Knowledge, curriculum, instruction. *Journal of Education for Social Work, 7,* 31–38.

Marks, R. B. (1972). Has social work failed? *Social Service Review, 46,* 427–431.

McNair, R. H., & Stewart, C. A. (1971) Long-range planning in schools of social work. *Journal of Education for Social Work, 7,* 31–38.

Meinert, R. G. (1978, Spring). Concentrations: Empirical Patterns and Future Prospects. *Journal of Education for Social Work, 15,* 51–58.

Menefee, D. T., & Thompson, J. J. (1994). Identifying and comparing competencies for social work management: A practice-driven approach. *Administration in Social Work, 18,* 1–25.

Meyer, H. J., Borgatta, E. F., & Jones, W. C. (1965). *Girls at Vocational High: An experiment in social work intervention.* New York: Russell Sage Foundation.

Mullen, E. J., & Dumpson, J. R. (1972). *Evaluation of social intervention.* San Francisco: Jossey-Bass.

Newman, E., & Turem, J. (1974). The crisis of accountability. *Social Work, 19,* 5–16.

Parsons, M. B., Reid, D. H., & Green, C. W. (1993). Preparing direct service staff to teach people with severe disabilities: A comprehensive evaluation of an effective and acceptable training program. *Behavioral Residential Treatment, 8,* 163–185.

Reid, D. H., Parsons, M. B., & Green, C. W. (1989). *Staff management in human services: Behavioral research and application.* Springfield, IL: Charles C Thomas.

Reid, J. W., & Shyne, A. W. (1969). *Brief and extended casework.* New York: Columbia University Press.

Rinn, R. C., & Vernon, J. C. (1975). Process evaluation of outpatient treatment in a community mental health center. *Journal of Behavior Therapy and Experimental Psychiatry, 6,* 5–11.

Roberts, R. W. (1973). An interim report on the development of an undergraduate-graduate continuum of social work education in a private university. *Journal of Education for Social Work, 9,* 58–64.

Rose, S. D., Cayner, J. J., & Edleson, J. L. (1977). Measuring interpersonal competence. *Social Work, 22,* 125–129.

Rothman, D., & Vililante, J. L. (1974). Curriculum planning in social work education. *Journal of Education for Social Work, 10,* 76–85.

Schinke, S. P., & Rose, S. D. (1976). Interpersonal skill training in groups. *Journal of Counseling Psychology, 23,* 442–448.

Schwartz, I. S., & Baer, D. M. (1991). Social Validity assessments: Is current practice state of the art? *Journal of Applied Behavior Analysis, 24,* 189–204.

Shepard, G., & Wahle, C. P. (1981). A competency-based approach to social work education: Does it work? *Journal of Education for Social Work, 17,* 12–20.

Smith, D. (1974). Integrating humanism and behaviorism: Toward performance. *Personnel and Guidance Journal, 52,* 513–519.

Stein, D. M., & Lambert, M. J. (1995). Graduate training in psychotherapy: Are therapy outcomes enhanced? *Journal of Consulting and Clinical Psychology, 63,* 182–196.

Stuart, R. B. (1971). Research in social casework and group work. *Encyclopedia of Social Work* (Vol. II). New York: National Association of Social Workers.

Wahle, L. P., & Shepard, G. (1981). A competency-based approach to social work education: Does it work? *Journal of Education for Social Work, 17,* 75–82.

Wodarski, J. S. (1975a, August). *Requisites for the establishment, implementation, and evaluation of social work treatment programs.* Paper presented at the Annual Program Meeting of the Society for the Study of Social Problems, San Francisco, CA.

Wodarski, J. S. (1975b). Use of videotapes in social work practice. *Clinical Social Work Journal, 3,* 120–127.

Wodarski, J. S. (1979). Critical issues in social work education. *Journal of Education for Social Work, 15,* 5–13.

Wodarski, J. S. (1979). Requisites for the establishment, implementation, and evaluation of social work treatment programs. *Journal of Sociology and Social Welfare, 6,* 339–361.

Wodarski, J. S. (1980a). Legal requisites for social work practice. *Clinical Social Work Journal, 8,* 90–98.

Wodarski, J. S. (1980b). Requisites for the establishment and implementation of competency-based agency practice. *Arete, 6,* 17–28.

Wodarski, J. S. (1981). *Role of research in clinical practice.* Baltimore, MD: University Park Press.

Wodarski, J. S. (1983). *Rural community mental health practice.* Baltimore, MD: University Park Press.

Wodarski, J. S. (1985). *Introduction to human behavior.* Austin, TX: PRO-ED.

Wodarski, J. S. (1986). *An introduction to social work education.* Springfield, IL: Charles C Thomas.

Wodarski, J. S., & Bagarozzi D. A. (1979a). A review of the empirical status of traditional modes of interpersonal helping: Implications for social work practice. *Clinical Social Work Journal, 7,* 231–255.

Wodarski, J. S., & Bagarozzi, D. A. (1979b). *Behavioral social work: An introduction.* New York: Human Sciences Press.

Wodarski, J. S., Bricout, J., & Smokowski, P. R. (in press). Making interactive videodisc computer simulation accessible and practice relevant. *Journal of Teaching in Social Work.*

Wodarski, J. S., & Feldman, R. A. (1973). The research practicum: A beginning formulation of process and educational objectives. *International Social Work, 16,* 42–48.

Wodarski, J. S., & Feldman, R. A. (1974). Practical aspects of field research. *Clinical Social Work Journal, 2,* 182–193.

Wodarski, J. S., Feit, M. D., & Green, R. K. (1995, March). Graduate social work education: A review of two decades of empirical research and considerations for the future. *Social Service Review, 69,* 108–130.

Wodarski, J. S., Filipczak, J., McCombs, P., Kousteins, G., & Rusilko, S. (1979). Follow-up on behavioral intervention with troublesome adolescents. *Journal of Behavior Therapy and Experimental Psychiatry, 10,* 181–188.

Wodarski, J. S., Pippin, J. A., & Daniels, M. (1988). Effects of graduate social work education on personality, values, and interpersonal skills. *Journal of Social Work Education, 24,* 266–277.

Younghusband, D. E. (1973). The future of social work. *International Social Work, 16,* 4–10.

CHAPTER 11

Development of Management Information Systems for Human Services: A Practical Guide

T he 1990s can be characterized as the decade of computer technology. Social and political events have demonstrated the necessity of establishing human services based on data that provide the rationale for the planning and delivery of services, evaluation of data, and fiscal support. Moreover, status indicators for the human services have changed. In the 1950s and 1960s, an agency had status if it employed a psychoanalyst as a consultant. Today, status is determined by the number of computers and the amount of data an agency collects.

Agencies are finding that lack of resources no longer prevents the introduction of computers. However, as in all fields, the application of technology often lags behind its development. This chapter addresses the development and implementation of data management systems pertinent to helping agencies provide appropriate services to clients. The role of management information systems in human service agencies is reviewed: managerial applications, client descriptive analyses, diagnosis, treatment planning, documentation of program implementation and effectiveness, research operations, specific clinical procedures, and educational functions. The chapter provides guidelines for establishing requisites for the development and selection of an adequate information system, dissemination of information, and application of relevant knowledge. Finally, the implications of management information systems for the field of social work are reviewed.

BASIC REQUISITES

In designing an information system, the first requisite is its compatibility with other systems. Compatibility among systems increases their utility. For example, client needs in mental health agencies might be compared with those of clients in family service agencies. A yearly evaluation of an information management system should be conducted. The evaluation should address how professionals use the system, what types of information are collected, and how the organization is structured to facilitate the use of data.

An agency must address the following questions: What type of data are needed? What kind of software is required? What forms are required to collect this data? Who collects the data? How are the data stored? How is the confidentiality of the data to be ensured? Is a data specialist needed? How can it be ensured that the appropriate individuals are involved in setting up the system and in its subsequent use?

The data to be collected in human service agencies should focus on the following phenomena: client traits, worker and treatment characteristics, and outcomes. Such data enable managers to see, for example, how many clients were tested, what type of worker served clients, and how many times clients were seen. These data enhance an agency's ability to conduct cost-benefit analysis in order to determine how much a service unit costs. An information system should prove invaluable to the assessment of a client as treatment, evaluation of services, documentation of intervention, and follow-up.

Individuals developing the data system must determine how many files should be free-form in contrast to fixed-form format. Free-form records are used to document client assessments, treatment, and follow-up. Such records are rich in descriptive information; however, they are difficult to condense and summarize. For example, if a practitioner wishes to view all the cases of potential suicide, the computer can be instructed to review all case documents and to list cases where this potential was indicated. Yet such an analysis is slow and costly.

A fixed-form record specifies the exact nature of the data to be collected. A typical example would be a structured interview schedule used to secure descriptive data on clients. The computer can quickly summarize the number of clients who received services during a particular period by their age, income, marital status, and number of children (Kreuger & Ruckdeschel, 1985).

Before an agency sets up an information management system, as many workers as possible should be involved to enlist their support for the system's utilization. This involvement of staff should take place at the earliest possible date. There should be joint decisions regarding the type of records needed. The agency must determine who will have access to the data and who will implement appropriate security measures to maintain clients' confidentiality. Securing a file is relatively simple with the technological developments in access coding (Naisbitt, 1982).

MANAGERIAL APPLICATIONS

The applications of computer technology address a wide range of problems and administrative tasks. One major area of application in the delivery of services is information management. Agencies are finding computers to be tremendous time savers in compiling service statistics, processing payrolls, and preparing financial reports. Moreover, computer technology makes possible forms of inquiry previously inconceivable, particularly because the computer permits more timely and expeditious use of sophisticated research techniques on routinely collected data.

Paperwork consumes an inordinate amount of time and energy in traditional human service agencies. The computer's word processing capability dramatically decreases paperwork in the production of reports, letters, memos, payrolls, tests, and forms. Once a draft of a document is written, there is significantly little time needed to modify the copy. Tailoring of different reports from the same store of information, outlining plans for worker development, and preparing budgets are other useful applications. Through word processing, these functions can be quickly completed (Boyd, Hylton, & Price, 1978). Considering the present economy, computer applications can ease an agency's billing, financial screening procedures, review and revision of fee schedules, and maintenance of accurate accounts of operating reserves to reduce cash flow problems (Goplerud, Walfish, & Bruskowski, 1985).

CLIENT DESCRIPTIVE ANALYSES

All agencies require descriptive data to document whom they have served and how. These data provide a rationale for the agency budget and help in planning for future needs. With appropriate intake forms, information is quickly and accurately gathered to determine (a) client to be served, (b) duration of service, (c) cost of service, (d) provider of the service, (e) follow-up results, and (f) additional service. Thus, an agency can benefit from knowing who its clients are and using these data in approaching the sources of support and gaining sanctions to extend the life of an agency. Once such a system is functional, an agency can conduct several cost-effectiveness analyses. This accountability requisite, evident in the 1980s, provides agencies with a means of deciding to alter, maintain, or expand services (Catherwood, 1974; Rapp, 1984).

DIAGNOSIS, TREATMENT PLANNING, AND DOCUMENTATION OF PROGRAM IMPLEMENTATION AND EFFECTIVENESS

In the last decade, a number of scales have been developed to facilitate obtaining information necessary for workers to make adequate assessments of their clients (Howing, Wodarski, & Gaudin, 1989; Newmark, 1985; Rittner & Wodarski, 1995). All inventories are computer scored to facilitate their use.

Multiproblem Screening Inventory

The multiproblem screening inventory (MPSI) (Hudson, 1992) is a 334-item self-report scale that measures 27 dimensions of family functioning. Subscales measure depression, self-esteem, partner problems, sexual discord, child problems, mother problems, personal stress, friend problems, neighbor problems, school problems, aggression, work associates, family problems, suicide, nonphysical abuse, physical abuse, fearfulness, ideas of reference, phobias, guilt, work problems, confused thinking, disturbing thoughts, memory loss, alcohol abuse, and drug abuse. Questions are answered on a 7-point Likert scale (from "none of the time" to "all of the time"). This scale is easily computer scored to develop additional subscales. (Available from: WALMYR Publishing Co., P.O. Box 24779, Tempe, AZ 85285-4779.) Table 11.1 lists other available Hudson scales.

Other Relevant Scales

Many personalized computer systems now aid in the administration of more than 50 assessment inventories. These can provide a wealth of information on which clinicians can base their assessment of the client and can plan subsequent treatment (Hedlund, Vieweg, & Cho, 1985). For example, National Computer Systems Professional Assessment Services (NCSPAS) has the capability to score assessment tests in the areas of (a) abnormal personality, (b) normal personality, (c) behavioral health and medicine, and (d) aptitudes and career/vocational interests. Table 11.2 lists other available NCSPAS tests.

By using the computer, practitioners can list goals, make progress notes, specify an intervention plan, and produce a timetable. It is possible to secure the documentation necessary to determine if goals have been met, and subsequently to analyze the data with respect to meeting

Table 11.1   Other Hudson Scales*

Child's Attitude toward Father	Index of Family Relations
Child's Attitude toward Mother	Index of Marital Satisfaction
Children's Behavior Rating Scale	Index of Parental Attitudes
Clinical Anxiety Scale	Index of Peer Relations
Computerized Scoring	Index of Self-Esteem
General Screening Inventory	Index of Sexual Satisfaction
Generalized Contentment Scale	Index of Sister Relations
The Global Screening Inventory	Nonphysical Abuse of Partner Scale
Index of Alcohol Involvement	Partner Abuse Scale: Nonphysical
Index of Attitudes toward	Partner Abuse Scale: Physical
Homosexuals	Physical Abuse of Partner Scale
Index of Brother Relations	Sexual Attitude Scale
Index of Clinical Stress	
Index of Drug Involvement	

* From Hudson, 1992.

Table 11.2   Other Available NCSPAS Tests

Adjective Checklist	Minnesota Multiphasic Personality
Bender Visual Motor Gestalt Test	Inventory (MMPI) Basic Service
California Psychological Inventory	MMPI—The Minnesota Report:
Career Assessment Inventory	Adult Clinical System
Clinical Analysis Questionnaire	MMPI—The Minnesota Report:
The Exner Report for the Rorschach	Personnel Selection System
Comprehensive System	Multidimensional Personality
General Aptitude Test Battery	Questionnaire
Giannetti Online Psychosocial	Myers–Briggs Type Indicator
History	The Rorschach Comprehensive System
Guilford–Zimmerman Temperament	Self-Description Inventory
Survey	Sixteen Personality Factors
Hogan Personality Inventory	Questionnaire
Millon Adolescent Personality	Strong–Campbell Interest Inventory
Inventory—Clinical	Temperament and Values Inventory
Millon Adolescent Personality	Vocational Information Profile
Inventory—Guidance	Word and Number Assessment
Millon Behavioral Health Inventory	Inventory

legal and administrative requisites (Carlson, 1985; Meldman, Harris, Pellicore, & Johnson, 1977). The amount of information provided by a computer analysis of the MMPI can truly facilitate the adoption of the scientific practitioner model (Hudson, 1992; Wodarski, 1986).

RESEARCH OPERATIONS

For research, computers are essential. Once information is organized and placed into the computer, complicated calculations become routine. Transformation of data, simple graphing of client goals, and modification of data for further analysis made easier. The frequently used SPSS and other statistical packages are now available for personal desktop computers (Butler, 1986). This innovation increases the capability of practitioners to execute basic statistical analyses on their cases. Thus, the ability to analyze different practice phenomena is enhanced. However, as with all technology, an adequate conceptual plan should guide the selection of appropriate analyses.

In summary, computers can assist human service workers in attaining the following clinical research goals:

1. Administration and scoring of tests
2. Interpretation and reporting:
    (A) Wechsler
    (B) Rorschach
    (C) MMPI
3. Client program planning and evaluation
    (A) goals
    (B) case progress
    (C) intervention plan
    (D) time table
4. Program documentation
    (A) data recording and illustration
    (B) data analysis
    (C) attainment of legal and administrative requisites
5. Research applications
    (A) client progress
    (B) calculations
    (C) transformation of data
    (D) graphing client and administrative variables
    (E) updating information in a database

SPECIFIC PRACTICE PROCEDURES
THAT CAN BE COMPUTERIZED

There are numerous concrete items that are easily computerized regardless of the practice context. Contracts formulated between client and workers can be checked for the inclusion of the following: purposes of the interaction, targeted problems and areas of difficulties to be worked on, various goals and objectives to be accomplished, client and therapist duties, delineation of administrative procedures, techniques to be used, duration of contracts and criteria for termination, and renegotiation procedures (Wodarski & Bagarozzi, 1979).

Agencies can use goal-setting forms that specify a client's problem, plans for therapy, short- and long-term goals, plans for termination, follow-up procedures, and so forth. These forms facilitate the evaluation of clients' progress in meeting their treatment goals. Additionally,

a summary form specifies the overall treatment plan, including termination and follow-up procedures. Access to these documentation should
improve the services offered to clients.

Other computer functions to improve evaluation include checking
to see if practice notes summarizing the major events of the client's
last visit are recorded within a reasonable time, such as 72 hr after the
session, and determining if the follow-up visits are executed when necessary and placed in the client's record within a reasonable time. Also
to be included are a letter to all third parties regarding treatment
plans and diagnosis, summary termination notes and follow-up procedures, and, if necessary, a letter to the referring professional or family
doctor regarding the termination of services, all within one week of
closing a case. In all instances, the energy and the time necessary to
complete the forms should be kept to a minimum (Rinn & Vernon,
1975). Computers facilitate the execution of these requisite clinical
tasks, by simplifying the record-keeping process.

Educational Functions

Through the use of educational programs, computers can help in
preparing the beginning practitioner to work with clients. Before working with parents who abuse their children, the worker might be trained
to assess adequately marital interaction, child management practices,
and social and vocational satisfaction, and to implement the appropriate intervention strategies according to the assessment.

To assess the worker's theoretical accuracy, an objective examination
or assessment battery—for example, on task-centered casework, family
therapy or behavioral social work—can be given. Once workers achieve
acceptable scores on an assessment battery, they can then move on to
implementing interventions based on the theoretical framework.

Practice skill levels can be determined by asking the worker to
review a contrived case, to make a diagnosis, to design an intervention
plan, and to describe the success of the plan to the satisfaction of practitioners who have already demonstrated their competencies. Education
exercises can be programmed and computed to help the practitioner
acquire competencies through repeated exercises.

Simulation

Simulation technologies are defined rather consistently throughout
the literature simply as an operating model of a real system; that is,

physical representations of reality (Cash, 1983). Simulation is a category within the general class of scientific tools known as models. Models are certain ways of representing reality, and students can compare the simulated experience to what they believe and experience in the real world (Wodarski, Bricout, & Smokowski, in press). Simulations are often used to promote participatory learning through acting out lifelike situations, thus allowing simulation participants to gain an understanding of problems they may encounter in their practice and encouraging a new perspective and problem-solving framework. Well designed simulations allow serendipitous, incidental learning as well as achievement of planned learning objectives.

There are many practical uses for simulations in the classroom setting. Theory can be applied immediately. Simulations can be used to break the ice, impart facts (though rarely used for this purpose alone), develop empathic sensitivity and values clarification, examine dimensions and dynamics of social problems, explore the future, and refine and immediately apply analytical research skills (Shay, 1980). Moreover, simulations heighten interest, change attitudes, facilitate skills acquisition, and assist in cognitive learning and personal growth (Faherty, 1983). Conclusive evidence, however, is available only for heightened interest. In skills acquisition, there is evidence to show that simulations aid in the integrative thought process (Shay, 1980).

One clear advantage simulation has over learning in real life situations is that the student is protected from the consequences of error in a real system. That is, practice skills can develop without negative consequences to a client. Another advantage of simulation over live practice is that in the early stages of training, stress can be removed and then replaced when the skill has been mastered (Lewis & Gibson, 1977).

As with any technology, however, there are several disadvantages to using simulation technologies in social work education. First, simulations are unpredictable; they only benefit certain students some of the time. There is also a lack of instructor control in many simulations. There can be a great investment of time, energy, and monetary costs in carrying out a simulation. Finally, there is a struggle between simplicity and complexity: Simple simulations are easier to use but are of less educational value, and complex simulations are too difficult to use. Despite limitations, however, the strengths of simulations outweigh its weaknesses.

Given the advantages and disadvantages of simulation use, when does one choose to do a simulation? The decision might be based on the following criteria: Will a simulation create a situation likely to be encountered in real life? Will it help prepare the practitioner to deal with ambiguities and complexities found later in life? The application of simulations is relatively unexplored. Only creativity limits the use of this teaching medium. Simulations integrate theory and practice.

For a simulation experience to be effective on any level, it must be relevant and have sound internal pedagogical elements and processes (appropriate learning objectives, related to and complementing lecture, self-reflection, and relevant student exercises). It must also facilitate achievement of specific learning objectives. The literature also suggests that the simulation experience heightens interest in the learning experience (Berven & Pope, 1980). This is especially true when the simulation is a computer simulation (Phillips, 1984a).

Types of Models

Different simulation model typologies are found in the literature. One useful typology classifies simulations as "person models," "person-machine models," or "pure machine models" (Faherty, 1972). The person model employs only human decision makers. These are usually simple or structured role plays, behavior games, sensitivity experiences, and many types of skills training. These simulations will not be reviewed in this book due to the extensive existing reviews in the literature. The person-machine model makes use of interaction of a person with a machine, usually a computer. New computer technologies make this the most exciting area to pursue in social work education. The third type of simulation is the pure machine model. These simulations include problem solving by machines and are pure mathematical models of reality. Their promise for human services has not yet been explored (Faherty, 1972).

Person–Machine Model

A person–machine model (e.g., computer simulations) employs high degrees of abstraction from reality. In computer simulations, all of the features of a real system are reduced to logical decision rules and operations, which are then programmed for computer manipulation (Meinert, 1972).

Computer technology is blossoming at a staggering rate. In fact, the computer is becoming so important that unless students become familiar with this machine, the student is destined to be unsuccessful in both school and the workplace (Green, 1984). Hence, it is imperative that computer interaction be required in the education of a social worker.

In discussing the utility of computer simulations for social work research, Fuller asserts that computer technology is now within the range of almost every practicing social worker (Fuller, 1970). Access to a computer and programming is as near as the extension service of a university's computer center. Even so, the literature regarding direct application of this technology on the social service agency and practitioner levels remains sparse (Wodarski, 1986).

The computer entered the counseling profession in the early 1960s, with practitioners exploring the use of technology in counseling. Throughout the 1960s and into the 1970s the computer was seen as an assistant to the counselor, and programs were developed that taught problem-solving skills and provided information. By 1970, two annotated bibliographies and two small volumes were written on computer technology in counseling professions. Recently, informational and diagnostic databases have been developed, and models of systematic interventions, mechanical clients with which to practice, and supervisory monitoring systems have all come into existence (Phillips, 1984a). As the use of the computer continues to make inroads into the helping professions, the use of the computer in education increases.

The computer has inherent value for education apart from the need to know how to use it in the work place. Phillips discusses the attractiveness of computers for education in the tasks and methods of individual instruction (Phillips, 1984a). It can be seen as an intelligent tutor, thus reducing the student–teacher ratio. Fascination with the medium is a plus; it may induce longer study time and greater learning. There are two ways by which a computer can help a trainee with skills acquisition. First, there is didactic presentation with examples of a skill, and there is simulation (Phillips, 1984b). Its use as a simulator has been compared to that of a cadaver for surgeons.

Self-Help Programs

Programs are now being written for the general public that can be used or adapted to social work education. These programs are called "life enrichment software" or "psycheware programs" and are designed to accept decision responses from one or more people. The programs allow multiple branching sequences. Programs include Eliza, which simulates a nondirective therapist; Mind Prober, which estimates another person's attitudes; Childpace and Discover Your Baby, produces improved parenting; and Coping with Stress and the Party, which teaches the adolescent about the effects of alcohol. Finally, Skip is a highly interactive program that allows users to learn about aspects of their own personality. According to White, there are enormous possibilities for computers in therapist education (White, 1984). There is also a danger, however, to the general public in these "self-help" programs. White compares them to the "self-awareness groups" of the sixties. Hence, it is important that social workers be familiar with these types of programs.

Simulated Counselor

Programs must be interactive to be of most use to social work education. Interactive programs have multiple branching-out contingencies that depend on the responses of the user. To be effective, the computer must be able to understand the client's natural language. The program also must be able to follow a therapeutic plan when dealing with a client. This can be problematic, but inroads into research on artificial language have been made. Eliza, for example, simulates a nondirective therapist; it analyzes each statement typed into the computer and then responds with a question or comment. This program is limited because it cannot recognize nonsense and it lacks intuition.

Morton is a computer-assisted therapy program that deals with the shortcomings of Eliza. Morton attends to depression and a related, specific psychological problem that has particular treatment strategies using a variety of cognitive and behavioral therapeutic techniques. This program uses multiple-choice items and case vignettes to aid the user in identifying dysfunctional thoughts. It deals with those thoughts that are assumed to be the major source of depression (Wagman & Kerber, 1984). Another interaction program, PLATO Dilemma Counseling System (PLATO DCS), is designed for the treatment of avoidance-avoidance problems. It teaches dilemmas counseling and solves specific problems. Because these programs must be exact, trainees learn to be precise throughout the therapeutic process. The programs facilitate learning and are patient, reliable, and efficient. Trainees can also experience what their future clients may feel like by using the systems.

Simulated Clients

The preceding programs all take on the role of the therapist. These simulations are helpful in teaching exactly "how to." However, there are other programs that simulate a client and allow trainees to practice their skills. One such program, as described by Lichtenberg is INTER-ACT (Lichtenburg, Hummel, & Shaffer, 1984). The assumption behind this program is that counseling is social interaction: It consists of a series of verbal and/or nonverbal exchanges. The INTERACT program analyzes the counselor-client transactions or response contingencies. It helps trainees learn how to elicit certain classes of responses that have been shown to contribute to favorable counseling outcomes. INTER-ACT also develops an awareness of the impact of those responses on their clients and the effects of their clients on their production of those responses.

A fascinating program described by Lichtenberg et al. is CLIENT 1 (1984). This is an interactive computer simulation of client behavior in an initial client interview. The model client is a 30-year-old who is verbal, motivated, and not overly resistant. The client can talk about several topics but they are not of equal importance; only one is his primary concern. Each topic is ranked from general to specific, and each statement is ranked according to threat value. The counselor's task is to move the client toward verbalization of a specific and threatening statement of his or her problem. Progress is defined as moving toward specificity and threat. The strength of the counseling relationship, the level of trust, is continually reevaluated by the computer. It is determined by the accuracy and appropriateness of the counselor's response. If the trainee is consistently inaccurate or inappropriate, a low "good counselor average" will occur and the session will be prematurely terminated.

Simulated client programs have many uses is social work education. They are flexible and allow a changing of variables and they can be used over and over again. CLIENT 1 is consistent and durable, and it will allow recognition of negative counseling habits. Counseling skills can be broken down into parts, and reflection on their use is possible. The clients can be made simple or complex, and they will not be harmed by the trainee's mistakes. This will allow the trainee to see the value in simply reflecting until good data are available. Finally, the trainee can move back to any portion of the interview and play "what if I had said. . . ." This option, which can be invaluable, is not available on any other training medium.

Video Technology

Video technology represents a combination of the person–model and the person-machine model. It can belong to either category depending upon its use. For instance, it can be used in conjunction with computer simulation, or it can be used as a way to confront one's own performance in a role-play process. Self-observation is the most frequent application.

Observation of oneself on videotape can be very beneficial to skill acquisition. For example, Hosford and Johnson (1983) performed an experiment on teaching techniques using video playback. They found that using "self-as-a-model" reduced almost all inappropriate behaviors by approximately 100%. Observation of self also helped improve performance, especially if feedback was provided by a supervisor or teacher. However, confrontation of one's image on tape can be anxiety producing for some people and may actually block learning. Thus, positive feedback is necessary.

Videodisc Simulation

In making the transition from informal simulations to laboratory modeling simulations, remember that this text discusses phases of development rather than distinct conceptual categories. The transition to what the literature refers to as "laboratory simulation" seems to indicate an increase in structure or structured task, which the earlier informal simulations lacked.

As technology has become more sophisticated and people have begun to be more creative, many new educational tools have become available. Interactive video is one such tool. Iuppa defines interactive video as any video system in which the sequence and selection of messages is determined by the user's response to the material presented (1984). There are computer languages and software packages that will allow a person who knows absolutely nothing about programming languages to create an interactive simulation (Hosie & Smith, 1984).

Interactive video requires the use of a video cassette recorder or a videodisc. The former are cumbersome and not very practical. Since they do not have random access to any segment of the recorded material as the disks do, video cassettes are too slow. With the videodisc's greater sophistication, there is not much in the way of coursework that could not be converted into a computer-controlled interactive videodisc (Pribble, 1985). For example, the Interactive Technology Groups, based in Sante Fe, New Mexico, has developed a five-disc course on human relation skills. Hence, a beginning has been made into this exciting and promising field (Pribble, 1985).

The videodiscs allow fast and random access to any part of the disc in less than a second. The discs hold up to 54,000 single video frames per side and can accommodate up to 30 min of moving imagery. Of course, the microcomputer controls the access, evaluates responses (as in the CLIENT 1 program), displays text, and even asks questions. Hence, the trainee can learn verbal and nonverbal skills before working with actual clients. The experience of video simulation should include as much video presentation of real images as possible. Interactive video allows trainees to see the consequences of their choices and this is the real strength of this type of learning medium.

There is some evidence of the effectiveness of videodisc training (Pribble, 1985). In 1984, the University of West Florida trained a group of welfare department employees in the administration of food stamps using a 16-hr interactive videodisc course. The trainees finished the training course 25% faster than the control group, which was taught in the traditional manner. Also, 66% of the interactive group passed the posttest while only 50% of the control group passed the posttest.

An authoring system for interactive computer simulations is available that can be adapted to simulations in social work education. The hardware and software of the authoring system was developed by the staff of the Interactive Videodisc for Special Education Technology (IVSET). IVSET had five criteria in developing their authoring system for the education of mentally retarded children. The programmer should be able to use the system regardless of computer experience, and flexibility of instruction is recommended. The system should collect data to analyze. A teacher should be able to author a program. Finally, the system should be capable of summarizing student data and monitoring students' progress.

INFORMATIONAL REQUISITES

The first requisite in developing an information management system is to determine how the data will be collected and which forms are necessary. It is essential that the collected data be reliable and valid.

Second, it is essential that the agency consider the number of files that will be necessary for the collection of these data. The more files that are needed, the more complicated and costly a management information system becomes. The files also should be evaluated for how much data they will contain, how they will interface with other systems, and whether the central processing unit can handle the numbers.

Selecting a Management Information System

The design of a management information system entails specifying an agency's needs and the purpose of the system. An assessment of financial and time resources is the next step, followed by a review of an agency's needs and resources with others knowledgeable about information systems. If available, a number of different management systems should be studied.

Second, consult various experts and others working with the system to see what they are doing with them. Visit a similar agency in which an information system is already operational; pilot test the system before full-scale implementation. Read journals that have sections devoted to the latest computer applications to human service agencies (i.e., *The Behavior Therapist* by the Association of the Advancement of Behavior Therapy and *Behavioral Assessment*). Finally, after selection and implementation, it is necessary to annually review the system to make modifications and improvements as needed.

The Dissemination of Information and Application of Relevant Knowledge

If practitioners are to participate in management information system research, which is a necessary condition in developing the treatment technology needed for the field, schools of social work must begin to teach the skills required. The ability to formulate questions, choose the data options needed to answer these questions, and make rational decisions based on the data—not on the vague criteria presently employed—are critical.

Another challenge will be implementing effective technologies as they are developed. A rational method for choosing change strategies to meet client needs should be a primary function of research in social work. In an area where tradition, authority, and "common sense" practice have ruled for years, a "databased" set of alternatives should facilitate the effective delivery of services. It would be a mistake, however, to assume that the availability of good empirical research will lead automatically to improved services. The history of knowledge utilization in other human services fields shows clearly that the change process is much more complicated than is implied by a simple linear model, which suggests that the production of knowledge leads naturally to its utilization. In fact, in most cases, the effective dissemination and use of new findings are as difficult as their production (Hartmann, Wood, & Shigetomi, 1981).

The problem of knowledge utilization can be seen as an adoption problem related to the issue of how to train practitioners to search for and evaluate research data when choosing intervention alternatives. In certain cases, practitioners may be capable of conducting their own evaluation, but in most cases, they must rely on information and conclusions reported by more qualified professional researchers and evaluators. Certainly, social workers should be trained to monitor personally the effects of their intervention and gather feedback on the direction and magnitude of change, interpret studies for their relevance, and implement time-series designs. But workers rarely possess the resources and skills of a professional evaluator which are necessary to perform a summary evaluation of the effects of a program or a change strategy (Tornatzky et al., 1983; Wodarski, 1981).

Even after practitioners are exposed to new techniques and show that they are employing aspects of a new treatment, evaluations suggest that they are practicing in the same manner as in the past but have merely labeled this activity differently (Mullen & Dumpson, 1972). Thus, to ensure that professionals are kept abreast of current treatment developments, and will implement them, the incentive structure of social work practice must be changed: Social workers will have to be rewarded.

ISSUES FOR THE FIELD

First, preparing human service workers to use computers in helping clients is essential. Even if information management systems become readily available and agencies implement them, technical expertise will be necessary to aid in the interpretation and summarization of the knowledge they produce. Moreover, experts should be prepared to summarize the data and disseminate them to other agencies that deal with similar clients. This process will add to the knowledge base of service providers. In the absence of such integration, chaos may ensue.

Second, yearly evaluations are required to update a data system as needed. Sufficient time should be spent in setting up an adequate system, since it is much more difficult and costly to change a data system once it is operational.

Third, the human service field must come to grips with defining outcomes and standards for service. When outcomes are ambiguous, standardizing them is impossible and comparisons across agencies are meaningless. Information systems can be utilized to plan and implement agency goals. For example, computers can (a) facilitate an empirical approach to the identification, collection, organization, and analysis of data and information about clients; (b) aid in the study of the component processes and outcomes of human service delivery systems; (c) clarify the state of human service needs and how practitioners can facilitate the strengths of clients; (d) aid in practitioners' learning theories and practicing various skills; and (e) facilitate the evaluation of different theories of behavioral change and intervention.

In essence, for informational management systems to facilitate the provision of relevant services to clients, the following recommendations are proposed: The field should develop standards for practice; data management systems should be developed so that human service agencies can interact with one another, such as mental health interfacing with criminal justice and child welfare programs; and, at the national level, a data system might be developed that would lead to the identification of how social policies of both federal and state governments affect clients.

The client change process and the interventions used to help clients are complex. Computers can facilitate an understanding of these processes, and, thus, enhance a practitioner's ability to tailor appropriate interventions built on a client's strengths.

REFERENCES

Bernstein, I. N., & Freeman, H. E. (1975). *Academic and entrepreneurial research.* New York: Russell Sage Foundation.

Boyd, L. H., Jr., Hylton, J. H., & Price, S. V. (1978). Computers in social work practice: A review. *Social Work, 23,* 368–371.

Butler, D. L. (1986). Statistics packages. *Contemporary Psychology, 31,* 485–487.

Butterfield, W. H. (1983). Computers: An overview. *Practice Digest, 6,* 3–5.

Carlson, R. W. (1985). Connecting clinical information processing with computer support. *Computers in Human Services, 1,* 51–66.

Cash, K. (1983). Simulation and gaming in social work education: A projection. *Journal of Education for Social Work, 19,* 111–118.

Catherwood, H. R. (1974). A management information system for social services. *Public Welfare, 32,* 56–61.

Faherty, V. E. (1983). Simulation and gaming in social work education: A projection. *Journal of Education for Social Work, 19,* 111–118.

Fuller, T. K. (1970). Computer utility in social work. *Social Casework, 51,* 606–611.

Goplerud, E. N., Walfish, S., & Bruskowsi, A. (1985). Weathering the cuts: A delphi survey on surviving cutbacks in community mental health. *Community Mental Health Journal, 21,* 14–27.

Green, M. S. (1984). Computer resources and terminology: A brief introduction. *Counselor Education and Supervision, 24,* 133–141.

Hedlund, J. L., Vieweg, B. W., & Cho, D. W. (1985). Mental health computing in the 1980s: I. General information systems and clinical documentation. *Computers in Human Services, 1,* 3–33.

Hosford, R. E., & Johnson, M. E. (1983). A comparison of self-observation, self-modeling, and practice without video feedback for improving counselor-interviewing behaviors. *Counselor Education and Supervision, 23,* 62–70.

Hosie, T. W., & Smith, C. W. (1984). Piloting. *Counselor Education and Supervision, 24,* 176–185.

Howling, P. T., Wodarski, J. S., & Gardin, J. M. (1989). Clinical assessment instruments in the treatment of child abuse and neglect. *Early Child Development and Care, 42,* 71–84.

Hudson, W. W. (1992). *The WALMYR assessment scales scoring manual.* Tempe, AZ: WALMYR Publishing Company.

Kreuger, L. W., & Ruckdeschel, R. (1985). Microcomputers in social service settings: Research applications. *Social Work, 30,* 219–224.

Lewis, J., & Gibson, F. (1977). The teaching of some social work skills: Towards a skill laboratory. *British Journal of Social Work, 7,* 189–209.

Lichtenburg, J. W., Hummel, T. J., & Shaffer, W. F. (1984). CLIENT 1: A computer simulation for use in counselor education and research. *Counselor Education and Research, 24,* 176–185.

McNaul, J. P. (1972). Relations between researchers and practitioners. In S. Z. Nagi & R. C. Corwin (Eds.), *The social contexts of research* (pp. 269-288). New York: Wiley.

Meldman, M. J., Harris, D., Pellicore, R. J., & Johnson, E. L. (1977). A computer-assisted, goal-oriented psychiatric progress note system. *American Journal of Psychiatry, 134,* 38–41.

Meinert, R. G. (1972). Simulation technology: A potential tool for social work education, *Journal of Education for Social Work, 8,* 50–59.

Mullen, E. J., & Dumpson, I. R. (1972). *Evaluation of social intervention.* San Francisco: Jossey-Bass.

Naisbitt, J. (1982). *Megatrends.* New York: Warner Books.

Phillips, S. D. (1984a). Contributions and limitations in the use of computers in counselor training. *Counselor Education and Supervision, 24,* 130–132.

Philips, S. D. (1984b). Computers as counseling and training tools. *Counselor Education and Supervision, 24,* 186–192.

Pribble, R. (1985). Enter the videodisc. *Training, 3,* 62–70.

Rapp, C. A. (1984). Information, performance, and the human service manager of the 1980s: Beyond "housekeeping." *Administration in Social Work, 8,* 69–80.

Rinn, R. C., & Vernon, J. C. (1975). Process evaluation of outpatient treatment in a community mental health center. *Journal of Behavior Therapy and Experimental Psychiatry, 6,* 5–11.

Rittner, B., & Wordarski, J. S. (1995). Clinical assessment instruments in the treatment of child abuse and neglect. *Early Child Development and Care, 106,* 43–58.

Shay, C. (1980). Simulations in the classroom: An appraisal. *Educational Technology, 20,* 11–15.

Tornatzky, L. G., Eveland, J. D., Boylan, M. G., Hetzner, E. C., Johnson, D., Roitman, D., & Schneider, J. (1983). *The process of technological innovation: Reviewing the literature.* Washington, DC: National Science Foundation

Wagman, M., & Kerber, K. W. (1984). Computer-assisted counseling: Problems and prospects. *Counselor Education and Supervision, 24,* 142–154.

White, A. (1984, October). *A sample of counselor educators about microcomputers.* Paper presented at the annual meeting of the Northern Rocky Mountain Educational Research Association.

Wodarski, J. S. (1981). *Role of research in clinical practice.* Baltimore: University Park Press.

Wodarski, J. S. (1986). The application of computer technology to enhance the effectiveness of family therapy. *Family Therapy, 13,* 5–13.

Wodarski, J. S., & Bagarozzi, D. (1979). *Behavioral social work.* New York: Human Sciences Press.

Wodarski, J. S., Bricout, J., & Smokowski, P. R. (in press). Making interactive videodisc computer simulation accessible and practice relevant. *Journal of Teaching in Social Work.*

CHAPTER 12

Developing and Formulating Quality Proposals

All researchers need to secure support for their activities (Lauffer, 1983; Wodarski, 1983, 1995). Social science research needs support in its attempt to answer complex and difficult questions. Such studies require large amounts of energy and resources. This chapter reviews the basics of securing support.

INFORMATIONAL EXCHANGE

All research proposals, whether federal and state agencies, private foundations, or business and industry, have similarities. The basic differences between the requirements of the various funding sources are the length of the proposal and the approach. Proposals to federal agencies usually are the most lengthy. State agencies, private foundations, and business and industry usually require a shorter proposal and the development of a relationship between someone at the university and an individual within the agency.

Many grant proposals fail because certain issues are not addressed by those formulating the grant. If the research proponent spends enough time dealing with these issues, having a successfully funded proposal is highly probable. As the purpose of grants is to solve significant problems, it is up to the researcher to identify such problems and to convince a review panel that the allocation of funds will contribute significantly to the solution of those problems. Each proponent has to develop sources on available grants. This will mean attending conferences and maintaining contacts with state and federal agencies, foundations, and business concerns. If such contacts are maintained, up-to-date information can be provided to facilitate a competitive grant proposal (Coley & Scheinberg, 1990; Wodarski, 1990).

KNOWLEDGE

It is essential that a prospective researcher knows the objectives and foci of the granting agency and tailors the proposal to meet the specific needs of the agency; that is, faculty needs matches funding sources interests. How the proposal addresses the major concerns of the agency should be elaborated through a relevant, clear, and concise review of the literature (Larsen, 1973; Locke, Spirduso, & Silverman, 1993).

PERSONAL CONTACTS

Before formulating a proposal, the applicant should contact an agency representative to learn what the agency needs. For federal and state agencies, this usually requires a telephone call. For private foundations, a brief letter outlining the project is sufficient. For business and industry, a phone call is also necessary. Introductions to key individuals are essential for state, industrial, and private foundation funds. For example, working with foundations is eased if a faculty member can secure an endorsement. Good working relationships between university research office personnel or department heads and agency representatives also helps to secure a grant.

Before contacting a funding agency, the principal investigator must isolate the following concerns: Is the research idea central to the agency's mission? Is the potential researcher on the cutting edge of research and theoretical development in that area? Is the researcher competent in the methodological and theoretical issues that face the field?

Whether the agency wishes to be approached by telephone or letter must be ascertained. A 5-min telephone conversation with an agency official to determine the agency's interest in an idea can save a principal investigator many months of hard work. The agency's interest can be evaluated by the length of the call made, and verbal and nonverbal enthusiasm communicated. Moreover, the agency official can indicate the particular areas of interest that might be addressed when developing a proposal, and the person usually will offer to help.

Before the telephone contact is made, researchers should practice delivering the central ideas of the proposal and how they will approach the idea. They should also formulate specific questions concerning the agency's focus. If the contact indicates that the idea is mutually beneficial, the last question usually asked is if the agency would like to review a 10- to 20-page concept paper. The concept paper must elucidate the general need addressed by the proposal, and it should include a specific demonstration of the researcher's knowledge in the area and his or her competencies with theoretical and methodological issues. *Every word in this concept paper is important.* The investigator must be concise; ambiguous statements must be clarified. Finally, the proposal should be reviewed by other colleagues before it is forwarded to the funding agency.

When an agency does not solicit telephone calls but will accept a 10- to 20-page letter, usually the same procedures as outlined above will apply. Written material from the agency can serve as a guide.

DEVELOPING A PROPOSAL

It is essential to obtain critiques from colleagues when developing a proposal. These critiques will facilitate a clearer writing style and will foster creativity in addressing theoretical and methodological issues.

As the development of the proposal proceeds, the investigator must feel free to call the agency for consultation. Program managers are more than willing to assist an individual in formulating a proposal with the latest research findings and outcome measures. Moreover, grant administrators desire contact with individuals in the field. After all, agencies must fund proposals to stay in business.

The proposals should outline the issue to address, the methodology to use, the tasks the proposal seeks to perform, the staff members who will perform the tasks, and a timetable to follow for the performance of these tasks.

PREPROPOSALS

It is necessary to be as succinct as possible in the preproposal or concept paper. The preproposal should elucidate the investigator's intentions to address the agency's needs through a relevant methodology and should indicate the investigator's sophistication with the theoretical and methodological issues in the field. If one receives permission to proceed after the preproposal is reviewed by agency personnel, a quality proposal should be executed. In some instances, agency personnel will consent to review a total proposal before it is submitted. Investigators should capitalize on such offers and should incorporate relevant suggestions into the final proposal.

Many agencies have prefunding conferences. If the topics are of interest to the researcher, he or she should definitely plan to attend. At these conferences, agencies explain the objectives of their programs and how grants are to be prepared. Conferences also are invaluable for making contact with key agency personnel to facilitate the submission of competitive proposals.

FOLLOW-UP

No news from the agency concerning a submitted proposal is usually good news. However, it is very acceptable to place a follow-up telephone call to check on the status of the proposal's review after the notification date has expired.

KEY CONTACT PERSONS

Foundations and businesses typically require a key contact be provided for an individual wishing to formulate a proposal. Foundations and businesses still operate on the "good old boy and girl" network; therefore, a key contact frequently is a prerequisite. After contact with the agency is made, the researcher must determine the agency's interest in reviewing a proposal. It is possible that the agency may only be interested in inflating the number of applications that are received.

THEORETICAL PROPOSALS

Theoretical proposals should not be submitted to business or industry. Experience demonstrates that business and industry emphasize products and solutions to applied problems; they are interested in supporting research that can develop technologies they can market (Wodarski, 1991). Theoretical research should be submitted to the appropriate federal agencies. Moreover, the researcher must be willing to deal with contracts, patents, and copyrights. Procedures for dealing with these are reviewed in Chapter 6 of *The University Research Enterprise* by John S. Wodarski (1990).

CRITICAL QUESTIONS

Do not prepare a proposal that the researcher cannot execute. Review boards are composed primarily of individuals who have written many proposals, and these individuals are not easily fooled. It is often helpful to choose a coprincipal investigator who complements the first principal investigator. Federal agencies focus on proposals of an interdisciplinary nature, because of the complexity of theoretical knowledge of the world.

Do not bluff! Review committee members have many proposals to read. There is nothing as disturbing as reading an endless proposal by an individual who is evidently not knowledgeable about the subject and who tries to fabricate his or her way through. Grant writers should realize the context of evaluation. Grant committees are composed of experts who usually meet to review and assign scores to proposals. Reviewers are knowledgeable, busy individuals who become angry with unpolished proposals that contain too much rhetoric. Budgets should be prepared with particular care, because all reviewers have had extensive budget experience; thus, it pays to justify relevant budget items. Moreover, to help in the main comprehension of ideas, a proposal should be executed with accurate typing, clear copies, and a definitive organizational style.

RESUBMISSION OF THE PROPOSAL

Receiving evaluation sheets from agencies is dreaded; however, it can be looked on as a corrective mechanism. If the methodological and theoretical issues outlined on the evaluation sheet are addressed, the probability of the grant applicant receiving funding for the revised proposal is extremely high. An investigator should address the evaluation sheet issues individually. Moreover, agencies prefer investigators to specify how the proposal has incorporated issues contained in the evaluation sheets. This is usually done in a cover letter. Aspects of the proposal, which are addressed as a reviewer's comments, should be highlighted.

One fatal mistake is assuming that a proposal will never be funded if it does not receive a positive, constructive critique. A proposal must be submitted to be funded.

FACTORS INFLUENCING PROPOSALS

The following factors have been determined to influence the funding of a proposal.

1. A proposal written in a clear and logical manner is expected to gain higher evaluations than a proposal that is rather vague and sketchy.
2. Although a solid and well-tried procedure leads to slightly higher ratings, an innovative and untested procedure is not necessarily detrimental.
3. A smaller, conservative project may be preferred over a large, ambitious project; however, a large project is not rated adversely due to its size.
4. The scientific relevance of the research is extremely important and is expected to have a strong, positive effect on evaluation.
5. The reporting of pilot data that clearly support the proposed research can be expected to increase favorable assessments of the proposal.
6. Although information that the researcher is highly respected in the field has a strong, positive effect, a new researcher who is perceived as promising is also expected to receive high ratings.
7. Information concerning the size and prestige of the research

facility is important. A proposal from a large, well-known laboratory is expected to receive a higher rating than that coming from a small, unknown lab.

TIPS FOR OBTAINING RESEARCH GRANTS

The following tips have helped in grant-proposal preparation:

1. Cultivate relationships with key staff members in foundations and governmental agencies that offer research grant funds. Personal contact, nurtured by correspondence, telephone conversations, and, most desirable, in-person meetings with the contact at conferences or in his or her office, are indispensable for obtaining guidance, advice, and feedback on all steps in the grant-application process. This can be done by agency or university research services office personnel, by faculty or staff assigned to facilitate the research function, or by individuals.

2. Find out which research areas are "hot" and timely through colleagues who are successful grant recipients and through agency contacts. Drug abuse and child abuse have become popular research areas in recent years. As the population continues to age, geriatric research will become more popular.

3. Develop the proposal in steps with the *active* collaboration of a knowledgeable and helpful staff person: (a) preproposal (ideas statement or concept paper), (b) preliminary proposal, and (c) final draft. Actively solicit input and feedback.

4. Develop local support as the proposal is formulated. Do not wait to obtain the "blessings" of administrators, collaborators, and consultants after the application has been forwarded. Cost-sharing agreements are particularly attractive to granting agencies.

5. Know who on the review committee will evaluate and judge the application. This may help the researcher "tailor" aspects of the design and method. Citing grant reviewers' research increases the probability of funding.

6. Write detailed and explicit justifications for all budget items, especially when outlining tasks, roles, and time involvement for each individual listed in the "personnel" category.

7. Write a focused and objectively balanced "background" section. This should be a scholarly, but not encyclopedic, review of literature that is pertinent and relevant to the proposed research. Keep interpretation and opinion to a minimum in this section, saving interpretive comments for the "rationale" and "significance" sections.

8. Write the "methods" section clearly and cogently because it is the critical segment of the application. Visual aids are a must to facilitate the reviewers' comprehension of main ideas. Include flow charts, timetables, figures, and tables to help the reviewers "see" exactly what is planned. For example, a table showing how dependent variables are organized to measure the anticipated effects of a treatment intervention conveys the investigator's grasp of the project.

9. Whenever possible in treatment research, specify what intervention will be presented, how therapists will be trained, what criteria of competency will be used, and how the therapy will be carried out with clients and patients. For example, the existence of a written treatment manual and criteria for evaluating the competence of therapists are assets to a grant application. Also helpful is a description of how the investigators will monitor the fidelity of the therapists and therapy to the treatment methods and concepts.

10. Consider whether the training and experience level of the therapists are appropriate to the demands of the methods and target population.

11. Keep project application design simple, and limit the number of hypotheses and questions being asked of the data. Be modest in prioritizing specific aims and objectives, acknowledging the limitations of the available subject pool (the "N"), the time to do the project, and the quality and quantity of data.

12. Consultants are valuable for what they will tangibly offer the project and for who they are.

13. Keep the text terse, neutral, tight, and free of jargon and biases. Write for the intelligent layman as well as for the fellow researchers; this achieves a proper balance. The reviewers rarely are as familiar with the area of research as the investigator, and the proposal will not receive favorable reactions if the material cannot be understood.

14. The investigator should try to arrange a site visit in order to more fully inform the review committee of plans and competence before the proposal is finally evaluated.

15. View grant writing as a learning experience, utilizing modeling and "trial-and-error" processes. Rarely will a novice receive a research grant award on a first try, but revisions and resubmissions based on review committee and staff feedback will yield positive results in the hands of a persistent researcher.

SUMMARY

The basics of preparing a quality proposal have been explained in this chapter. It should be emphasized that developing a quality proposal requires substantial time and energy. The probability of securing funds increases when research activities are aimed toward the solution of a significant problem that society faces. To get funding, the researcher must prepare many proposals and resubmit rejected proposals. The difficulty should not be underestimated, but the rewards are substantial.

REFERENCES

Coley, S. M., & Scheinberg, C. A. (1990). *Proposal writing*. Thousand Oaks, CA: Sage.

Larsen, P. T. (1973). Why project proposals are rejected. *Journal of the Society of Research Administrators, 4,* 3–6.

Lauffer, A. (1983). *Grantsmanship*. Thousand Oaks, CA: Sage.

Locke, L. F., Spirduso, W. W., & Silverman, S. J. (1993). *Proposals that work: A guide for planning dissertations and grant proposals* (3rd ed.). Thousand Oaks, CA: Sage.

Wodarski, J. S. (1983). Establishing and maintaining a research center: A case example. *Journal of Social Services Research, 7,* 79–94.

Wodarski, J. S. (1990). *The University Research Enterprise*. Springfield, IL: Charles C Thomas.

Wodarski, J. S. (1991). Technological transfer activities: Benefits and costs. *Research Management Review, 5,* 56–58.

Wodarski, J. S. (1995). Guidelines for building research centers in schools of social work. *Research on Social Work Practice, 5,* 383–397.

CHAPTER 13

The Research Practitioner: The Formulation of Process and Educational Objectives

Т

he increased interest in research ultimately will necessitate schools of social work to strengthen and integrate their training in research methods at all levels of the educational process. However, with the exception of certain doctoral programs, few guidelines are given to facilitate the training of those who will execute research functions for empirical social work practice (Rosen, 1978; Reid, 1978a; Wodarski, 1995; Wodarski & Feldman, 1973).

Educational objectives for training empirical practitioners must be identified if social work is to produce personnel capable of planning and evaluating adequate service-delivery systems, delineating targets for intervention, and deriving practice principles from the burgeoning research base of social work and the social sciences, and disseminating research knowledge to social workers. Hence, this chapter addresses the elaboration of research training at the undergraduate and master's levels. The formulations presented are derived from experiences of students participating in ongoing studies conducted by the author. Learning objectives, developmental sequences, types of assignments used in training research practitioners, and process of teaching the formulation of research questions that enhance the knowledge base of social work practice are discussed. Issues involved in offering such training are discussed in this chapter.

Basic courses in research should be offered at the undergraduate level. These should include introductory research courses and a course on the use of research methodology in social work practice. Additionally, all students should have an introductory statistics course to help them understand the role of statistics in the research process. This is an ideal situation, but such preparation is necessary if practitioners are to be trained as consumers of research. Early learning experiences in the use of research to attain practice objectives are critical in assuming that practice must be based on knowledge derived from a research base.

Instruction at the bachelor's and master's levels should incorporate a research base. The instruction would include study of the literature, derivation of practice principles, and evaluation of empirical support for the principles. Such a focus is essential for all courses in the curriculum. Students at the master's level who do not possess necessary skills should be provided the opportunity to obtain them through supplemental instruction.

COURSES FOR INCLUSION IN THE UNDERGRADUATE CURRICULUM

Introduction to Research

This course is concerned with the identification and formulation of problems for research and includes the study of various design strategies and techniques for gathering, analyzing, and presenting data with emphasis on causal analysis procedures. The purpose of the course is to provide an opportunity for students to learn the elements of the scientific method and to develop research competence relevant to individual interests, background, and professional concerns.

Course Objectives

1. To understand the nature of the scientific method, its relevance to professional practice in social work, and the implications of the view that research competence and scientific thinking are an essential part of the professional role definition.

2. To develop the ability to review literature, synthesize information, and understand its relationship to the formulation of a significant research question.

3. To learn the elements of the research process. These include not only the techniques of gathering data, but also the relationship of the components of the research process to each other, such as combining the appropriate question with the necessary measurement process, design, statistical analysis, and data presentation through tables and graphs.

4. To learn how to analyze and to present data with emphasis on table construction, interpretation, and causal analysis.

Outline of Topics Covered

1. Introduction to science
2. Ethics and rights of human subjects involved in research
3. Aspects of the research study
4. Different types of studies
5. Facts, concepts, theories, events
6. Definition of a problem and formulation of a hypothesis
7. Use of time-series designs in research and relation of time-series designs to classical experimental designs
8. Use of classical experimental designs in research
9. Introduction to measurement scales
10. Reliability and validity
11. Rival hypotheses
12. Statistical procedures
13. Data interpretation
14. Computer application
15. Practical aspects of research
16. Research reporting in manuscript form

Simulation Exercises

These should be used with the introductory course to facilitate the comprehension of various concepts. These might include:

1. Debates on "social work practice—the science" versus "social work practice—the art."
2. Reality exercises illustrating the difficulty in establishing consensus among observers of the same phenomenon.
3. Small-group discussions concerning what are relevant, researchable practice problems, and subsequent discussions concerning methodological aspects of the proposed investigation.
4. Completion of various scales designed to measure an attribute and then assessment of the merits of such means to study the phenomenon.
5. Experience in securing data on a concept through various means, such as questionnaires, interview schedules, and behavioral observations.
6. Visits to a computer center and subsequent execution of data analyses by the computer.
7. The steps in building practice technologies on research findings. With the use of simulated exercises, students can relate how the concepts of structure and goal setting facilitate behavioral change, and how they derive their rationales from accumulated research data on task-centered casework, brief and crisis-oriented psychotherapies, behavioral practice, and group social work (Bednor & Kaul, 1978; Butcher & Koss, 1978; Douglas, 1979; Reid, 1978b).

Performance Criteria

1. Students should develop basic skills in
   (A) Identifying problems
   (B) Formulating hypotheses or questions
   (C) Locating information relative to the problem of interest
   (D) Operationalizing outcome variables adequately
   (E) Formulating logical designs
   (F) Analyzing and digesting data
   (G) Formulating and interpreting conclusions
   (H) Understanding limitations of studies
   (I) Criticizing research reports
   (J) Understanding survey data analysis
2. Students should master the presentation of research-related material in proper form and style.
3. Students should follow the foregoing criteria in preparing a research proposal.

Research Methodology in Empirical Social Work

This course, dealing specifically with the elements of practice research, operates within the framework of the scientific method like any research. It gives emphasis to those design considerations and techniques that are most appropriate for the development of practice knowledge and evaluation of practice techniques through research.

Course Objectives

1. To acquire the ability to translate behavioral science knowledge into practice principles.
2. To develop the skills necessary to assess a study through its internal and external validity and its implications for social work practice.
3. To develop the ability to evaluate empirically any intervention procedure and outcome and to formulate intervention strategies when the original ones have proven ineffective.

Outline of Topics Covered

1. Relationship between science and practice
2. Critique of traditional experimental evaluation
3. Special problems in the assessment of behavioral change and deterioration
4. Empirical bases of practice
5. Methodological issues in evaluative research
6. Requisites for the establishment of services
7. Implementation of change strategy: by whom, why, and how long?
8. Organizational factors pertinent to the creation and evaluation of social work services
9. Baselines
10. Self-measures
11. Behavioral observations of client and worker
12. Designs for practice evaluation
13. Statistical evaluation procedures
14. Data requisites for competency-based agency practice
15. Documentation of practice research for publication
16. Practice research and its relationship to social policy

Performance Criteria

Students are required to design a study that evaluates the effectiveness of a practice intervention. The project must contain an empirical rationale for the intervention, means to measure the intervention, rationale for the choice of outcome criteria, appropriate design and reliable means of measurement, data presentation and statistical interpretation, and implications for practice based on the results of the investigation. Students present the project to fellow students for feedback at the conclusion of the course. This process enables students to share difficulties in operationalizing a concept and in dealing with agency constraints. Students learn how various constraints affect research and see the variety of applications of different designs that can be used to evaluate the different types of practice.

After the conclusion of the above courses, additional training can occur through coursework involving experimentation with social interventions, evaluative research, qualitative research, seminars in measurement, and macrolevel policy research, and through participation in research projects at undergraduate and master's levels. These projects may entail a student and a faculty member working on independent studies involving research and thesis research. These research experiences can become particularly relevant if the student works on topics related to practice interests. In one case, a student placed in a halfway house for abused wives reviewed the literature to isolate the factors involved in abuse, and subsequently worked on a prediction scale that would assess the potential for violence between spouses.

Students should be encouraged to take research courses in other departments to gain different perspectives on the research process by seeing how other fields use research methods to facilitate the provision of services. It is also an opportunity for experiences that are not currently available in schools of social work. For example, most schools of social work cannot provide extensive training in computer programming and statistical procedures, such as factor analysis. The number of research offerings in schools of social work usually is directly related to how large the school is.

LEARNING OBJECTIVES FOR THE EMPIRICAL PRACTITIONER

Learning objectives are conceptualized on a continuum of experiences. Beginning competencies should develop at the undergraduate level, with the final mastery at the graduate level. Fieldwork should in all instances involve the provisions of relevant experiences.

1. Optimally, learning experiences should be broad enough to enable students to participate in the entire range of activities required of a social work research practitioner. These research activities include the delineation of a research question, conceptualization and operationalization of that question, formulation of a research plan, and execution and evaluation of that plan. These experiences should also enable a student to determine how research relates to effective practice, how practice principles can be derived from behavioral science knowledge, and how the application and evaluation of such practice principles may be accomplished.

2. The student also should have an opportunity to experience and to cope with the practical aspects of research. These include organizational concerns, such as assessment of agency characteristics, coordination of research activities, interpretation of research to agency staff, collaboration with other agencies, treatment of negative attitudes toward research, selection of appropriate terminology, and effective monitoring of research activity (Wodarski & Feldman, 1973).

3. Technical aspects of research should be emphasized. Basic research terminology associated with concepts, such as baselines, randomization, experimental group, control group, and t statistics, should be learned as concepts to be applied in practice.

4. Students should be given the opportunity to apply concepts through simulation exercises or through participation in an actual study. This essential process is analogous to social work training often called "learning by doing."

5. Students should be prepared to assess critically the strong and weak points of various studies through the application of specific social work research and practice criteria mentioned in Chapter 2.

6. Students should learn to recognize the interrelationship of all parts and phases of a research study and the interdependence of each part and phase on the successful implementation of the others. Even though the parts of a research study may overlap substantially, students should see that studies consist of at least four discrete phases: planning, execution, evaluation, and documentation.

7. Students should develop the ability to assess current social work knowledge and to formulate new directions for research and practice technology. Students should appreciate how crucial this process is to the qualitative and quantitative growth of social work's knowledge base.

SPECIFIC PRACTICUM GOALS: MASTER'S DEGREE

Becoming Acquainted with Practice Research

An adequate introduction to various research concepts—randomization, experimental group, control group, and *t* statistics—represents an essential foundation for social work research. This can be accomplished usually through formal coursework followed by practicum exercises and mutual discussions among the students and instructor. If practicum instructors are engaged in ongoing research, they can present examples from their own studies to help students visualize the practical application of research concepts, and the relationship of the research process to the development and refinement of practice technologies.

For example, while working with the author on a study (funded by a private foundation) on the effects of divorce on children's academic and social behavior, students were able to see the rationale for the study and the subsequent proposed therapeutic interventions in the study.

Organizational Factors

Concurrently, students should be helped to see how the context of a study influences its outcomes. In one study, participating students had the opportunity to compare the research design presented in the original grant proposal with the one subsequently implemented. This experience enabled the students to see how original plans must be altered to accommodate various administrative considerations of the research site. The students saw the effects of the context of a study on the types of questions that can be asked, the types of designs that can be employed, the measuring devices that can be utilized, and the constant negotiations that occur regarding original plans and practical aspects of executing a study.

Execution of the Study

If a research practicum is associated with a larger research study, students may choose to investigate a selected aspect or ramification of that study and to use their ingenuity in developing a relevant substudy. For instance, in a large investigation on the evaluation of a community-based treatment program for antisocial children, students chose subtopics dealing with integrating antisocial children into prosocial groups at summer camp and at the agency, with evaluating the efficiency of different self-inventories in prediction of antisocial behaviors, and with determining how antisocial and prosocial children perceive themselves. Likewise, students might devise an evaluation of the case they are currently working with.

Outlining a study and carrying it through helps the student to follow the research sequence from the formulation of a question to its operationalization, collection of data, and the final writing. These are the most essential aspects of practice research, which, if planned in such a manner, provide the student with first-hand experience in all stages of the research and in the relationship of research to social work practice.

Throughout this entire process, great demands will be placed on the practicum instructor. Students will desire feedback in the formulation stages. The instructor and students, therefore, should constructively criticize various aspects of the question formulation and should point out overlooked ideas. The instructor also will have to help students in the actual operationalization, the choice of different statistical measures, the collection and analysis of data, the documentation, and the interpretation of the relationship of research to practice interventions. Throughout all the phases, the students should obtain feedback not only from the instructor but also from fellow students. In the ideal practicum, students present various aspects of their studies as they move through the different stages, thus providing themselves and their fellow students with the benefit of each other's experiences.

The practicum should conclude by assessing the merits of various theories postulated to account for social work practice and the relevance of behavioral science knowledge to practice. Development of skills in phrasing future research questions is crucial to further the expansion of social work knowledge. Relevant considerations include the reliability and the validity of theoretical predictions, the empirical evidence that supports these predictions, the adequacy of evidence, and the order of future research projects. For example, in one practicum, discussion focused on the ways that different practice theories influence a worker to explain and predict a client's behavior, to anticipate how much change can be achieved by a client, and to select interventions to be used in working with the client. The discussion concluded with questions such as the following: (a) To what extent are the various theories valid in their explanations and predictions of behavior? What amount of change that these theories hypothesize can take place in the client? What are the interventions that these theories propose to alter a client's behavior? (b) What evaluative research is available to show whether methods have different success rates with clients? And, (c) what evaluative research should be conducted next?

ISSUES RELATED TO TRAINING RESEARCH PRACTITIONERS

Offering the research training with a faculty member who is presently engaged in practice research or within a project involving several researchers has many merits. In such situations, students have the opportunity to use the researcher as a model who will exhibit various behaviors necessary for conducting a research project. Moreover, students gain first-hand knowledge of the practical aspects of research and see how an empirical practitioner translates behavioral science knowledge into relevant practice principles. This is especially pertinent for those in social work, or for that matter, for any social scientist who will engage in research relevant to helping people. This type of experience balances textbook learning and field experience, a seldom attained goal of social work education.

Students should be able to complete an experimental evaluation of a chosen case. It may be difficult to complete other types of research projects within the school's required time frame for the practicum. For example, projects requiring random assignment of participants to an experimental condition and substantial administrative coordination of agency personnel may be impractical. The first 4 or 5 months may be used in preparing the agency to do the research: communicating basic ideas and preparing staff for their roles. Certain practicum students have devoted a year and a half to the attainment of their research objectives. It is evident, then, that research learning cannot be constrained within rigid time frames. Circumstances may arise that prevent students from completing their practicums as planned. For example, development of skills in computer programming may take longer than expected, or unexpected difficulties may arise in data collection and interpretation. If research projects are to be time structured, the student should keep in mind that the quality of the research may be sacrificed in order to meet the schedule. It is possible, however, to streamline the training of empirical practitioners by incorporating a substantial portion of the technical research knowledge into regular classroom sessions offered at the undergraduate level. This procedure prepares students to undertake a research study shortly after beginning the practicum in the master's program and entails close coordination between the classroom experience and fieldwork.

Coordination of the research training with the doctoral requirements can measurably reduce the time required for completion of the doctoral program. This arrangement also provides an excellent pool from which potential doctoral students can be recruited and selected on the basis of appropriate performance criteria.

SUMMARY

The idea of training researchers apart from practitioners may be detrimental to the goals of the profession. Research should be interwoven throughout any social work curriculum. Development of all the basic research skills described here should be emphasized at all levels of social work education. Training empirical practitioners able to operationalize social work practice goals and able to assess whether such goals have been achieved is a must for the profession to ensure quality of services provided to clients. For this development to take place in the near future, it will be necessary for the ideas expressed in this chapter to be elaborated and sequenced in a curriculum, in which students can learn the necessary behaviors to execute the functions involved. Such training no doubt would improve the services offered to clientele.

REFERENCES

Bednor, R. L., & Kaul, T. J. (1978). Experimental group research: Current perspectives. In S. Garfield & A. Bergin (Eds.), *Handbook of psychotherapy and behavior change: An empirical analysis* (2nd ed.). New York: Wiley.

Butcher, J. N., & Koss, M. P. (1978). Research on brief and crises-oriented psychotherapies. In S. Garfield & A. Bergin (Eds.), *Handbook of psychotherapy and behavior change: An empirical analysis* (2nd ed.). New York: Wiley.

Douglas, T. (1979). *Group process in social work.* New York: Wiley.

Reid, W. J. (1978a). Some reflections on the practice doctorate. *Social Service Review, 52,* 449–455.

Reid, W. J. (1978b). *The task-centered system.* New York: Columbia University Press.

Rosen, A. (1978). Issues in educating for the knowledge-building research doctorate. *Social Service Review, 52,* 437–448.

Wodarski, J. S. (1995, July). Guidelines for building research centers in schools of social work. *Research on Social Work Practice, 5,* 383–398.

Wodarski, J. S., & Feldman, R. A. (1973). The research practicum: A beginning formulation of process and educational objectives. *International Social Work, 16,* 42–48.

Empirical Practice

Bellack, A. S., & Hersen, M. (1993). *Handbook of behavior therapy in the psychiatric setting.* New York: Plenum.

Bloom, M., & Fischer, J. (1982). *Evaluating practice: Guidelines for the accountable professional.* Englewood Cliffs, NJ: Prentice Hall.

Garfield, S. E., & Bergin, A. E. (1994). *Handbook of psychotherapy and behavior change: An empirical analysis,* (4th ed.). New York: Wiley

Gottman, J. M., & Leiblum, S. R. (1974). *How to do psychotherapy and how to evaluate it.* New York: Holt, Rinehart, & Winston.

Kazdin, A. E. (1980). *Research design in clinical psychology.* New York: Harper & Row.

Posavac, E. J., & Carey, R. G. (1989). *Program evaluation: Methods and case studies* (3rd ed.). Englewood Cliffs, NJ: Prentice Hall.

SUGGESTED READINGS

Research Methods

Adams, G. R., & Schvaneveldt, J. D. (1991). *Understanding research methods* (2nd ed.). London: Longman.

Black, J. A., & Champion, D. J. (1975). *Methods and issues in social research.* New York: Wiley.

Katzenberg, A. C. (1975). *How to draw graphs.* Kalamazoo: Behaviordelia.

Kerlinger, F. N. (1986). *Foundations of behavioral research.* New York: Holt, Rinehart, & Winston.

Kuhn, T. S.. (1970). *The structure of scientific revolutions* (2nd ed.). Chicago: University of Chicago Press.

McGain, G., & Segal, E. M. (1988). *The game of science* (5th ed.). Monterey, CA: Brooks/Cole.

Rubin, A., & Babbie, E. (1993). *Research methods for social work* (2nd ed.). Pacific Grove, CA: Brooks/Cole Publishing Company.

CHAPTER 14

Emerging Trends and Issues

P revious chapters reviewed the basic conceptual and methodological processes practitioners need to incorporate behavioral science knowledge and research in their repertoires for evaluating their practices. The major aspects of training empirical practitioners and the requisites for competency-based agency practice have also been outlined.

This chapter addresses the emerging trends and issues in social work practice research. The reader learns evaluation of practice; importance of research in education, rapid assessment techniques, simulation technology in social work education, prevention, and deinstitutionalization; organizational aspects of research; researchers versus practitioners; the researcher's distance from clients; incentives for research; dissemination of information; and application of relevant knowledge.

EMERGING TRENDS

Evaluation of Practice

More emphasis will be placed in the future on assessment of practice interventions with clients. Practitioners will continue to combine research skills in developing practice technology and conceptual advancement in the understanding of human behavior. Data systems that facilitate the execution of research pertinent to the practitioner's needs are being developed by agencies. More sophisticated research questions will be posited. There will be a move from polemic questions, such as "Is casework effective?" to "What technique, type of worker and client, treatment contexts, duration, and relapse-prevention procedures interact to produce the greatest client change?" The main question will be: "Were the services offered the client instrumental in a change for the better?"

Components of successful treatment packages will be analyzed. In task-centered casework (Paul, 1969), essential aspects of the model that elicit specific client behaviors will be identified, such as structure, expectations, enhancing commitment procedures, planning task implementation, analyzing obstacles, modeling, rehearsal, guided practice and summarizing. These aspects will provide data for answering six complex questions of a practice technology explained in Chapter 2.

Research should help resolve critical legal dilemmas regarding practice that plague the profession at this time. If left unresolved by the profession, it will be up to the courts to set guidelines. For instance, what are the traditional acceptable standards of practice? What is adequate treatment and where should it be provided? What qualities should the change agent possess? How long should treatment be provided? What happens if there is no change in the client? (Bernstein, 1978; Johnson, 1975; Wodarski, 1980).

Moreover, if accumulated data attest to the efficacy of particular treatment approaches, those treatment technologies that restrict the client's civil liberties the least and demonstrate superior effectiveness over the other approaches will have to be utilized. Under the legal doctrines of equal protection and least restrictive environment, all individuals are constitutionally entitled to the same privileges or social services. Thus, if two or more technologies achieve the same results, the technology that restricts the client's liberties the least, in such terms of personal resources as money, time, and energy, must be used. Judges have based their rulings concerning treatment issues on these two criteria (Martin, 1974, 1975; Wodarski, 1976).

Role of Research in Education

The role of research in social work education will increase dramatically at all degree levels with initial training in the relevance of research in social work practice at the baccalaureate level (Baer & Federico, 1978). The curricula will include courses based on empirical knowledge, the practice techniques derived from a verifiable empirical base, and the relevant practice issues that can be resolved through research. More faculty will engage in research relevant to practice and will move to knowledge development with applications. Moreover, students and beginning practitioners will begin to integrate research findings substantially into practice.

As discussed above, new variables must be isolated and new types of theories must be developed to alter complex human behavior effectively. Another development will be the incorporation not only of task-centered casework theory in social work practice, but of empirically based theories of human behavior and behavior change: on accurate empathic understanding, nonpossessive warmth, and genuineness (Truax & Carkhuff, 1967; Parloff, Waskow, & Wolfe, 1978). Many graduate programs in social work will incorporate into their curricula current theories of interpersonal attraction, attribution, and relationship formation; game theory and decision theory; effect of organizations on behavior; and nonverbal communication.

Future research will likely unravel the complex relationship between societal experiences and human behavior. For example, an issue which will be addressed in the future but which the field has virtually ignored is how to construct a society using macrolevel interventions versus individual interventions to prevent or facilitate certain prosocial behavior.

In the past, employment opportunities for social workers in criminal justice, marriage and family counseling, and human services were uncontested. Now social workers must compete with colleagues in nontraditional human services programs using empirical theories. The curricula of social work schools must, therefore, incorporate knowledge bases of social psychology that will provide an empirical base for practice techniques.

Rapid Assessment Techniques

Accurate assessment of client, worker, and agency attributes is essential for effective practice (Wodarski, 1981, 1985). Unfortunately, there are few accurate assessments of clients available to professionals (Steever, Wodarski, & Lindsey, 1984).

The goal of social work education is to equip the practitioner with the fundamental tools necessary for accurate assessment, an essential element of effective intervention at all levels of social work practice, whether it be at the individual, group, organizational, or societal level.

Rigorous training in assessment is considered to be a *sine qua non* for qualitative training and social work practice. No matter what powerful techniques the change agents possess, insufficient time spent on assessment results in ineffective or irrelevant intervention because an accurate assessment of the client's difficulties are not accurately assessed.

In the last decade, a number of rapid assessment scales have been developed to facilitate obtaining information necessary for workers to make adequate assessments of their clients (Rittner & Wodarski, 1995). The measurement instruments and procedures, designed to provide ongoing feedback, and to assess and to document client change during the helping process will be incorporated in social work education.

Simulation Technology in Social Work Education

Educators today are faced with the interesting, yet alarming, situation of information overload. Knowledge and skills are essential to efficacious social work practice; yet how to impart to students this vast and continually increasing knowledge poses a formidable challenge. There is debate in the literature as to the effectiveness of current teaching methods of social work theory and skills (Wodarski, Feit, & Green, 1995). Simulation technology, a recent product of the knowledge explosion in the social and the physical sciences, has been proposed to address this challenge.

Researchers and theorists generally find simulation techniques beneficial in both model building and experimentations, on both the micro- and macrolevels. Modeling contributes to theory building by replicating experience with alternate systems and conceptualizing holistically. Simulation, whether it be informal role-play, videotaping with focused feedback, other variations of micromodeling, or computer simulations, permits more complete control over the variables than does any other experimentation method. Computer simulation, in particular, supplies unique techniques for generating large numbers of synthetic observations from which conclusions can be drawn.

Future research related to education for social work practice must address the question: "What practice behaviors are most effectively taught by which training methodologies and with what learner characteristics?" There seems to be no argument that with the advent of more portable, less expensive, and relatively simplistic audiovisual taping equipment, this particular technology will continue to be included as a basic tool in the training of social work practitioners. Programs now using or contemplating the use of this and related laboratory model-ing techniques should consider the literature about relative advantages and disadvantages of simulation technology (Wodarski, Bricout, & Smokowski, in press).

Simulation technology benefits social work education by providing students with training to improve analytic prowess of systems of all types, as well as helping design new social arrangements that may advance and enhance field science. Perhaps the greatest limitation is the difficulty involved in specifying the relevant interrelated variables at play in the real system under simulation. Even if relevant variables are identified, it is very difficult to assign them their proper relative weights in the physical model. Thorelli and Graves (1964) suggest two dimensions on which all simulations should be evaluated are: their ability to aid in understanding real systems and their ability to predict accurately devel-opments in the realistic situation.

The rise of simulation technologies, such as computers, can be quite beneficial to social work educators. As people become aware of the benefits of simulation technology to education, better educational sim-ulations can be developed. In the near future, it is plausible that voice-activated computers will easily understand natural conversations and will be used to enhance prepracticum interpersonal skills. The day of the impersonal computer teaching people to be more personable is drawing nearer. We hope that educators will become aware of and use this great educational tool to raise social work to the realm of science.

Videodisc Computer Simulation

Accountability in delivering of social services ought to be a primary goal of social work practitioners and students alike. The key to greater accountability is the use of objective and standardized measures and evaluation procedures (Wodarski, 1986a). Interactive video program-ming can be centered on a series of steps corresponding to competency requirements. As students demonstrate that they have made the maxi-mum competency requirements, they can proceed to the next level of advancement. Mastery of interpersonal skill development and cognitive abilities for that level is a prerequisite for progress to the next level (Wodarski, 1986a). Interpersonal skills are at the core of all practice competencies and can be developed through interactive videodisc (IVD) for undergraduate students, graduate students, and professionals engaged in continuing education. The IVD program for accountable practice should exemplify certain key practice concepts, which Wodarski (1986a) calls the "social-psychological approach to interpersonal helping" (p.35). Each concept can be integrated into the demonstrations on interpersonal skills in the IVD program. The concepts can be both explicitly stated and implicitly modeled in video, text, and programmed feedback. The are seven key concepts to integrate into the program: client-worker relationship, communication, positiveness, mutuality, reciprocity, repetition (mastery), and evaluation (Wodarski, 1986a).

There have been exciting developments in social work education around interactive computer technology, most especially around interactive videodisc instruction. Computer simulations with applications for social work education began in the early to mid-1980s. Until 1985, the focus of simulation was on diagnosis, treatment planning, and evaluation (Wodarski, 1986b). Applications were basically database or research oriented. Wodarski (1986b) proposed that beginning practitioners use computer simulations to assess their clinical thinking and choices using contrived cases. Since then, many authors have explored the possibilities of videodisc simulation (Carlson, Bogen, & Pettit, 1989; Falk, Shepard, Campbell, & Maypole, 1992; Maynes et al., 1992; Maypole, 1991; Pardeck, Umfrets, & Murphy, 1987; Seabury & Maple, 1993; Wodarski, 1990; Wodarski & Kelly, 1987).

Interactive videodiscs promise to be an effective medium for practice instruction. A high degree of realism is possible with IVD, particularly in practice applications, such as interviewing, facilitation, and counseling (Carlson & Falk, 1990; Carlson et al., 1989). Learner responses can be recorded, and even self-taped, for later evaluation with an instructor or supervisor (Carlson et al., 1989).

The effectiveness of computer simulations in teaching quantitative research skills has already been established in other disciplines (Oliver & Huxley, 1988). These findings were later replicated in social work education (Falk et al., 1992). There is some evidence of IVD success in human service training as well (Wodarski, 1985b; Wodarski & Kelly, 1987; Wodarski, 1990). Two major studies of IVD training and social work education have been conducted. Seabury and Maple (1993) studied 293 social work students and 57 practitioners who looked at learning programs in group treatment, crisis counseling, and interviewing. Falk and colleagues (1992) studied 28 students (19 graduate, 9 undergraduate) who focused on three different learning programs: statistics, understanding groups, and human diversity. Both studies showed IVD a success as rated by student and practitioner satisfaction. Students in both studies and practitioners in Seabury and Maple were extremely satisfied. The Falk graduate students, however, found a three-hour IVD lab too long, and the Seabury and Maple students preferred IVD with a lecture to IVD alone.

IVD technology permits a flexible, self-paced interactive learning session. It has proven to be an effective learning tool for expanding knowledge and for acquiring and augmenting quantitative and clinical practice skills (Carlson et al., 1989; Finnegan & Ivanoff, 1991; Ives, 1992; Maypole, 1991; Sharf & Lucas, 1993; Wodarski et al., in press; Wodarski, 1986b; Wodarski & Kelly, 1987). Interactive video is an appropriate tool for concrete and abstract learning (Carlson & Falk, 1990; Reeves, 1986). Highly realistic computer simulation, which can involve high-order, conceptual learning, is possible with IVD. For teaching social work practice skills and concepts, IVD promises to be a medium capable of supporting complex learning tasks. In most schools of social work, there has been computer education (Caputo & Canan, 1990; Pardeck et al., 1987); however, little of this technology has been applied to practice skills refinement.

Interactive computer technologies provide a new tool for meeting the learner at their level of competence. These technologies offer a self-paced, noncompetitive platform for learning, which gives immediate feedback and, in clinical applications, allows for the exploration of differing responses without penalizing the client who depends on the learner's professional competence (Seabury & Maple, 1993).

Social work students and educators find interactive computer technology a highly desirable learning tool (Falk et al., 1992; Seabury & Maple, 1993). In human services, trainees using IVDs have achieved higher scores in less time than have controls using more traditional learning formats have achieved (Maypole, 1991). Furthermore, the interactive learning format is not just simply suited for inexperienced learners, who reported more satisfaction with interactive field simulations than those with less field experience.

Students may come to see IVD as much as a practice tool as an academic tool. This type of theory/practice–feedback loop reinforces social work's traditional blending of academic knowledge and practice experience. Involving practitioners in the development of IVD for classroom and practice environments bolsters practice–education links.

The potential for interactive computer education in social work is great. The portability, power, and flexibility of this learning tool make educational programming desirable. Interactive programs with broad-branching applications can be devised based on educational needs of learners. Ultimately, a life-long learning record may be designed for social workers as they develop their practice knowledge. Clients will be assisted by a more accountable, self-aware, and up-to-date practitioner who combines ongoing interactive learning with professional experience.

Prevention

Social work will stress prevention (Wodarski & Wodarski, 1993). The helping professions have a history of dealing with individuals only after they have exhibited behavior problems. To resolve this deficiency, the social work profession should facilitate thorough research on the preventive and educative roles that can be assumed by social workers, and criteria should be developed for early intervention. Prototypes of this approach may be found in courses on parental effectiveness, sex education, and marital enrichment. Parental effectiveness courses should focus on helping parents develop better communication and consistent child management skills, two variables that research has shown are necessary conditions for successful child rearing (Hoffman, 1977). Likewise, sex education and marital enrichment programs should prepare young adults for the requisites of marriage with effective communication skills, problem-solving strategies, and conflict resolution procedures (Collins, 1971; Ely, Guerney, & Stover, 1973; Lederer & Jackson, 1968; Rappaport & Harrell, 1972; Satir, 1967).

In another example, adolescents identified as high risk for poor coping with daily life could be taught a problem-solving approach based on the works of D'Zurilla and Goldfried (1971), Goldfried and Goldfried (1975), and Spivack and Shure (1974). The general components emphasized are

1. How to generate information
2. How to generate possible solutions
3. How to evaluate possible courses of action
4. How to choose and implement strategies through the following procedures:
   (A) General introduction to how the provision of certain consequences and stimuli can control problem-solving behavior
   (B) Isolation and definition of a behavior to be changed
   (C) Use of stimulus-control techniques to influence rates of problem-solving behavior

    (D)   Use of appropriate consequences to either increase or decrease a behavior
5. How to verify the outcome of the chosen course of action

Deinstitutionalization

One of the most perplexing yet critical problems confronting social work professionals is the effective implementation of deinstitutionalization procedures. What individuals can be placed in the community through adequate assessment? What socialization processes are necessary? What community characteristics may be matched with individuals' attributes to facilitate placement and enhancement of the individuals' functioning? What support systems are available to enhance placement? And how can the provision of an integrated social services system facilitate community maintenance? All are questions to be resolved before the clients are placed in the open community. Yet the community mental health social worker is ill prepared to address these issues, largely due to lack of research knowledge on the issues. Well-developed assessment techniques based on empirical knowledge from relevant social science disciplines and made available to social workers will help prepare these workers to implement deinstitutionalization procedures.

Development of these tools is essential to enable community mental health practitioners to utilize efficacious and cost-effective procedures to isolate physical, psychological, and social factors, leading to successful placements, such as:

1. Assessment of individual attributes, such as dependence, social skills, substance abuse, homelessness, employment, and economic resources, and community attributes, such as homogeneity of population, social cohesion, and employment possibilities.

2. Preparation of the community through enlistment of social networks, such as family, peers, ministers, and public employees to provide necessary support.

3. Preparation of the individual by emphasizing appropriate social behaviors that will be rewarded and will facilitate integration into the social structure of the community.

4. Education of the individual about available support services and whom to contact, and gradually introducing the individual to the new living context and to appropriate available social support systems.

5. Maintenance placement or monitoring placement and making

necessary alterations to facilitate successful placement through the use of relevant diagnostic aids; that is, determining whether the individuals are maintaining themselves physically and socially by working, receiving appropriate medical care, and socially interacting frequently to prevent social isolation and depression (Brook, 1976; Fields, 1975; Keskiner, 1977; Lamb, 1976; Levine & Kozloff, 1978; Miller, 1977; Morrissey, 1965; Segal, 1978; Swann, 1973; Wood, 1976).

Family Intervention

Data indicate that parents whose adolescents are at risk face multiple social and psychological difficulties. The clearest empirical finding about adolescents at risk is the lack of knowledge by the parent or parents and the consequent lack of effectiveness in managing the child's behavior in a manner that facilitates his or her psychological and social development. It has also been pointed out that another common feature of relationships between parents and adolescents at risk is unrealistic expectations by the parents on what is appropriate behavior for their child (Cowen & Work, 1988; Howing, Lishner, Catalano, & Howard, 1986; Patterson & Forgatch, 1987; Wodarski & Thyer, 1989).

Another empirical finding of note has been the high degree of strain evident in families. Family interaction patterns have been characterized as primarily negative; that is, parents engage in excessive amounts of criticism, threats, negative statements, physical punishment, and a corresponding lack of positive physical contact, and so forth (Bock & English, 1973; Brandon & Folk, 1977; Brennan, Huizinga, & Elliott, 1978; Hildebrand, 1968; Robin & Foster, 1989; Robinson, 1978; Suddick, 1973; Vanderloo, 1977). In view of this finding, a comprehensive prevention approach should include appropriate interventions that teach family members about the problems adolescents face, substance-use issues, communication skills, problem solving, and conflict resolution.

ISSUES IN CLINICAL RESEARCH

The Organizational Aspects of Research

Research is frequently based on the assumption that it takes place in a static, unchanging agency. Even though research in social work meets all the requirements of a well-designed study, the researcher faces the problem of executing the study in environments characterized as being fluid or turbulent and having high staff changeover, client dropout, and strikes. These organizational characteristics and different administrative styles, level of worker training, and number of years of experience affect practice research. Procedures must be developed to evaluate the confounding effect of the organizational aspects of the agency where the research takes place. A minimal requisite of any research study is the adequate specification of the characteristics of the organization in which the study is conducted to permit consumers of the research to determine the applicability of findings to their particular organization. This knowledge will also provide clues on how organizational variables interact to affect worker behavior (Feldman & Wodarski, 1974; Wodarski & Feldman, 1974).

Researchers versus Practitioners

The division of research and practice has proven detrimental to practice research because one cannot effectively operate without feedback from the other. Detachment of those professionals engaged only in research and those engaged only in practice precludes possible exchange of information needed for research of practice problems. However, this structural problem in social work is one that is not easily overcome. For instance, in the education of social workers, research and practice instruction are seldom intermixed. This dysfunctional aspect of professional training would be alleviated by integrating aspects of research that are relevant to practice at all levels of social work education. If the profession is to improve services offered to clients through use of research, there must be a substantial increase in the number of research practitioners who will be able to operationalize social work practice goals, and assess through collected data whether such goals have been attained (Broskowski & Schulberg, 1975; Perloff, Perloff, & Sussna, 1976; Schinke, 1979; Sechrest, 1975; Wodarski & Feldman, 1973).

The Researcher's Distance from Clients

There must be minimal distance between the investigators and the population to be served for research to be relevant to client needs. This situation can be accomplished by (a) placing clients on the review boards of granting agencies, (b) hiring clients to conduct various aspects of the research, (c) having the empirical practitioner spend time with the clients in the clients' environment, and (d) training practitioners in research methodology relevant in evaluating their daily practice. Large sums of money are being spent now on research to improve the criminal justice system. However, unless researchers gain relevant input concerning client needs, their research endeavors may prove nonproductive. Surely one cannot expect significant studies to be designed in the ivory towers of university settings without the proper fieldwork (Argyris, 1975; Bard, 1975; Elmo, 1975; Gadlin & Grant, 1975; Smith, 1973).

Incentives for Research

The means by which various federal agencies presently provide grants lead to dysfunctional social work research. For example, many agencies and universities are interested in conducting research; however, but their purpose oftentimes is not to evaluate service but, unfortunately, to secure money for overhead costs. Moreover, many researchers are motivated to secure funds to enhance professional stature through publication of their work and financial gain; research goals often reflect these motives rather than the desire to develop services to meet client needs. These dysfunctional aspects of research would be minimized if the granting agency monitored the research goals more closely to ascertain that they were attained. Likewise, universities should change their incentive structure for promotion. Rather than providing the incentives for undertaking those projects that make relevant contributions to meeting client needs—although costly in time, energy, and money—the present incentive structure reinforces researchers to execute projects that can be published expeditiously, thus enhancing the prestige of both the university and the researcher (Ben-David & Sullivan, 1975; Coelho, Rubenstein, Bauer, Snow, & Hilgard, 1971; Hall, 1972; Patterson, 1972).[1]

Therefore, if the profession desires the production of research, the incentives for such professional contributions will have to be made through recognition, budgets that include secd funds for initial projects, and release time to engage in research. Moreover, incentives

---

[1] This process is especially characteristic of the discipline of social psychology (Jung, 1969, 1971; Kelman, 1967; Ring, 1967; Schultz, 1969) that Jung (1971) described as a "psychology of college sophomores." This population is a captive one and, thus, can supply the large subject pools needed to conduct expeditious studies. Additionally, the costs and energy involved in carrying out such studies are minimal, as is its relevance, except for its use as a test of preliminary theoretical hypotheses.

must be provided for practitioners to keep abreast of developments in the behavioral sciences by reading journals and reporting to staff, attending and presenting papers at conferences, and undertaking research and publishing articles relevant to practice (Wodarski, 1995).

The Dissemination of Information and Application of Relevant Knowledge

If practitioners are to participate in practice research, which is a necessary condition in developing the treatment technology needed for the field, schools of social work must begin to teach the skills required, such as the ability to formulate questions, decide on various data options needed to answer the questions, and make rational decisions on the basis of data and not on the vague criteria presently employed. Likewise, practitioners must be capable of evaluating research endeavors of others.

Even if practitioners develop the appropriate research skills, there will still be the problem of information dissemination when the profession begins to isolate the crucial variables in social work practice. This problem is intensified when those who practice social work do not spend adequate time reading timely publications to obtain the information necessary to apply new knowledge (Fischer, 1978a, 1978b; Rosenblatt, 1968; Weed & Greenwald, 1973).

Another problem will be the implementation of various efficacious technologies as they are developed. A primary function of practice research in social work should be to provide a rational method for choosing change strategies to meet client needs. In an area where tradition, authority, and "common-sense" practice have ruled for years, a databased set of alternatives should facilitate the delivery of more effective services. It would be a mistake, however, to assume that the availability of good practice research information will automatically lead to improved services. The history of knowledge utilization in other human services fields shows clearly that the change process is much more complicated than is implied by a simple linear model leading from production to utilization of knowledge. In fact, in most cases, the effective dissemination and use of new findings is as difficult as their production (Martinez-Brawley, 1995).

For the purpose of analysis, the problem of knowledge utilization can be seen as an adoption problem: how to train social work students and practitioners to search for and to evaluate research data when choosing intervention alternatives. In some cases, practitioners may be capable of conducting their own evaluation, but in most cases, they may rely on information and conclusions reported by more qualified professional researchers or evaluators. Certainly, social workers should be trained to personally monitor the effects of their intervention and to gather feedback on the direction and magnitude of change, interpret studies for their relevance, and implement time-series designs. However, social workers rarely possess the resources and skills required of a professional evaluator, which are required to perform a comprehensive evaluation of the reliable outcomes of a program or a change strategy.

Data suggest that even after practitioners are exposed to new techniques and that practitioners employ aspects of the newer interventions, evaluations reveal that workers have been practicing in the same manner as in the past and that they have merely labeled it differently (Mullen & Dumpson, 1972). Thus, to ensure that professionals will keep abreast of current treatment developments and, moreover, will implement them, the incentive structure of social work practice must be changed. For practitioners to exhibit these behaviors, they will have to be rewarded for them.

The problem with the adoption of change strategies that have been scientifically verified is effective communication between the practitioner and the evaluator (Bernstein & Freeman, 1975; McNaul, 1972). More information is needed about the informational mechanisms used by social workers before any progress can be made. Although researchers communicate through professional journals and meetings, it is not likely that practitioners rely heavily on these mechanisms. To reach the practitioner, advocates of research need to include knowledge of the informational mechanisms and informal networks of the practitioner in their studies, and possibly have the practitioner and researcher work on studies together for one solution and then make use of those studies to disseminate knowledge. The change agent in education usually resides in the superintendent of schools or in other administrative positions. The research-evaluation work on innovative procedures and products usually is done often in a university or a research and development setting and reported in journal articles or technical reports, which are read by only a small minority of the school administrators. Administrators typically rely on reports from colleagues and on their own professional organizations and publications for their information on new procedures and products. Researchers and evaluators in education are beginning to realize that they must be able to supply their information to the channels used by the administrators if they want their stories to be told. The same procedure will likely hold for the dissemination of practice research in social work.

SUMMARY

The use of research techniques offers the social worker the exciting possibility of evaluating practice on empirical data and not on the basis of faith and practice authority. As the demand for competent social workers increases, the training of empirical practitioners will have to be formalized and competency criteria developed. Where practitioners should be trained and what level of skills must be acquired at each educational degree level are yet to be determined. What are the basic training functions at the undergraduate level, at the master's level, and the doctoral level (Wodarski et al., 1995)? Entrance criteria for students who will become empirical practitioners and appropriate objectives for training must be developed. Also, testing procedures will have to be developed and incorporated into training programs to ensure that practitioners meet appropriate standards. Such an assessment process will ensure that the individuals who call themselves empirical practitioners are really competent to engage in research and development of practice technology (Arkava & Brennen, 1975; Armitage & Clark, 1975; Grant, 1979; Peterson, 1976). Furthermore, new confidence in the change methods being employed should help alleviate the crisis of credibility in social work practice. The incorporation of research can lead only to improvement of services offered clients.

REFERENCES

Argyris, C. (1975). Dangers in applying results from experimental psychology. *American Psychologist, 30,* 469–485.

Arkava, M. L., & Brennen, E. C. (1975). Toward a competency examination for the baccalaureate social work. *Journal of Education for Social Work, 11,* 22–29.

Armitage, A., & Clark, F. W. (1975). Design issues in the performance-based curriculum. *Journal of Education for Social Work, 11,* 22–29.

Baer, B. L., & Federico, R. (1978). *Educating the baccalaureate social worker: Report of the undergraduate social work curriculum development project.* Cambridge, MA: Ballinger.

Bard, L. (1975). Collaboration between law enforcement and the social sciences. *Professional Psychology, 6*, 127–134

Ben-David. J., & Sullivan, T. A. (1975). Sociology of science. In A. Inkeles, J. Cademan, & N. Smelser (Eds.), *Annual review of sociology.* (Vol. 1). Palo Alto, CA: Annual Reviews.

Bernstein, B. E. (1978). Malpractice: An ogre on the horizon. *Social Work, 23*, 106–112.

Bernstein, I. N., & Freeman, H. E. (1975). *Academic and entrepreneurial research.* New York: Russell Sage Foundation.

Bock, R., & English, A. (1973). *Got me on the run.* Boston: Beacon.

Brandon, J. S., & Folk, S. (1977). Runaway adolescents' perception of parents and self. *Adolescence, 12*, 175–187.

Brennan, T., Huizinga, D., & Elliott, D. S. (1978). *The social psychology of runaways.* Lexington, MA: D.C. Health.

Brook, B. (1976). Community families: An alternative to psychiatric hospital intensive care. *Hospital and Community Psychiatry, 27*, 195–197.

Broskowski, A., & Schulberg, H. C. (1975). A model training program for clinical research and development. *Professional Psychology, 5*, 133–139.

Caputo, R. K., & Cnaan, R. A. (1990). Information technology impacts on increasing cultural awareness in education for human services. *Journal of Social Work Education, 2*, 187–198.

Carlson, H. L., Bogen, D., & Pettit, J. K. (1989). Designing the human factor into videodiscs for human service professionals. *Educational Technology, 32*, 41–43.

Carlson, H. L., & Falk, D. R. (1989). Effective use of interactive videodisc instruction in understanding and implementing cooperative group learning with elementary pupils in social studies and social education. *Theory & Research in Social Education, 17*, 241–258.

Carlson, H. L., & Falk, D. R. (1990). Interactive models using videodiscs in college inservice instruction. *Computer in Human Services, 7*, 277–293.

Coelho, G. V., Rubenstein, E. A., Bauer, R. A., Snow, J. A., & Hilgard, E. R. (1971). Can psychology be socially relevant? *Professional Psychology, 2*, 105–128.

Collins, J. D. (1971). *The effects of the conjugal relationship modification method on marital communication and adjustment.* Unpublished doctoral dissertation, Pennsylvania State University.

Cowen, E., & Work, W. (1988). Resilient children, psychological wellness, and primary prevention. *American Journal of Community Psychology, 16*, 591–607.

D'Zurilla, T. L., & Goldfried, M. R. (1971). Problem solving and behavior modification. *Journal of Abnormal Psychology, 78*, 107–126.

Elmo, A. C. (1975). The crisis of confidence in social psychology. *American Psychologist, 30*, 967–976.

Ely, A. L., Guerney, G. G., & Stover, L. (1973). Efficacy of the training phase of conjugal therapy. *Psychotherapy: Theory, Research and Practice, 10*, 201–207.

Falk, D. R., Shepard, M. F., Campbell, J. A., & Maypole, D. E. (1992). Current and potential applications of interactive videodiscs in social work education. *Journal of Teaching in Social Work, 6,* 117–136.

Feldman, R. A., & Wodarski, J. S. (1974). Bureaucratic constraints and methodological adaptations in community-based research. *American Journal of Community Psychology, 2,* 211–224.

Fields, S. (1975). Breaking through the boarding house blues. *Innovation, 16,* 2–10.

Finnegan, D. J., & Ivanoff, A. (1991). Effects of computer training on attitudes toward computer use in practice: An educational experiment. *Journal of Social Work Education, 27,* 73–82.

Fischer, J. (1978a) Does anything work? *Journal of Social Service Research, 1,* 215–243.

Fischer, J. (1978b) *Effective casework practice: An eclectic approach.* New York: McGraw-Hill.

Gadlin, H., & Grant, I. (1975). Through the one-way mirror: The limits of experimental self-reflection. *American Psychologist, 30,* 1003–1009.

Goldfried, M., & Goldfried, A. (1975). Cognitive change methods. In F. Kanfer and A. Goldstein (Eds.), *Helping people change.* New York: Pergamon Press.

Grant, G. (1979). *On competence.* (Ed.). San Francisco: Jossey-Bass.

Hadley, S. W., & Strupp, H. H. (1977). Evaluations of treatment in psychotherapy: Naiveté or necessity? *Professional Psychology, 8,* 478–490.

Hall, R. L. (1972). Agencies of research support: Some sociological perspectives. In S. Z. Nagi & R. C. Corwin (Eds.), *The social contexts of research.* New York: Wiley.

Hildebrand, J. A. (1968). Reasons for runaways. *Crime and Delinquency, 14,* 42–48.

Hoffman, M. L. (1977). Personality and social development. In M. R. Rosenzweig & L. W. Porter (Eds.), *Annual review of psychology* (Vol. 28). Palo Alto, CA: Annual Reviews.

Howing, P. T., Hawkins, J. D., Lishner, D. M., Catalano, R. F., & Howard, M. O. (1986). Childhood predictions of adolescent substance abuse: Toward an empirically grounded theory. *Journal of Children in Contemporary Society, 8,* 11–48.

Howling, P. T., Wodarski, J. S., & Gaudin, J. M. (1989). Clinical assessment instruments in the treatment of child abuse and neglect. *Early Child Development and Care, 42,* 71–84.

Ives, W. (1992). Evaluating new multimedia technologies for self-paced instruction. *Education and Program Planning, 15,* 287–296.

Johnson, F. M. (1975). Court decisions and the social services. *Social Works, 20,* 343–347.

Jung, J. (1969). Current practices and problems in the use of college students for psychological research. *Canadian Psychologist, 10,* 280–290.

Jung, J. (1971). *The experimenter's dilemma.* New York: Harper & Row.

Kelman, H. C. (1967). Human use of human subjects: The problem of deception in social psychological experiments. *Psychological Bulletin, 67,* 1–11.

Keskiner, A. (1977). Determinants of placement outcomes in the foster community project. *Diseases of the Nervous System, 38,* 439–443.

Lamb, H. (Ed.). (1976). *Community survival for long-term patients.* San Francisco: Jossey-Bass.

Lederer, W., & Jackson. D. (1968). *The mirages of marriage.* New York: Norton.

Levine, S., & Kozioff, M. A. (1978). The sick role: Assessment and overview. In R. H. Turner, J. Coleman, & R. C. Fox (Eds.), *Annual review of sociology* (Vol. 4). Palo Alto, CA: Annual Reviews.

Martin, R. (1974). *Behavior modification: Human rights and legal responsibilities.* Champaign, IL: Research Press.

Martin, R. (1975). *Legal challenges to behavior modification.* Champaign, IL: Research Press.

Maynes, B., McIntosh, G., & Mappin, D. (1992). Experimental learning through computer-based simulations. *Alberta Journal of Educational Research, 38,* 269–284.

Maypole, D. E. (1991). Interactive videodiscs in social work education. *Social Work, 36,* 239–241.

McNaul, J. P. (1972). Relations between researchers and practitioners. In S. Z. Nagi & R. C. Corwin (Eds.), *The social contexts of research.* New York: Wiley.

Miller, M. (1977). A program for adult foster care. *Social Work, 22,* 275–279.

Morrissey, J. (1965). Family care for the mentally ill: A neglected therapeutic resource. *Social Service Review, 39,* 63–71.

Mullen, E. J., & Dumpson, J. R. (1972). *Evaluation of social intervention.* San Francisco: Jossey-Bass.

Nietzel, M. T., & Moss, C. S. (1972). The psychologist in the criminal justice system. *Professional Psychology, 3,* 259–270.

Oliver, P. J., & Huxley, P. T. (1988). The development of computer-assisted learning materials for teaching and testing mental health social work in Great Britain. *Journal of Teaching in Social Work, 2,* 21–34.

Orcutt, B. A., & Mills, P. R., Jr. (1979). The doctoral practice laboratory. *Social Service Review, 53,* 633–643.

Pardeck, J. T., Umfrets, K. C., & Murphy, J. W. (1987). The use and perception of computers by professional social workers. *Family Therapy, 14,* 1–8.

Parloff, M. B., Waskow, I. E., & Wolfe, B. E. (1978). Research on therapist variables in relation to process and outcome. In S. L. Garfield & A. E. Bergin (Eds.), *Handbook of psychotherapy and behavior change: An empirical analysis* (2nd ed.). New York: Wiley.

Patterson, C. H. (1972). Psychology and social responsibility. *Professional Psychology, 3,* 3–10.

Patterson, G. R., & Forgatch, M. S. (1987). *Parents and adolescents living together. Part 1: The basics.* Eugene, OR: Castalia.

Paul, G. L. (1969). Behavior modification research. In C. M. Franks (Ed.), *Behavior therapy: Appraisal and status*. New York: McGraw-Hill.

Perloff, R., Perloff, E., & Sussna, E. (1976). Program evaluation. In M. Rosenzweig & L. W. Porter (Eds.), *Annual review of psychology* (Vol. 27). Palo Alto, CA: Annual Reviews.

Peterson, G. W. (1976). A strategy for instituting competency-based education in large colleges and universities: A pilot program. *Educational Technology, 16,* 30–34.

Rappaport, A., & Harrell, J. (1972). A behavioral exchange model for marital counseling. *The Family Coordinator, 21,* 203–212.

Reeves, T. C. (1986). Research and evaluation models for the study of interactive video. *Journal of Computer-Assisted Learning, 7,* 96–103.

Reid, W. J. (1979). The social agency as a research machine. *Journal of Social Service Research, 2,* 11.

Ring, K. (1967). Experimental social psychology: Some sober questions about some frivolous values. *Journal of Experimental Social Psychology, 2,* 113–123.

Rittner, B., & Wodarski, J. S. (1995). Clinical assessment instruments in the treatment of child abuse and neglect. *Early Child Development and Care, 106,* 43–58.

Robin, A. L., & Foster, S. L. (1989). Negotiating parent-adolescent conflict: A behavioral family systems approach. *Behavior Therapist, 13,* 69.

Robinson, P. A. (1978). Parents of "beyond control" adolescents. *Adolescence, 13,* 109–119.

Rosenblatt, A. (1968). The practitioner's use and evaluation of research. *Social Work, 13,* 53–59.

Satir, V. (1967). *Conjoint family therapy*. Palo Alto, CA: Basic Books.

Schinke, S. P. (1979). Bridging the accountability gap. *Practice Digest, 1,* 28–29.

Schultz, D. P. (1969) The human subject in psychological research. *Psychological Bulletin, 72,* 214–228.

Seabury, B. A., & Maple, F. F. (1993). Using computers to teach practice skills. *Social Work, 38,* 430–439.

Sechrest, L. (1975). Research contributions of practicing clinical psychologists. *Professional Psychology, 6,* 413–419.

Segal, S. (1978). *The mentally ill in community-based sheltered care: Study of community care and social integration*. New York: Wiley-Interscience.

Sharf, R. S., & Lucas, M. (1993). An assessment of a computerized simulation of counseling skills. *Counselor Education and Supervision, 32,* 254–266.

Smith, M. B. (1973). Is psychology relevant to new priorities? *American Psychologist, 28,* 463–471.

Spivack, G., & Shure, M. B. (1974). *Social adjustment of young children*. San Francisco: Jossey-Bass.

Streever, K. L., Wodarski, J. S., & Lindsey, E. W. (1984). Assessing client change in human service agencies. *Family Therapy, 11,* 163–173.

Suddick, D. (1973). Runaways: A review of the literature. *Juvenile Justice, 24,* 46–54.

Swann, R. (1973). A survey of a boarding-home program for former mental patients. *Hospital and Community Psychiatry, 24,* 485–486.

Thorelli, H. B., & Graves, R. L. (1964). *International operations simulations.* Glencoe: The Free Press.

Truax, C. B., & Carkhuff, R. R. (1967). *Toward effective counseling and psychotherapy training and practices.* Chicago: Aldine.

Vanderloo, M. C. (1977). A study of coping behavior of runaway adolescents as related to situational stresses. *Dissertation Abstracts International, 38,* 2387–2388B. (University Microfilms No. 5-B).

Weed, P., & Greenwald, S. R. (1973). The mystics of statistics. *Social Work, 18,* 113–115.

Wodarski, J. S. (1976). *Recent supreme court legal decisions: Implications for social work practice.* Paper presented at the 103rd Annual Forum, National Conference on Social Welfare, Washington, D.C.

Wodarski, J. S. (1979a). Requisites for the establishment, implementation, and evaluation of social work treatment programs for antisocial children. *Journal of Sociology and Social Welfare, 6,* 339–361.

Wodarski, J. S. (1979b). Critical issues in social work education. *Journal of Education for Social Work, 15,* 5–13.

Wodarski, J. S. (1980). Legal requisites for social work practice. *Clinical Social Work Journal, 8,* 90–98.

Wodarski, J. S. (1981). Comprehensive treatment of runaway children and their parents. *Child Welfare, 60*(1), 51.

Wodarski, J. S. (1985). An assessment model of practitioner skills: A prototype. *Arete, 10*(2), 1–14.

Wodarski, J. S. (1986a). *An introduction to social work education* (pp. 33–59). Springfield, IL: Charles C Thomas.

Wodarski, J. S. (1986b). The application of computer technology to enhance the effectiveness of family therapy. *Family Therapy, 13,* 5–13.

Wodarski, J. S. (1990). Practical computer applications in the psychotherapy process. In J. T. Pardeck & J. W. Murphy (Eds.), *Computers in human services* (pp. 21–34). London: Harrwood Academic Publishers.

Wodarski, J. S. (1991). Promoting research productivity among university faculty: An evaluation. *Research on Social Work Practice, 1,* 278–288.

Wodarski, J. S. (1995). Guidelines for building research centers in schools of social work. *Research on Social Work Practice, 5,* 383–398.

Wodarski, J. S. (in press, a). Cognitive and behavioral treatment: Uses, issues, and future directions. In D. K. Granvold (Ed.), *Cognitive and behavior social work treatment.* Belmont, CA: Wadsworth Publishing Company.

Wodarski, J. S. (in press, b). The empirical and legal bases of intervention provided by social workers. In B. Thyer (Ed.), *Controversial issues in social work practice.*

Wodarski, J. S., Bricout, J., & Smokowski, P. R. (in press). Making interactive videodisc computer simulation accessible and practice relevant. *Journal of Teaching in Social Work.*

Wodarski, J. S., Feit, M. D., & Green, R. K. (1995, March). Graduate social work education: A review of two decades of empirical research and considerations for the future. *Social Service Review, 69,* 108–130.

Wodarski, J. S., & Feldman, R. (1973). The research practicum: A beginning formulation of process and educational objectives. *International Social Work, 16,* 42–48.

Wodarski, J. S., & Feldman, R. (1974). Practical aspects of field research. *Clinical Social Work Journal, 2,* 182–193.

Wodarski, J. S., & Kelly, T. (1987). Simulation technology in social work education. *Arete, 12,* 12–20.

Wodarski, J. S., & Thyer, B. A. (1989). Behavioral perspectives on the family: An overview. In B. Thyer (Ed.), *Behavioral Family Interventions.* Springfield, IL: Charles C Thomas.

Wodarski, J. S., & Wodarski, L. A. (1993). *Curriculums and practical aspects of implementation: Preventive health services for adolescents.* Lanham, MD: University Press of America.

Wood, P. (1976). A program to train operators of board-and-care homes in behavioral management. *Hospital and Community Psychiatry, 27,* 767–770.

Index

ABAB design
    antisocial behavior, 111–112, 114
    case illustration, 115–116
    characteristics of, 109–111
    interventive methods, 114
    nonsocial behavior, 112–114
    prosocial behavior, 112–113
Acceptance of client, 43
Accountability, significance of, 3–4, 32,
    169, 185, 208
Active control group, 131
African Americans, social myths about,
    47, 49
Aging, attitude toward, 45
Aid to Families with Dependent
    Children (AFDC), 10
Alcoholism, 46
Alternate forms reliability, 77
ANCOVA, 147
Anglo-American population, social
    myths about, 47
ANOVA, 145–146, 154–155
Antisocial behavior, 110–112, 114
Applied social psychology, 20
Asian American population, social
    myths about, 49
ASP Tutorial and Student Guide,
    163–164
Assertiveness training, 2, 53, 56

Assessment
    of agency characteristics, 166–169
    of client behavior, 79–84
    of competencies, 196–198
    emerging trends in, 248–249
    of interpersonal skills, 191–194
    positive, 16–20
    of practice skills, 194–195
    of theoretical knowledge, 195–196
    of worker behavior, 79–84
Assumptions, statistical correlations
    and, 143
Atmosphere, in treatment setting,
    64–65
Attitude
    about research, 172
    testing, 197
Audiotapes, in practice sessions, 194,
    196–197

Bachelor's-level practitioners, 2, 22,
    247–248
Barrett–Lenard inventory, 194
Baseline
    measures, 33, 75–77
    period, 174–175
Behavioral observation
    of children, 79–80
    one-way mirrors, 176–177

Behavioral observation *(continued)*
  significance of, 3
  of therapists, 81–82
Behavioral Observational Scale for
  Children, 111
Behavioral rating scales, 34
Behavioral Social Work, 54
Behavior modification, 13, 32
Bias, in research studies, 170, 173
Brief therapy, 6

Canonical correlation (CC), 160–161
Casework
  empirical practice in, 12–13
  problem-solving, 134
  professional, 13
  task-centered, *see* Task-centered
    casework
Change agent, 11–16, 32, 259–260
Childpace, 215
Child's Checklist, 82–83
Choice-of-outcome measures
  adequate specification of behavior
    and baselines, 75–76
  choice of measures, 75
  client behavior, 73
  client outcomes, 72–73
  criterion, single *vs.* multiple, 74
  evaluation measures criteria, 77–79
  worker behavior, 73
Classical experimental design,
  132–133
Client(s), generally
  civil liberties of, 247
  simulated, 216–217
Client–counselor relationship, 44–45
CLIENT 1, 217, 219
Client behavior, measures of
  adequate specification of behavior
    and baselines, 75–76
  assessment procedures, 79–84
  choice of, 75
  criterion, single *vs.* multiple, 74
  evaluation criteria, 77–79
  types of, generally, 73

Client variables, social myths
  age, 44–45
  practice recommendations and, 52
  race/ethnicity, 46–48
  sex, 45–46
  socioeconomic status (SES), 48–50
  YAVIS *vs.* Non-YAVIS, 50–52
Clinical research
  incentives for, 257–258
  information dissemination, 258
  knowledge utilization, 258–260
  organizational aspects of, 255–256
  researcher's distance from clients,
    256–257
  researchers *vs.* practitioners, 256
Code of ethics, 8
Collaboration
  in research, 171–172, 174
  on research grants, 229, 231
Communicability, measurement of, 30
Communication
  nonverbal, 31, 42–43, 248
  positive, 41–42
  verbal, 42–43
  with worker, 41
Community-Oriented Program
  Environment Scale (COPES), 64
Competency-based agency practice
  assessment of competencies,
    196–198
  development of, 185
  implementation issues, 198–199
  improvement of, 198
  practice competencies, 191–196
  procedures, evaluation of, 190–191
  securing practitioner's agreement,
    186, 190
Competency-based education (CBE)
  accountability and, 185
  criticisms of, 184
  curriculum issues, 184
  defined, 183
  elements of, 183–184
  future research, 185
Competency-based social work, 3

Computer programs, types of, 36, 161, 196, 210
Computer simulation, 249
Computer technology, impact of, 205, 215; *see also* Management information systems
Concurrent validity, 78
Confidentiality, of data, 176
Conscience, 9
Consistency, reliability and, 77
Construct validity, 78–79
Content relevance, 42
Content validity, 78
Continuing education, 4; *see also specific degree levels*
Contract, therapeutic, 8, 53
Control groups, 131–132
Convergent validity, 78
Conversational distance, in treatment setting, 60–61, 65
Coordination, of research, 169–170
Coping with Stress, 216
Cost containment issues, 4
Counselor, simulated, 216
Counterbalanced design, 135–136
Covariance, analysis of, 146–147
Credibility
  of interviewer, 62
  of worker, 41, 43
Curriculum, generally
  competency–based, 3
  graduate, 248
  planning challenges, 184–185
  sociobehavioral and systems theory in, 1
  undergraduate courses, 235–239

Daily practice evaluation
  ABAB design, 109–111
  behavioral categories, 111–117
  emerging trends in, 246–247
  multiple baseline design, 117–124
  types of, generally, 107–108
Deinstitutionalization, 254–255
Delayed reinforcement, 36, 58

Delinquency studies, 143
Dependent variables, in empirical studies, 10–13, 15
Depression, 46, 216
Diagnostic and Statistical Manual of Mental Disorders (DSM-IV), 5
Discover Your Baby, 215–216
Discriminate analysis, 155
Discriminative validity, 78
Distracting behaviors, 78
Doctoral-level practitioner, 22
Drug dependency, 46

Eating disorders, 46
Educational/learning objectives
  emerging trends in, 248–249
  for empirical practitioner, 239–240
  for master's degree, 241–243
  purpose of, 234–235
  training for research practitioners, 243–244
  undergraduate curriculum courses, 235–239
Efficacious therapeutic program
  adequate specification of behaviors and baselines, 33
  conceptualization/operationalization of treatment, 32
  duration, 33
  measures of client/therapist behaviors, 33–34
  rationale for service provided, 32–33
Elderly, worker perception of, 44–45
Eliza, 215–216
Emerging trends
  in assessment techniques, 248–249
  in clinical research, 255–260
  in deinstitutionalization, 254–255
  in family intervention, 255
  in practice evaluation, 246–247
  in prevention, 253–254
  role of research in education, 247–248
  in simulation technology, 249–250
  in videodisc computer simulation, 250–253

Empathic understanding, 248
Empathy, 41–42, 191
Empirical practice
   change agent, 11–16
   changes needs, 8–11
   minimal use of, 1
   plausible studies of, 7–8
   positive assessment criteria, 16–20
   rationale for, 2–5
   research functions, 5–7
Empirical practitioner
   competencies of, 21–22, 46–47
   function of, 20–21
   learning objectives of, 239–240
Equipment/materials, in treatment
      setting, 63
Ethnicity, influence of, 46–48
External validity
   defined, 127
   multiple treatment interference, 131
   pretesting, effects of, 131
   reactive effects of, 131
   selection biases and, 130–131

Face validity, 78
Factor analysis (FA), 157–159
Factorial design, 134–137
Family intervention, trends in, 255
Family therapy, 5
Feedback
   in coursework, 242
   for empirical practitioner, 21–22
   peer, 57
   research interpretation and, 170
   significance of, 170–171, 259
Fixed-form records, 206–207
Follow-up, significance of, 3, 36–37
Free-form records, 206–207
Furniture, in treatment setting, 62, 65

Gender differences
   therapeutic relationship and, 45
   in treatment setting, 60, 62
Genuineness, 42, 191, 248
Goal-setting forms, 190, 211

Graphs, 36
Gross motor behavior, 78
Group therapy, 5
Guided practice, 247

Hispanic population, social myths
      about, 49–50
Home visits, 58
Human resource training, 191

"Ideal" clients, 50–52
Incentive programs, 221, 257–258
In-course training, evaluation of, 196
Independent variables, in empirical
      studies, 10–15
Informed consent, 176
INTERACT, 217
Interactive Technology Groups, 218
Interactive videodisc (IVD) program,
      250–253
Interactive Videodisc for Special
      Education Technology (IVSET), 219
Interior design, in treatment setting,
      62–63
Internal consistency, 30
Internal validity
   defined, 127
   experimental mortality, 130
   historical effects, 128
   maturational effects, 128
   measurement procedures, 129
   statistical regression effects,
      129–130
   subjects, selection of, 130
   testing procedures, 129
Interpersonal process recall, 191
Interpersonal research-helping process,
      1, 35
Interpersonal skills
   assessment of, 191–194
   mastery of, 250–251
Interpretation, of research, 170–171
Interreliability, 77
Interrupted Case Test (Benjamin Rose
      Institute), 195

Interviews
    client behavior, 83–84
    competency assessment, 197
    schedules, 75
Intimate distance, 61
Intrareliability, 77

Knowledge
    bases, 1, 22–23
    utilization, 258–260

Learning by doing, 240
Learning Programs, computer-assisted,
    162–163
Life enrichment software, 215–216
Litigation, see Malpractice litigation
"Loaded" training, 184

Malpractice litigation, 3–4
Managed health care, 4, 53
Management information systems (MIS)
    basic requisites, 206–207
    client descriptive analyses, 208
    diagnosis, 208–210
    documentation, of program imple-
        mentation and effectiveness,
        208–210
    field issues, 221–222
    information requisites, 219–221
    managerial applications, 207–208
    practice procedures, overview,
        211–219
    selection of, 220
    research operations, 210–211
    treatment planning, 208–210
Manifest Aggression Scale, 149
MANOVA, 154–155
Manuals
    for treatment intervention, 11, 14
    treatment plans, in grant proposals,
        232
Marital enrichment programs, 253
Master's degree
    curriculum for research, 248
    practicum goals, 241–243

Master's-level practitioners, 2, 12, 22
Mean, 36, 141
Median, 36, 141
Medical treatment, 13
Mexican American population, social
    myths about, 47
Microcase program, 163
Microcounseling, 191
Micromodeling, 249
Miller's Analogy Scores, 78
Mind Prober, 215
Minimax principle, 19
Minorities, social myths about;
    see specific minority groups
MMPI (Minnesota Multiphasic
    Personality Inventory), 210
Mode, 36, 141
Modeling, 247, 249
Morton, 216
Multicriteria measurement, 33–34
Multiple baseline design, case study
    methodology, 120–123
    previous research and, 119–120
    purpose of intervention, 117–118
    results of study, 123–124
    theoretical rationale for intervention,
        118–119
Multiproblem screening inventory
    (MSI), 208–209
Multivariate analysis, 150, 154–155

National Computer Systems
    Professional Assessment Services
    (NCSPAS), 209–210
Native American population, social
    myths about, 50
Nonsocial behavior, 110, 112–114
Nonverbal communications, 31, 42–43,
    248
NYBMUL computer program,
    147–148

Obesity, 46
Objectives, see Educational/learning
    objectives

Odd-even reliability, 77
One-way mirrors, 176–177

Parenting skills programs, 11, 56, 253
Parsimony, 30
Party, 216
Path analysis (PA), 155–156
Performance-based education,
    see Competency-based education
    (CBE)
Personal distance, 61
Personality disorders, 46
Person–machine models, 214–215, 217
Person models, 214, 217
Physical contact, 78
Placebo problem, 40
PLATO Dilemma Counseling System
    (PLATO DCS), 216
Positive assessment, criteria for, 16–20
Poverty, impact on therapy, 49
Practice notes, 190, 212
Practice skill(s)
    assessment of, 194–195
    levels of, 212
Predictive validity, 78
Prejudice, impact on therapy, 46, 50
Preproposals, 228
Pretest sensitization hypothesis, 129,
    133
Prevention, emerging trends in,
    253–254
Problem-solving
    casework, 134
    skills, 11, 13, 53, 56
Procedural clarity, 31
Professional casework, 13
Proposals
    critical questions for, 229
    development of, 227–228
    follow-up, 228
    influential factors, 230–231
    informational exchange, 225–226
    key contact persons, 228–229
    knowledge and, 226
    personal contacts, 226–227

preproposals, 228
research grants and, 231–232
resubmission of, 230
theoretical, 229
Prosocial behavior, 110, 112–113
Psycheware programs, 215–216
Psychodynamic theory, 9
Psychology of college sophomores, 257
Psychopathology, 45
Public distance, 61

Questionnaires, 75

Race, of client/worker, 46–48
Random assignment
    in daily practice, 108
    importance of, 35, 57
    in traditional experimental design,
        127–129, 132–133
Reality exercises, 237
Recordkeeping
    computerized systems, 211–212
    documents for, 190
Referrals, 73
Regression analysis, 149–150
Rehearsal, 247
Reinforcement schedules, 36, 58
Relapse-prevention procedures, 6, 12, 31
Relationship enhancement, 2
Relaxation training, 2–3, 11, 14, 56
Reliability, choice-of-outcome
    measures, 77
Remission, 40
Replication, 13
Research, generally
    clinical, *see* Clinical research
    functions of, 5–7
    preparation process
        agency characteristics assessment,
            166–169
        attitude toward research, 172
        collaboration, 171–172
        coordination of research, 169–170
        evaluation, structural components
            for, 176–180

interpretation of research, 170–171
methodological procedures, implementation of, 174–176
supervision, consistency of, 173–174
terms, choice of, 173
technology, 15
Research grants, 231–232; *see also* Proposals
Research practitioners, training issues, 243–244
Response enumeration, 193
Response evaluation, 193
Review boards/committees, for research grants, 229, 231–232
Rival factors, 30
Rival hypotheses, 35, 127–128, 130
Role plays, 192, 194, 214, 218, 249
Role theory, 9
Room size, in treatment setting, 61–62, 65

St. Louis Conundrum Effective Treatment of Antisocial Youth, The, 72, 79
Seating arrangements, in treatment setting, 60, 65
Schizophrenia, 63
Scientific criteria, research studies evaluation
generally, 29–31
for social work practice, 31–32
Self-awareness groups, 216
Self-control
importance of, 55
procedures, 36, 58
Self-disclosure, 46
Self-exploration, 46
Self-help programs, 215–216
Self-inventories
advantages of, 75
behavioral rating scales *vs.*, 34
of children, 82–83
drawbacks of, 75
positive assessment, 16

by significant adults in child's life, 83
Self-management procedures, 53
Self-sufficiency, 56
Sex education programs, 253
Simulations, generally, 192
Simulation technologies
emerging trends in, 249–250
types of, 212–214
Single-case study, 35, 108; *see also* ABAB design
Situational analysis, 193
Situational specific hypotheses, 144
Skip, 216
Social learning theory, 56
Social myths, 43–52
Social policy changes, 57
Social skills training, 2, 11
Social toys, 63
Socioeconomic status (SES), as therapeutic influence, 48–50
Sociofugal space, 60
Sociopetal space, 60
Solomon four-group design, 133
Solution-focused therapy, 13
Split-half reliability, 77
SPSS, 161, 210
Standard deviation (SD), 142
Standards for practice, 222
Statistical packages, computer-assisted, 162–163
Statistical regression, 129–130
Statistical significance myth, 17–18
Statistical techniques
advanced, overview, 153–164
basic statistical functions, 143
canonical correlation, 160–161
covariance analysis, 146–149
data description and, 141–143
discriminate analysis, 155
factor analysis, 157–159
multivariate analysis, 150, 154–155
path analysis, 155–156
regression analysis, 149–150
statistical correlations, 143–144

Statistical techniques *(continued)*
  structural equations, 159–160
  t tests, 144–145
  variance analysis, 145–146
Stimulation value, 30
Strengths perspective, 13
Structural equations, 159–160
Subsumptive power, 30
Suicidal behavior, 46
Summary form, 190, 211
Supervision, consistency of, 173–174
SYSTAT, 162–164
Systematic desensitization, 11, 14, 56

Task-centered casework
  in daily practice, 118–119
  defined, 53–54
  emerging trends, 247
  traditional experimental design and,
    134
Task implementation sequence (TIS),
  54, 119
Termination, of treatment, 212
Testability, 30
Test–retest reliability, 77
Theoretical accuracy, 212
Theoretical knowledge, assessment of,
  195–196
Therapeutic alliance, 40
Therapist's Checklist, 82–83
Therapy, generally
  brief, 6
  family, 5
  group, 5
  length of, 33, 53
  solution-focused, 13
Time sampling
  of children, 79–80
  of therapists, 81–82
Time-series studies
  ABAB design, 109–111
  benefits of, 108
  generally, 35
  multiple baseline design,
    117–124

Traditional experimental designs
  applications of, 127–128
  classical design, 132–133
  control group characteristics,
    131–132
  external validity and, 130–131
  factorial design, 134–137
  generally, 35
  internal validity and, 128–130
  multiple group design, 133–134
  Solomon four-group design, 133
Trait, situation-specific hypothesis *vs.*,
  144
Training programs
  assertiveness training, 2, 53, 56
  in-course, 196
  in human resources, 191
  loaded, 184
  relaxation, 2–3, 11, 14, 56
  for research practitioners, generally,
    243–244
  in social skills, 2, 11
Treatment components
  behavior acquisition, 53–54
  behavioral approaches, 54–56
  behavioral change, generalization
    and maintenance of, 58
  change strategy
    individual *vs.* group treatment,
      56–57
    macrolevel intervention, 57–58
  length of therapy, 53
  practice recommendations, 58–59
Treatment context
  atmosphere, 64–65
  conversational distance, 60–61, 65
  equipment and materials, 63
  furniture, 62, 65
  interior design, 62–63
  practice recommendations, 64–65
  room size, 61–62, 65
  seating arrangements, 60, 65
Treatment efficacy, evaluation criteria
  designs, 35
  reliable measures, 35

statistics, 36
treatment monitoring, 34–35
Treatment goals, 190, 211
Trust, establishment of, 41
t tests, 144–145
Tulane Assessment Scale, 195

Unconditional positive regard, 191
Undergraduate curriculum courses
    introduction to research, 236–237
    research methodology, 238

Validity, choice-of-outcome measures,
    77–78
Value judgments, 8, 15, 19
Variance, analysis of, 145–146
Verbal behavior, 42
Verbal congruence, 42–43
Verbalizations, 78
Verbal Language Development Scale,
    120–121
Videodisc simulation
    defined, 218–219
    emerging trends in, 250–251
Videotapes, in research studies
    behavioral observations of children,
      79–80
    of clinical interaction, generally, 3,
      111, 196–198, 249

potential benefits of, 179–180
purpose of, 173, 177–178
staff concerns, 178–179
Video technology, impact of, 217–218

Waiting-list control group, 131–132, 134
WALMYR Publishing Co., 209
Ward Atmosphere Scale (WAS), 64
Warmth, 41–42, 248
Word processing systems, 207–208
Worker behavior, measures of
    adequate specification of behavior
      and baselines, 75–76
    assessment procedures, 79–84
    choice of, 75
    criterion, single *vs.* multiple, 74
    evaluation criteria, 77–79
    types of, generally, 73
Worker characteristics
    communications, 41
    positive communications, 41–42
    practice recommendations, 42–43
    professional *vs.* paraprofessionals,
      40–41
    similarity of client and worker, 40

YAVIS (young, attractive, verbal,
    intelligent and successful) syndrome,
    50–52

Springer Publishing Company

Total Quality Management in Human Service Organizations
Toward the 21st Century
John Gunther, DSW and Frank Hawkins, DSW

The total quality management (TQM) paradigm presents a unique opportunity for human service professionals to break away from traditional management approaches. In this useful supplemental text, the authors provide a clear overview of the tenets of TQM, as well as illustrative and extremely detailed case studies in an array of human service settings, including health care, public welfare, and educational. The authors include two useful chapters on the emerging practices of benchmarking and reengineering. This text supplies the reader with a brief guide on how to implement TQM, as well as a useful glossary of terms for management students.

Partial Contents:

Overview of Total Quality Management. Total Quality Management and Human Service Organizations • Total Quality Management: A Model of Implementation • The Tools of Total Quality Management

Applied Total Quality Management in Human Service Organizations. Health Care. The St. Joseph's Health Center Story • Freeport Hospital Health Care Village • Public Welfare • "Quality Oklahoma" and the Oklahoma Department of Human Services

Emerging Practices. Benchmarking • Reengineering • Epilogue

Appendix A: Total Quality Management in Human Service Organizations: A Guide to Implementation • Appendix B: State of Oklahoma, Executive Order 92.3 • Appendix C: "Quality Oklahoma" Strategic Plan • Appendix D: A Brief History of "Quality Oklahoma"

1996   264pp   0-8261-9340-4   hardcover

536 Broadway, New York, NY 10012-3955 • (212) 431-4370 • Fax (212) 941-7842

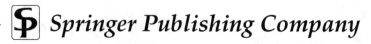 **Springer Publishing Company**

Multicultural Perspectives in Working with Families

Elaine P. Congress, DSW

Professionals must develop new skills in working with culturally diverse clients and their families due to an increasing number of families from backgrounds other than Western Europe. To address this issue for social work students, the Council on Social Work Education has updated their curriculum policy to mandate content on cultural diversity. Dr. Congress has developed a major textbook that focuses on multiculturalism and populations at risk, in order to expand the knowledge of practitioners as well as students.

The purpose of this book, which contains the latest information, research, and practice examples about culturally diverse families, is to decrease stereotypes and promote non-biased thinking. The author addresses many timely topics within the family including HIV/AIDS, homelessness, substance abuse, domestic violence, and child sexual abuse. This volume is written for social work practitioners, as well as social work educators and students.

Partial Contents:

Assessment—Micro and Macro Approaches. Use of the Culturagram to Assess and Empower Culturally Diverse Families • Managing Agencies for Multicultural Services

Culturally Diverse Families Across the Life Cycle. The Child, the Family, and the School: A Multicultural Triangle • Working with Poor Ethnic Minority Adolescents and Their Families: An Ecosystemic Approach • Multicultural Dimensions of the Third Shift: Employees, Mothers and Students • The Aging Family: Ethnic and Cultural Considerations

Selected Culturally Diverse Populations. Motherless Children: Family Interventions with AIDS Orphans • Working with Immigrant Families in Transition • Working with Soviet Jewish Immigrants • Redefining the Family: The Concept of Family for Lesbians and Gay Men • Machismo, Manhood and Men in Latino Families

Springer Series on Social Work
1997   376pp (est.)   0-8261-9560-1   *hardcover*

536 Broadway, New York, NY 10012-3955 • (212) 431-4370 • Fax (212) 941-7842

Springer Publishing Company

Evaluating Your Practice
A Guide to Self-Assessment
Catherine F. Alter, PhD
Wayne Evens, MSW

This easily accessible text provides step-by-step guidelines for choosing and implementing self-assessment research. Featuring a wealth of case histories and examples, the book emphasizes data collection and analysis methods, and spans the three levels of social work practice: direct practice, administration and community organization.

Springer Series on Social Work

Evaluating Your Practice

A Guide to Self-Assessment

Catherine F. Alter
Wayne Evens

Contents:

- Self-Assessment Research
- Designing Self-Assessments
- Analysis of Data
- Qualitative Designs
- Quantitative Designs
- Social Work Practice and Research
- Appendices: The Self-Assessment Checklist
- 100+ Outcome Measures
- Annotated Bibiliography of Books of Scales
- Microcomputer Software for Self-Assessments
- Creating Templates for Statistical Tests
- Human Subjects Review

Springer Series on Social Work
1990   208pp   0-8261-6960-0   hardcover

536 Broadway, New York, NY 10012-3955 • (212) 431-4370 • Fax (212) 941-7842

Springer Publishing Company

Program Evaluation in the Human Services
Michael J. Smith, DSW

"Smith has written an outstanding introductory program evaluation text for students of the human services. He effectively balances presentation of the major technical concepts in evaluation research with good advice about how program evaluation should be done. Particularly effective are the examples drawn from his personal experiences as an evaluation researcher."

—Francis G. Caro, PhD, *University of Massachusetts*

Contents:

- An Introduction to Program Evaluation
- A Comprehensive Definition of Program Evaluation
- The First Step: Describing the Program
- The Second Step: Defining the Program Goals
- The Third Step: Designing the Study
- The Fourth and Fifth Steps: Implementing the Program Evaluation
- The Sixth Step: Conclusions, Implications and Recommendations
- Appendices

Springer Series on Social Work
1990   168pp   0-8261-6590-7   hardcover

536 Broadway, New York, NY 10012-3955 • (212) 431-4370 • Fax (212) 941-7842